The Common Sense Manifesto

THE

COMMON
SENSE

MANIFESTO

(WITH A NOD TO THOMAS PAINE, NOT KARL MARX)

MAX J. SKIDMORE

Westphalia Press
An Imprint of the Policy Studies Organization
Washington, DC
2020

Westphalia Press
An imprint of Policy Studies Organization
1527 New Hampshire Ave., NW
Washington, D.C. 20036
info@ipsonet.org

ISBN: 978-1-63391-493-3

Cover and interior design by Jeffrey Barnes
jbarnesbook.design

Daniel Gutierrez-Sandoval, Executive Director
PSO and Westphalia Press

Updated material and comments on this edition
can be found at the Westphalia Press website:
www.westphaliapress.org

This book is dedicated to a perfect couple,

Joey and Iryna,

and to

Jacqueline, Max, and Hannah

★ Table of Contents

Introduction ix
Common Sense in Paine's World,
and in the World of Trump

Chapter I 1
Travesty and Tragedy: The Political History of American
Conservatism and the Republican Party Since 1968

Chapter II 53
Common Sense in Voting; Does the Majority Rule?

Chapter III 65
Two Inside Views of a Bizarre Election, with
Forthright Comments from the Outside

Chapter IV 91
Why Does Poverty Still Exist in the World's Richest Country?

Chapter V 125
Modern Political Economy and Public Policy

Chapter VI 143
Crafting Public Policy in a Modern Political Economy

Chapter VII 187
Republican Policies for Minority Rule

Chapter VIII 219
Conservative Goal: Maximum Feasible Inconvenience

Chapter IX 235
Common Sense Action Appendix

Chapter X 243
A Selective Appendix: Quick and Easy Reference
to Decades of Republican Malfeasance

Chapter XI 257
Appendix on Common Sense Self-Protection:
Fighting is Wrong; Learn to Fight

Index 267

Common Sense in Paine's World, and in the World of Trump

"Call me Republican," I once might have said to begin this book. I was born in a family that came from a long line of Republicans in an area of southwest Missouri that was dominated by the GOP. I lived my first two decades there, and as an undergraduate, I was president of a local chapter of College Republicans.

One member of that family was the exception, Betrenia Bowker, "Aunt Teeny." She was the maverick, a talented writer—playwright and poet—and New Deal Democrat. We discussed, and argued, politics all my young life. Throughout her life, she was my favorite. She prepared me intellectually for an eventually opened mind that would welcome common sense and new information.

Later, no doubt thanks to her, I found that studying history, politics, and literature broadened my views and gradually made them far less ideological. Still, I could not have predicted the changes that were to come over the next few decades. My Republican Party had professed to be thoroughly American, hard right in its conservative views, and fiercely anti-communist. It tended to share the racist attitudes of most white Americans (attitudes which, happily, my upbringing caused me never to share), but nonetheless the party looked with disdain at racist southern Democrats and their heritage of slavery, segregation, and bigotry.

I could not have foreseen (if I had even been aware of them) that the seeds the New Deal planted soon would have sprouted when a Democratic president, Harry Truman, finessed a Congress controlled by southern Democrats and desegregated the military by executive order. Nor could I have anticipated that those sprouts might flower, and the Democratic Party ultimately would be the one that responded to a powerful civil rights movement. With support from some northern Republicans, LBJ was able to sign not only the landmark Civil Rights Act of 1964, but also the potent Voting Rights Act of 1965. Almost immediately, bigoted southern Democrats morphed into bigoted southern Republicans.

As painful as it is to condemn the party that I once found to represent "Truth, Justice, and the American Way" (to borrow from Superman of the 1940s and 1950s), that party no longer exists— if in fact it ever did. The Republican Party of today has not been corrupted by Trump. Its corruption grew, at least from Nixon onward, until it enthusiastically embraced the most obviously corrupt, arrogant, boastful, militantly ignorant, and selfish presidential contender in American history, simply in order to regain and retain power. The party was ethically dead before Trump came on to the scene as the logical conclusion of the party's increasing corruption.

Owing more to a non-Republican, the angry populist and not really conservative George Wallace, than to its first presidents, the magnificent Abraham Lincoln and the admirable—and deliberately misrepresented—Ulysses S. Grant, spokesmen for today's Republican Party attack the very notion of *Truth*. Ripping children from their parents' arms for political gain while working vigorously to distribute wealth upward and deny the populace decent healthcare, calling for political opponents to be "locked up," hanged, or given the electric chair the party has certainly departed from any notion of *Justice*. Openly seeking to secure Russian meddling in American elections by a former KGB thug to benefit and elect its presidential candidate, then soliciting assistance from another country to besmirch an opponent and work to the advantage of that Republican president's re-election, it has departed from American values, and no longer maintains more than a bare pretext of favoring *the American Way*.

Common sense, combined with a bit of observation, suggests that the modern Republican Party recognizes no limits on what it will do to achieve its goal to make the government work for them, not the people. It has transgressed any line that once might have restrained its conduct and seems to redefine "conservatism" (which always failed in any case[1]) as anything, however outrageous, that Donald Trump might do on a whim.

At best, the party has marched boldly, by any common-sense definition, to the brink of treason; at worst, it has gone beyond. Its actions have reflected an increasing willingness to cast aside accepted limits. Could any reasonable person expect more from a party that has thrown in completely with a figure such as Donald Trump? Others have issued warnings as well.

"The greatest threat to our democracy today is a Republican Party that plays dirty to win." So begins an especially perceptive op-ed piece in *The New York Times*, by Steven Levitsky and Daniel Ziblatt.[2] The authors, two Harvard political science professors, also wrote *How Democracies Die*.[3]

Republicans across the country, the authors point out, have sought and are seeking to preserve their power using "any means necessary." As examples, they cite the stolen Supreme Court seat, the tactics in 2016 and 2018 that Republicans adopted in Wisconsin and North Carolina to try to minimize the power of incoming Democratic governors, the attempt in Pennsylvania to impeach judges of the state's supreme court after they struck down a Republican gerrymander, and most recently, using a surprise vote in the North Carolina House to override a gubernato-

---

1   See Max J. Skidmore, *Unworkable Conservatism* (Washington: Westphalia Press, 2017).

2   Steven Levitsky and Daniel Ziblatt, "Why Republicans Play Dirty," *The New York Times* (September 21, 2019), A27.

3   Levitsky and Ziblatt, *How Democracies Die* (New York: Broadway Books 2019).

rial veto of a budget bill, a vote that they had promised would not be held while Democrats attended a commemoration ceremony for the victims of 9/11. Fundamental to all this are the GOP's fervent attempts to keep Democratic voters away from the polls, attempts that are cynically and deliberately corrosive to popular government.

The reason for the dirty tactics, the authors say, is pure fear. Republicans are terrified that if they ever lose power, they will never regain it. The party is becoming smaller and less and less diverse: older, more Christian, and whiter. The result is, they say, "constitutional hardball," but electoral math is not the sole cause. "White Christians" are losing more than the ability to win elections; they are losing their dominance of the entire culture. Trump shouts that if Republicans lose, they can never win again "because you are going to have people flowing across the border."

The only remedy Levitsky and Ziblatt see is a Republican Party that becomes more diverse and is able to appeal to younger, urban, and nonwhite voters. For many reasons, that is hardly likely.

To appeal to a broader range of groups, the Republican Party would have to become far less Republican: it would have to become more diverse ideologically. It would need to shed the fanatical "political fundamentalism" that, at least rhetorically, has become its distinguishing characteristic. The rigid "conservative" principles that the party professes violate common sense, can rarely be implemented, are unsatisfactory even when they are implemented, and are uniformly praised even while duplicitous officeholders ignore them—apparently even fooling themselves.[4]

Until that unlikely development, the brilliant illustration that accompanies the op-ed in the *Times* will continue to be appropriate, unless the party disintegrates. That illustration takes the GOP's abstract elephant logo, and transforms it into a set of brass

---

4   Again, see Skidmore, *Unworkable Conservatism.*

knuckles. Hardly any visual representation could better capture the spirit of the contemporary Republican Party—its violence, cruelty, and fear—than this.

The 2016 election results were the most dangerous in America's modern history—perhaps the most dangerous of all time. The Electoral College aberration that year demonstrated that what had appeared to be the sound, sturdy, representative institutions of the world's most successful democratic republic were indeed far less stable than they had seemed.

In fact, it exposed those institutions as fragile. Trump exposed the apparently impregnable supports of American civic life to be vulnerable to the destructive antics of a crude and malevolent buffoon, a bully that no rational, well-functioning, political structure could ever have allowed anywhere near a position of authority.

We find the same phenomenon regarding the vulnerability of apparently sturdy institutions at work elsewhere. The USSR, one of the modern era's two great superpowers, crumbled during the George H. W. Bush administration. That instance reflected the inherent weaknesses in the Soviet Union, weaknesses that often affect dictatorial regimes.

Among international governments, the United States is not alone in having difficulties. Another great democratic state, the United Kingdom, faces turmoil because of an ill-advised, Russian-and-demagogue-influenced vote on "Brexit," which brought about attempts to depart from the European Union.

In Britain's case, Boris Johnson was cast in the role of malevolent buffoon that Trump so perfectly played in America. For Johnson the outcome was the same. He became Prime Minister.

Within the American system, two years passed before there could be any correction. When that correction took place, as a result of the 2018 midterms, it could only partially address the first true existential danger since the Great Depression and the Second World War, a danger that presented the greatest threat since the Civil War itself. It was the greatest danger, that is, if one assumes that those in charge of countries with nuclear weapons are rational, as they seem to have been—at least until January 20, 2017.

The most pressing concern about nuclear proliferation has always been that someday these fearsome weapons could fall under the control of an irrational ruler, likely a tyrant in an obscure foreign state. No one predicted that instability would emerge within the government of the most stable and powerful entity on earth. Even less could it have been anticipated that one of that superpower's two dominant political parties would quickly fall into lockstep support of the clearly irrational, completely unqualified, and notably unprincipled choice of the antiquated Electoral College; a selection mechanism that, with the assistance of voter suppression, social media, and foreign meddling, overruled the undeniable choice of the majority of the people.

America's ruling party withdrew from an agreement with Iran that was restraining, for a time, that country's pursuit of nuclear weapons; Iran, in response, has renewed its weapons program. This was the direct result of an irrational American action that broke an official promise from one country to another.

The same American party, in another irrational action, has withdrawn the United States from climate accords, and denied the clear scientific consensus regarding the effects of human activities on the planet's climate. All the while saying it favors clear air and water, that party relaxes controls over atmospheric emissions, over discharging dangerous chemicals near sources of drinking water, and over environmental regulation of automobiles that even the car manufacturers favor. Whatever motivates the Trump administration, it is certainly not scientific knowledge or even common sense.

Thus, the requirement for this manifesto—or plea for rational thought. It stresses the need for common sense but does not pretend that it is a panacea. Common sense is a prerequisite for viewing things rationally, but it is not enough. In a non-technological society, common sense might suggest that the Earth is flat, that the sun revolves around the Earth, or that an action is necessarily responsible for the conditions that follow it. What seems to be common sense can be wrong, so caution is always necessary before coming to a conclusion. Following common sense is a necessary way to begin, but it is only a beginning.

Sound conclusions usually require additional thought and observation, even if "common sense" would seem on its own to mandate a certain conclusion. If something offends "common sense," though, it absolutely should trigger such additional examination automatically. In modern American politics, common sense is so routinely offended that entire groups of people are conditioned to believe what—even to the most casual objective observer—is obviously nonsense.

Regarding the America of his day, Thomas Paine had written at the very beginning of "The Crisis," that those were "the times that try men's souls." Today, his words are equally appropriate and echo powerfully. Although much of the current danger is subtler than it was when Paine wrote or when the Civil War threatened the nation's very existence, the potential for harm has never been greater.

What should be painfully obvious is that Paine's warnings are as strongly needed now as they were during revolutionary times. When he issued his ringing call, he lit the spark of the American Revolution. Where is our Thomas Paine today? At the risk of sounding partisan, common sense will reveal that today's Paine-like figures have indeed emerged. They are among the Democratic aspirants for the presidential nomination. Nearly all of them are sounding Paine's warnings, and any one of them, bar none, would be far better in office than Donald Trump.

Paine actually called his message "Common Sense," and it was enormously powerful: a skilled propagandist's most brilliant piece of political propaganda. It immediately became one of the most effective cries for political action in all of history. He said that if common sense became the normal habit of thought, it could be the cure for the crisis. A habit of "not thinking a thing wrong gives it a superficial sense of being right."

So it is today, thoughtless people may assume that things today are not wrong, and therefore, they are right—whether it be violence at rallies where an American president openly incites it, children ripped cruelly from the arms of grieving parents pursuant to that president's policy, the spectacle of an American president openly enriching himself directly from his private business, or even the shocking spectacle of a president openly soliciting help from tyrants abroad against the interests of his own country. Common sense tells thoughtful people that things are very wrong.

Some things are technical and nuanced, so that what appears to be common sense may simply be misunderstanding. It remains, though, the first step toward an intelligent conclusion. We need constitutional lawyers, highly trained and skilled surgeons, pilots, and other technical specialists. What may appear to be a plain reading of a text may be less plain than it might seem to the uninformed, but the beginning must involve common sense.

Whenever something offends common sense, it requires examination. Without application of sense at the beginning (common or not), all subsequent conclusions can be wrong. Admittedly, things are complicated.

Even a well-informed public could find it difficult to ignore misleading comments when they permeate the news and form the substance of dire predictions from politicians and others.

Much of the American public is especially challenged in this regard, because it is not well informed. In the United States, there is constant bombardment from presidential tweets, talk radio, Fox News, and right-wing sources in general, supplemented by thoughtless repetition in more mainstream news sources. Conditions make it especially difficult for Americans to develop political sophistication.

- Think, for example, of the "weapons of mass destruction!" in Iraq that were not there.

- Think of the imminent "bankruptcy of Social Security!" that is not going to happen.

- Think of the projected depletion of the Medicare Trust Fund. The 2019 Medicare Trustees' Report shows depletion in seven years, 2026.[5] Now compare it with something I wrote *twenty years ago*:

    ... the heavily publicized predictions in 1995 and 1996 that Medicare would go bankrupt in seven years or so are merely a link in a long chain of such predictions spreading back for decades—predictions each time that the system had only seven years left.[6]

    They still are at it. Those seven years are like the vanishing point on a long, straight highway; the depletion date always stays about the same distance away. Doesn't common sense suggest caution in accepting such "information" as definitive?

- Regarding Medicare, think of its nature. It is enormously popular. It is built upon the American system of private medicine,

5   Office of the Actuary, "Medicare Trustees Report Shows Hospital Trust Fund Will Deplete [*sic*] in 7 Years," *Press Release, CMS.Gov* (April 22, 2019).

6   Max J. Skidmore, *Social Security and its Enemies* (Boulder CO: Westview Press, 1999), 148.

retaining private physicians and other providers. It has been highly successful. Yet Republicans, and conservative Democrats as well, have been successful in creating a conventional wisdom that Medicare for All is radical and extremist; not a workable, conservative, solution to fixing America's broken healthcare delivery system.

- Think of the "existential threat" from a group of refugees who just before the 2018 elections morphed into "a powerful military force attacking the United States," but evaporated immediately thereafter.

- Think of the "completely unreasonable (Witch Hunt!)" investigation into an "entirely acceptable request" to the Russians (broadcast live on TV by a presidential candidate) to assist a presidential campaign; a request that *within hours,* the Russians honored by beginning to hack Democratic emails.

- Think of the "greatest threat that America ever faced" from— what?—"Hillary Clinton's emails!" Neither Clinton nor Obama now holds any office, nor does Joe Biden, for that matter, but propaganda treats them as if they hold supreme power and present continued existential threats to "decent Americans."

Note that Clinton's private server was not hacked and seems to have been more secure than other, more "official" servers. Note also that there was and is little to no concern whatsoever regarding private servers of the many Republicans who use them. Nor is there concern for Mr. Trump's complete lack of concern for his own security breaches that include the cavalier treatment of documents and secret information, and his use of unsecured, personal mobile phones (anywhere, anytime, including at an unsecured private club). Trump, of course, actually does hold real power.

More basically, think of two things: first, ever since the New Deal, fiscal conservatives have been warning about threats to

America's future by "out-of-control" spending, deficits, or the debt. Consider that the warnings have been repeated for some three-quarters of a century, while America has grown prosperous and powerful. Common sense would suggest that the warnings need examination.

Second, consider the constant repetition primarily, but not only, from Republicans, that "the people" voted for policies of the Trump administration or that—possibly because Democrats presumably ignored "the heartland" and its down-to-earth people—the nation's people "wanted" whatever Trump may be doing at the moment to happen. Apply common sense. The Electoral College may have chosen Trump, but the "American people"—clearly and most assuredly—did not. Nearly three million more of them voted for Mrs. Clinton than for Mr. Trump, and Democrats gained seats that election in both houses of Congress.

When actual developments do not support their fevered warnings, the "pundits" simply proceed to other topics. Nevertheless, their breathless support for the unsupportable combined with dire economic predictions that the United States cannot afford to continue its "tax and spend" policies.

However plausible they may seem to a bewildered public, all such assertions are completely wrong. They deserve nothing better than to be rejected, or even scorned. Americans need to be reminded of how it is that we came to be where we are.

Decades ago, I heard Norman Cousins give a powerful speech warning of the threat from nuclear weapons. He likened the public's reaction to an experience he once had on a flight from Hawaii to California—this was on an old propeller airplane before the advent of the more reliable jetliners. Just after passing the famed "point of no return," when his flight had flown more than half the distance from Hawaii to the Mainland, the airliner developed engine trouble. There was concern that it might not be possible to maintain altitude the rest of the way to the destination. The pilots had no alternative but to continue on over the ocean. Returning was not an option.

For the first hour or so, the passengers were terrified. Many prayed. Presently, however, the fear wore off, and they began to talk and even joke with one another. The danger was no less real, and perhaps was becoming even greater, but it had become normalized and no longer dominated their thoughts. Most of those on board had been able to put it out of their minds long before they landed safely.

So it was, said Cousins, with nuclear weapons. They were no less a threat, but their existence had become accepted, normalized. Many people appeared to have lost the sense of danger that they presented.

The same is true regarding nuclear power (the "peaceful atom" of the 1950s), despite Three-Mile Island (1979), Chernobyl (1986), and Fukushima (2011)—to list them chronologically— along with many other incidents that received little or no publicity to the public (the records are easily obtainable online). Obviously, as these incidents demonstrate, accidents are possible, as are terrorist attacks and the unsolved, and likely unsolvable, troubles presented by nuclear waste.

As early as 1975, a nuclear physicist and safety expert, Carl J. Hocevar, of the Union of Concerned Scientists, wrote, "no matter how much diligence is exercised in the design, construction, and operation of a nuclear reactor things can and do go wrong. Design errors occur, the unexpected happens, human error is a very real possibility."[7] The three incidents mentioned above all took place after Hocevar's warning. Many others had occurred earlier.[8]

---

7   Carl J. Hocevar, "Foreword," John G. Fuller, *We Almost Lost Detroit* (New York, Ballantine Books, 1975), vi-vii.

8   See, e.g., John G. Fuller; *ibid*.

Hocevar's wisdom applies across the board. Consider the flawed software design of Boeing's 737 Max that resulted in two tragic airline crashes after it had been certified safe by Trump's FAA, an agency that because of ideology and depleted staffing delegated much of the determination to the manufacturer; never a good idea. Nuclear power is not the only area in which errors can occur—only the most dangerous.

Terrorist and completely irrational acts have not as yet happened with regard to nuclear plants and waste, but a sitting American president, according to widespread reports, can muse (in a terrifying manner) about "nuking" a hurricane to ward it off.[9] Also, the world otherwise certainly has not become safer since those early warnings.

In fact, those early warnings came before the United States became the center of mass shootings (thanks to the Republican response to fierce lobbying by the National Rifle Association, which has made the most dangerous firearms widely available to anyone with a grievance), before the world had adjusted to the frequency of mass killings by suicide, which reflect increasing levels of religious and political fanaticism. Nuclear power offers perhaps the most potent medium for the fanatics.

To return to contemporary American politics, many actions that at one time would have created a sense of outrage are so common that they no longer have the ability to generate mild concern. This is true even for actions that would seem to be clear instances of disloyalty to the country, if not worse. Normalization would seem to be the new routine. Consider, for example, the cavalier attitude among Republicans concerning the amply documented cyber assault by the Russians on America's 2016 election, the absence of any protest by the Trump administration (quite the op-

---

9   This was widely reported; see, e.g., "Nuclear Weapons and Hurricanes Don't Mix, NOAA Advises," *BBC News* (August 26, 2019), https://www.bbc.com/news/world-us-canada-49471093 (accessed September 15, 2019).

posite in fact), and the apparent lack of any plan to prevent such foreign assaults from being repeated in 2020 and beyond.

An extensive examination of the American political economy is in order. Accordingly, this Common Sense Manifesto seeks to provide at least the necessary beginning.

★ CHAPTER I

Travesty and Tragedy: The Political History of American Conservatism and the Republican Party Since 1968

I t may seem as though Donald Trump leapt into the political world from the outside, seizing one of America's major political parties, twisting it to his personal whims, and corrupting everything he touched. That is not what happened.

The Republican Party's march toward Trump as its inevitable (although then not yet recognized) goal left many rules broken, ethical boundaries erased, and principles discarded. Each transgression may have seemed acceptable at the time to those committing it, but once the Republicans ignored or discarded rules of accepted political behavior, such instances quickly began to come relatively rapidly and ultimately became normalized—at least to the perpetrators. The accumulation built until it soon became overwhelming. That corruption had been building for decades and was there, ready to be seized by a demagogue.

Far too few observers detected that Republican conservatives had been spending years carefully and methodically chipping away at American institutions, leaving them ready to welcome a destroyer. Trump is only the logical conclusion of trends then obscure, but clearly obvious in retrospect: trends that ultimately opened the system to anyone willing to cast aside all restraints, question the very existence of truth and reality, dispute scientific findings, demonstrate contempt for the country and its institutions, and operate solely for his own aggrandizement.

The record is clear. Decades of conservative Republican efforts culminated in bringing the United States to the most perilous position it has faced since the Great Depression and the Second World War. Party leaders and rank-and-file members alike delighted in, or at least acquiesced to, bringing to power and then wholeheartedly supporting a recognized swindler, who paid $25 million to settle lawsuits arising from his fraudulent Trump "University," which as widely disparate journals as *National Review* and *The New Yorker* exposed as a scam.[1]

Trump was a figure well known—notorious, in fact—for a total lack of integrity or experience, incompetence, ignorance, contempt for others, cruelty, sexual assault, bullying, defaults on his obligations, questionable connections, laziness, and an insouciant disregard for everything non-Trump. Despite witnessing him openly inviting Russian meddling on his behalf in the election, the Republican rank and file still noisily ("Lock Her Up," they bleated) derided Hillary Clinton and—oblivious to the implications of his outrageous invitation to the Russians—warmly supported him.

Katy Tur was the reporter covering Trump as he made that astonishing (but now almost normal for Republicans) request. She gave him an opportunity to walk it back, but, instead, he reiterated it.[2] Regardless of whether it met the strict legal definition of criminality, that, by itself, should be enough to demonstrate a willingness to collude—or to conspire—especially since the Russians hacked into Democratic emails immediately afterward.

In spite of all this and regardless of his arrogance that can only

---

1 See Ian Tuttle, "Yes, Trump University Was a Massive Scam," *National Review* (February 26, 2016), https://www.nationalreview.com/corner/trump-university-scam/; John Cassidy, "Trump University: It's Worse Than You Think," https://www.newyorker.com/news/john-cassidy/trump-university-its-worse-than-you-think (both accessed February 13, 2019).

2 This has been widely reported. For Tur's comments, see Katy Tur, *Unbelievable: My Front Row Seat to the Craziest Campaign in American History* (New York: Harper Collins, 2017), 241; for further discussion, see Chapter III.

be described as colossal—in fact, one is tempted to conclude *because* of all this—Trump received an enthusiastic welcome from party members as the new embodiment of the Republican Party. He also received the imprimatur of his handpicked attorney general and foremost henchman, William Barr, who—contrary to the content of the report—asserted that in his opinion, the results of the Mueller investigation contained insufficient evidence to take any action against Trump. This could have been anticipated. Barr, in June of 2018, before being Trump's chosen one, had sent an unsolicited memorandum to Congress calling the Mueller investigation "fatally misconceived."[3]

The ultimate release of the redacted Mueller Report and the testimony from Mueller himself made clear that Barr completely misrepresented what the report said. Neither he nor Trump, who claimed that the report exonerated him, was telling the truth. Despite their comments and the echoing murmurs from a variety of Republicans and right-wing broadcasters, the report was damning.

Reviewing the history of the party that brought the country to such a sad state is painful but essential. If this were a game, the aim would be to determine which of the actions discussed below were merely indications of bad faith, which ones were inexcusably destructive of the fundamental institutions of a democratic republic, and which ones, if any, actually went so far as to cross the line into open treason (not necessarily under the constitutional definition, since under the current interpretation, it seems as though we would need to be at war, but the more popular, and perhaps common sense, understanding of selling out America's interests for personal gain). This is far more serious, though, than a game.

---

3   Sadie Gurman and Aruna Viswanatha, "Trump's Attorney General Pick Criticized an Aspect of Mueller Probe in Memo to the Justice Department," *Wall Street Journal* (March 26, 2019).

The Sins of Richard M. Nixon

President Lyndon B. Johnson, whose presidency had been severely damaged by his conduct of the war in Vietnam, had announced that for the sake of national unity, he would not run in 1968 for another term. The 1968 presidential race, therefore, did not include LBJ on the ticket. It pitted his Vice President, Hubert Humphrey, against a former Vice President, Richard M. Nixon.

Nixon's previous political career had already brought him the nickname "Tricky Dick." However much he had earned the title, as things turned out, by far the worst was yet to come. This applies not only to Nixon's administration, but also to the present and everything in between. Except for Gerald Ford, every one of Nixon's Republican successors was worse than his predecessor, until the ultimate outrage, when the Electoral College overruled the substantial popular vote and installed the ineffable Trump.

A significant third-party candidate was also in the 1968 race, Alabama Governor, George Wallace. Wallace introduced strident segregationist themes to the contest. He did not come close to winning, and he was not a Republican. Nevertheless, Republicans learned from his example. Wallace's candidacy had long-term effects, making racist code words acceptable—even attractive—to Republicans in American politics and in laying the foundation for their "Southern Strategy," which has shaped (and corrupted) their party ever since.

Nixon first and then Ronald Reagan pioneered that strategy most effectively. Their Republican successors refined and strengthened the Southern Strategy still more, incorporating it into their own campaigns and administrations. That strategy involved directing appeals on race to white Southerners who previously had been Democrats.

Nixon's repertoire of reprehensible tactics did not rely solely on appeals to Southern racism. Anna Chennault was the widow of the late Major General Claire Chennault, who had won fame before and during World War II with his "Flying Tigers" against the Japanese. She was prominent in Washington social circles and an ambitious and influential Republican fundraiser with numerous connections in Asia. Nixon used her for his purposes and then shunned her completely, causing her to vanish into history without honors or political appointments.

Nixon's henchmen, at his direction, used Chennault as a go-between, attempting to convince the Thieu government of South Vietnam to boycott the planned Paris Peace Talks. She promised that a President Nixon would give more favorable treatment to the government of South Vietnam than it could expect from a President Humphrey. The purpose was to prevent an "October Surprise," or the possibility of an end to the Vietnam War prior to the November elections. Nixon thought an end to hostilities might increase Vice President Humphrey's chances for victory.

LBJ learned of Nixon's covert efforts to sabotage the peace talks and challenged Nixon directly. The Johnson Presidential Library has taped telephone conversations between LBJ and Nixon and between LBJ and Senator Everett Dirksen, then the Senate's Republican leader. Nixon expressed horror at the suggestion, and said he would never do such a thing. Johnson knew better, but did not have proof, so he did not go public with the information. He did, however, complain in a telephone call to Senator Dirksen, "his old friend. 'This is treason.' 'I know,' Dirksen said mournfully."[4]

All this was rumored for years, but it is now definite that it is true. Nixon did attempt to keep the Paris Peace Talks from succeeding. In 2007, historian John Farrell reviewed papers at the Nixon

---

4   John A. Farrell, "Nixon's Vietnam Treachery," *The New York Times* (December 31, 2016), https://www.nytimes.com/2016/12/31/opinion/sunday/nixons-vietnam-treachery.html (accessed February 9, 2019).

Presidential Library that it had just opened to the public. Farrell was preparing a book on Nixon and uncovered previously unknown notes from Nixon's key aide, H. R. Haldeman. In these notes, Haldeman revealed that Nixon gave him direct orders to "monkey wrench" the talks. Regarding the Southern Strategy, Haldeman also revealed that Nixon made promises "to Southern Republicans, that he would retreat on civil rights and 'lay off pro-Negro crap' if elected president." Farrell revealed these "gems," as he described them, in a *New York Times* op-ed on New Year's Eve, 2016.[5]

Farrell's extensive Nixon biography came out the following year. It includes the same information that is in his op-ed, and of course much more as well.[6]

The Thieu government refused to participate in the talks, and the talks collapsed. To be sure, they could have failed anyway. The Vietnamese may have refused to participate in any case. Moreover, had the talks proceeded with South Vietnamese participation, they certainly still could have failed. What is absolutely certain, though, is that in order to gain political advantage, Richard Nixon not only was willing to prolong the war—with many Americans, Vietnamese, and others dying daily—he gave explicit orders to do whatever could be done to make it happen to keep the war going, all for personal political gain. This was the beginning of a long train of Republican perfidy, culminating in Trump's most corrupt administration in American history.

As Peter Baker of *The New York Times* wrote very shortly after Farrell published his account in *The Times*, he agreed with Farrell that Nixon's actions were "beyond the normal political jockeying." There were lives at stake. Both agreed that "potentially, this is worse than anything he did in Watergate."[7]

---

5   *Ibid.*

6   Farrell, *Richard Nixon: The Life* (New York: Doubleday, 2017).

7   Peter Baker, "Nixon Tried to Spoil Johnson's Vietnam Peace Talks in '68,

Was it worse than Watergate? To be sure, and in no way should anyone minimize Watergate, which was an attempt to subvert America's electoral system by sabotaging political campaigns of opponents, committing multiple burglaries and other felonies, and otherwise throwing off all restraints in order to win an election. It led to a threatened impeachment of a president—impeachment was something that had happened only once before—then brought about a bipartisan effort, which culminated in that president's resignation. At this writing, Nixon retains the distinction of being the only president who has ever resigned the office. He was pushed to do so, not only by Democrats, but also by conscientious Republicans, who then still put country above party.

In the meantime, the corruption was clearly evident, and not just within the inner circle of Nixon and his aides. His Vice President, Spiro T. Agnew, elected in 1968 and re-elected with Nixon in one of the greatest landslide victories ever in 1972, had been corrupt when he was county executive of Baltimore County, Maryland, when he was governor of the State of Maryland, and when he was Vice President of the United States. Regardless of the huge victory, investigations of corruption continued until there was clear evidence of Agnew's guilt and he was in serious jeopardy. Under pressure, and to keep from serving time in prison, Agnew agreed to resign, leaving office on October 10, 1973.

That gave President Nixon a vacancy to fill. He had the authority, under the terms of the rather new Twenty-Fifth Amendment, which had never before been used, to nominate a new vice president who would take office after confirmation by *both* the Senate and the House. (All other presidential appointments require only senatorial confirmation; filling the vice presidency is unique in that respect; prior to the Twenty-Fifth Amendment, a vacancy in

Notes Show," *The New York Times* (January 2, 2017), https://www.nytimes. com/2017/01/02/us/politics/nixon-tried-to-spoil-johnsons-vietnam-peace-talks-in-68-notes-show.html (accessed February 9, 2019).

the vice presidency could not be filled until the next presidential election.) Nixon nominated the popular Republican leader in the House, Gerald Ford.

Most Republicans at the time were still devoted to the country and its welfare and would not put party considerations ahead of the public good. In fact, Mr. Republican himself, Senator Barry Goldwater, the fierce firebrand who was crushed by LBJ in the presidential election of 1964, went to Nixon to tell him he had lost his party's confidence and should resign his office.

Contrast that with the nearly unanimous support of congressional Republicans for Donald Trump, who makes Nixon look like a solid pillar of the establishment. Whatever Nixon's sins—and they were legion, including shaking the foundations of the constitutional order, colluding with a foreign power to prolong a war, and conspiring to commit felonies from the Oval Office—Nixon still had feelings for the country. However much he attempted to escape consequences, he did respect the law and accepted that laws applied to him. At his best, he did marvelous things as President. Substantial figures in his party, however, recognized that he could not stay in office and were ready to impeach and remove him if he did not resign. Nixon did depart, leaving the presidency on August 8, 1974, in the second year of his second term, more than two years before the next election. Today's Republicans, by shocking contrast, by and large concede almost openly that they would be furious if Clinton or Obama did what Trump does, and yet they will not turn on one of their own.

At the time Congress received the nomination for Gerald Ford to be the new Vice President, most knowledgeable figures in both parties were aware that chances were strong that President Nixon would not complete his second term. Knowing that Nixon's resignation or removal was likely, congressional Democrats could have refused to confirm anyone he nominated to be Vice President. Leaving the position vacant would have meant that when

Nixon left his office, Speaker of the House, Carl Albert, became president. Albert was a Democrat. Thus, the Democrats could have "stolen the presidency," just as the Republicans blatantly stole a Supreme Court seat when they refused to confirm any Obama nominee during the President's last year in office.

Although the Democrats could have easily engaged in the theft of the presidency, they did not do so. Speaker Albert and the Democratic leaders decided that it would be highly improper to seize the presidency, when Republicans had won it through a fair election; it would not be the honorable thing to do. The people had voted for a Republican president, they concluded, and the people deserved to have their votes respected. The Democrats of both the House and the Senate thus confirmed Ford, who subsequently succeeded to the presidency when Nixon resigned. One would be hard-pressed to find an example of modern Republicans putting honor ahead of expedience on any issue, especially one that involved power.[8]

Leaping ahead to that controversy, Republicans in 2016 cynically said that Supreme Court vacancies were never filled in a president's last year. Chairman Grassley of the Senate Judiciary refined the comment, saying it had not happened in the previous 80 years. Unquestionably, it has happened numerous times in American history, sometimes *very late in a president's last year*— in fact, President Van Buren filled a Court vacancy *in his last week* in office, as did President Tyler. President Jackson had a Supreme Court justice confirmed that he nominated on his *very last day* as president! At the exact time that Senate Republicans refused to seat President Obama's nominee, the Court had a sitting member appointed in a president's last year in office: Associate Justice Anthony Kennedy. President Reagan, a Republican, had nominated Kennedy in Reagan's last year as president. The Senate that con-

---

8   See Skidmore, *Unworkable Conservatism*, 136–137.

firmed Kennedy had been Democratic. Among those senators voting to confirm Kennedy were Senator Grassley and the Republican leader, Mitch McConnell. There is no doubt that they were well aware that their explanation was merely pretense.

They could argue, correctly, that Reagan had tried previously to fill the vacancy, and the Senate had rejected his nominee. That rationalization was irrelevant, as Republicans were quickly to demonstrate. Grassley, McConnell, and Republicans in general were merely seeking excuses not to confirm an Obama nominee. Other Republicans made this obvious, commenting that, should Hillary Clinton win the election, Senate Republicans should refuse to confirm anyone she nominated. They would leave the seat open until a Republican president could fill the vacancy, however long that might take. Senators Cruz of Texas, McCain of Arizona, and Burr of North Carolina were among those identified as making such comments.[9] There was no doubt whatsoever that Republicans would have quickly confirmed any nominee Donald Trump might send forward, whoever it might be, whenever the nomination might originate, and *whatever lack of judicial temperament that nominee might display.* This has been borne out. That is what, in fact, they did as soon as they had the opportunity. In effect, Republican senators were saying that no Democratic president could ever fill a Court vacancy, so long as they were able to prevent it and that they would apply no restrictive criteria to any Trump nominee. See the Kavanaugh hearings for textbook behavior that amply documents Kavanaugh as lacking judicial temperament.

If there had ever been any doubt regarding the duplicity of McConnell and Senate Republicans, McConnell himself gleefully set it

---

9   See, David A. Graham, "What Happens if Republicans Refuse to Replace Justice Scalia?" *The Atlantic* (November 1, 2016), https://www.theatlantic.com/politics/archive/2016/11/whats-the-opposite-of-court-packing/506081/ (accessed February 10, 2019).

to rest. He made it plain that all the varying excuses for holding the Scalia seat open were nonsense. The only "principle" at work was political advantage. When asked in 2019 at the end of May what he would do if another seat opened up in Trump's last year in office, he did not even have the grace to be embarrassed. Rather, he smirked, and said, "Oh, we'd fill it."[10] Of course they would.

Gerald Ford, a Welcome Relief

Gerald Ford, a conservative Republican, was a decent man and president. He pardoned President Nixon on his own initiative and as a result, suffered a massive wave of criticism. In retrospect, though, it seems to have been a wise move. It was not "justice done," nor did Nixon "deserve" his pardon. What the country deserved, though, was to heal. Nixon had been a source of great turmoil. He likely would have continued to tear the country apart the rest of his life had Ford not exercised good judgment as he did, by disregarding political considerations and pardoning Nixon. Historian Stephen Ambrose put it well, when he wrote that he was among the millions of Americans "furious" that Ford had issued the pardon. After seventeen years had passed, however, he had come to recognize that Ford had been "both wise and courageous" to do so.[11] As he put it, the last thing the country needed was to continue to be torn apart by Richard Nixon.

Ford also exercised good judgment at great political cost by ordering the massive NIIP (National Influenza Immunization Program), or the Swine Flu Program, which subjected him to withering criticism from both Reagan and Carter supporters when no pandemic developed. Knowing what he knew, however, it was far

---

10   See, e.g., Russell Berman, "Mitch McConnell's Grand Plan was Obvious," *The Atlantic* (May 30, 2019).

11   Stephen Ambrose, *Nixon: Volume Three, Ruin and Recovery, 1973-1990* (New York: Simon and Schuster, 1991), 462.

better to have the program without a pandemic than to have had a pandemic with no such program.[12]

One charge against Ford has some validity, although it was inadvertent; he could hardly have known what the future would bring. He brought to power Richard Cheney and Donald Rumsfeld, giving them the stature to cause great harm under the later presidency of George W. Bush—which they rapidly proceeded to do.

The Sins of Ronald Reagan

Ford's campaign to win his election was damaged by former California Governor Ronald Reagan, who waged a fight to take the nomination from him. Reagan failed in that effort, but because Ford lost his race to former Georgia Governor Jimmy Carter, Reagan was able to spend the next four years building his strength to become the Republican nominee in 1980. Counter-factual history can never be precise, but it is likely that, had Ford won the election in 1976, Reagan's political career would have been over. A second term President Ford likely would have seen to that.

As it was, Carter's presidency was fatally damaged by a number of circumstances, many over which he had no control. Reagan was able to use Carter's troubles to his advantage. Had Ford won, though, he likely would have been succeeded in 1981 by a Democrat or a moderate Republican, and the "Reagan Revolution," which brought "movement conservatives," who were right-wing extremists, into power and normalized their positions, might have been headed off. Most people seem to have forgotten, or never knew, that prior to his nomination as the 1980 Republican presidential candidate, Reagan was almost universally considered to represent the far-right fringe of American politics. Even his most

---

12 See, Max J. Skidmore, *Presidents, Pandemics, and Politics* (New York: Palgrave Macmillan, 2016), Chapter 6.

fervent Republican supporters would have agreed, because that was precisely the kind of candidate they had in Goldwater and wanted again in Reagan.

The Iranian students who seized the US embassy in Teheran landed the most forceful blow to the Carter administration. Carter simply had the bad luck to be in office when it took place. To be sure, he gave Iranians angry at "the Great Satan" their excuse, but their fury dated back a quarter century to the Eisenhower administration, which unleashed the CIA to overthrow the elected Prime Minister and install the Shah.

After the revolution, Carter admitted the exiled Shah to the US for cancer treatment. Regardless of the humanitarian considerations, the Iranians who attacked the embassy perceived it as a direct insult to their people.

That was consistent with Carter's luck throughout his presidency. When he sent a rescue mission to free the hostages, still held at the embassy, an unanticipated sandstorm arose. The military had selected helicopters not equipped to handle such conditions, and the mission failed. Carter, in fact, was the only American president who served a full term to have no opportunity to fill a vacancy on the Supreme Court (despite Donald Trump's ignorant boast that he was able to fill two vacancies in his first two years—as though that were a personal triumph—when "many presidents don't get a chance to put one on"[13]). Even presidents who served less than a full term—such as Ford, Kennedy, Harding, and Garfield—appointed justices to the Court. In fact, other

---

13   Comment Trump made in an October 24, 2018 speech in Mosinee, Wisconsin; see Louis Jacobson, "Donald Trump Said Many Presidents Don't Get a Chance to Appoint a Justice. He's Wrong," *Politifact* (October 25 2018), https://www.politifact.com/truth-o-meter/statements/2018/oct/25/donald-trump/donald-trump-said-many-presidents-dont-get-appoint/ (accessed February 15, 2019). One should note that Trump is profoundly, even proudly, ignorant regarding most subjects, especially American history.

than Carter, the only presidents who did not were William Henry Harrison (who died in office after only one month), Zachary Taylor (who died in office after only about a year and a half), and Andrew Johnson (who served nearly a full term after succeeding the slain Abraham Lincoln—but who was also at odds with Congress, which reduced the size of the Court so that he would not have a vacancy to fill).

Carter's presidency was flawed, partly because he was not a politician sufficiently skilled to handle the political forces of Washington, DC; however, he had substantial accomplishments and was (and remains) a man of integrity. His administration appears to many to have been mediocre but will likely be more favorably recognized when an able and favorable biographer pens a work that attracts attention, as David McCullough did for Harry Truman.[14] Carter should be lauded for placing human rights at the center of American foreign policy—however erratic his application of the principle may have been—and for his energy program. The Reagan forces, of course, rejected both.

Additionally, the Reagan administration proceeded with the Southern Strategy that Nixon had employed so effectively. Early in his campaign as the Republican nominee for president, Reagan chose to speak at the Neshoba County Fair in Mississippi. As Bob Herbert of the *New York Times* put it, Reagan, a master of symbolism, knew what he was doing. The venue was a few miles away from the small town of Philadelphia, a source of Mississippi shame, where the Klan had murdered Andrew Goodman, Michael Schwerner, and James Chaney in 1964 during the Civil Rights Movement. Reagan, said Herbert, in his speech praising states' rights, "was tapping out the code." Stressing "states' rights" in Mississippi at that time to a white audience was the same as saying "when it comes down to you and the blacks, we're with you." Reagan, he said, throughout his career had not only been

---

14   David McCullough, *Truman* (New York: Simon and Schuster, 1992).

wrong regarding race but had been "insensitive and mean-spirited on civil rights and other issues important to black people. There is no way," he wrote, "for the scribes of today to clean up that dismal record."[15]

Few things could be more symbolic of Carter's presidency, and of Reagan's, than what took place regarding energy policies. Carter had solar panels installed on the White House. Their effect on America's energy use was of course insignificant, but they represented the determination of the Carter administration to direct the country toward energy independence, which meshed with the emerging concern for the environment. After Reagan assumed the presidency, one of his first acts was to have the panels removed, which was consistent with his reduction in funding for the Department of Energy and his changes to tax policy that removed Carter's incentives for home owners to install equipment that would reduce energy usage. The actual removal resulted from the need to repair the roof, but Reagan refused to have the panels re-installed, despite the fact that they had been giving good, continuous service. The engineer who had installed them for Carter was later quoted as having said that Reagan's chief of staff Donald Regan called the system "a joke."[16] Maine's Unity College, however, subsequently acquired the panels that had been in storage. The panels that had been called a "joke" continued to work and provided the campus with free and clean energy from the sun.

Solar panels were absent from the White House until Barack Obama became president. He announced in 2013 that a new (and much more ambitious) system would be installed. The current status of that system is unclear, but it is reasonable to assume

---

15   Bob Herbert, "Righting Reagan's Wrongs?" *New York Times* (November 13, 2007), https://www.nytimes.com/2007/11/13/opinion/13herbert.html (accessed February 17, 2019).

16   John Light, "The White House Gets Solar Panels (Again)," *Bill Moyers Spotlight* (August 19, 2013), https://billmoyers.com/2013/08/19/the-white-house-gets-solar-panels-again/ (accessed February 17, 2019).

that it continues to function and has not come to the attention of the Trump administration. Trump is notorious for his emphasis on fossil fuels, especially coal, but also for lack of attention to detail. His administration, similarly, is permeated with unfilled positions and thus also unlikely to be able to concentrate on such issues (or on many others).

To be fair to George W. Bush, despite his reputation as being unreceptive to issues of the environment (except for protection of huge areas of the Pacific Ocean, where he excelled), there were solar panels installed on the grounds of the White House during his presidency. The National Park Service administers the grounds and has maintained environmentally friendly policies. These included the installation of solar panels on a maintenance building to provide both hot water and electricity for the grounds. There is no indication that this even came to the administration's attention; regardless, the installation took place while Bush was president.

One bit of mischief that the Reagan administration accomplished had far-reaching—and perhaps highly destructive—effects, despite being almost forgotten. That was to kill the Fairness Doctrine. If remembered at all, the doctrine may be presented as a rather quaint and outmoded policy of a simpler time. The rationale for eliminating it was that electronic media were proliferating, cable was burgeoning, without using airwaves, and the doctrine was portrayed as more likely to inhibit than foster free speech.

Some sort of fairness requirement for broadcasting had been in effect since the Radio Act of 1927. Because the airwaves are public and limited, broadcasting needed to be regulated and should operate in the public interest. In 1949, the Federal Communication Commission mandated that broadcasters include matters of public interest in their programming and that they do so with fairness. In 1987, the FCC under the Reagan administration eliminated the doctrine. Congress that year passed a bill requiring fairness, but President Reagan vetoed it. Conservatives applauded the elimination, and certainly there would be complicated issues raised by applying regulation of content to satellite and cable.

One can argue that the doctrine needed to be revised to accommodate a vastly more complicated situation and to ensure against suppression of speech. The immediate proliferation of extremist talk radio, however, along with the rise of Fox News as a de facto arm of the Republican Party, a virtual state television when Republicans are in power (or, with the presidency of the gullible Donald Trump, the driver of administration policy), demonstrates that the public good requires some way to regulate the melding of news and party politics. The current conditions represent direct threats to the ability of the political system to function in a democratic manner, especially when those of great wealth are privileged in speech as well as in lifestyle.

Regarding the allegations that Nixon sacrificed the country's interests for political gain, it took many years to prove that they were true: the verification that Nixon sought to continue the Vietnam War to improve his electoral chances came after his death, long after his presidency. It was the first such overt incident ever documented of an American president. Sadly, it was not the last. It was the beginning of a chain of outrageous actions by Republican presidents to help them gain or solidify their hold on power.

Considering Ronald Reagan's status as the "patron saint" of the modern Republican Party (at least before the advent of Trump), it should be especially shocking to discover that he, too, possibly——one might say probably—did something similar. There long have been allegations that in the 1980 campaign, Reagan was behind similar negotiations that sought to prevent the release of the American hostages held prisoner by Iranian students in the US embassy in Teheran. Thus far, there has been no "smoking gun," as there has been for Nixon; thus, Reagan's guilt has not been verified, unlike Nixon's.

THE COMMON SENSE MANIFESTO

The case against Reagan is that, just as Nixon sought to avoid an "October Surprise," so too did Reagan's aides, by making a deal with the Iranians—in this instance, by promising to supply them arms, if they did not release the American hostages until Carter left office. Gary Sick, who had been on the National Security Council in the Carter administration, conducted an investigation that led him to conclude that there had been an arrangement between the Reagan campaign and the Iranians. He admitted that he found no direct proof.[17]

Despite the lack of direct proof, and regardless of whether Sick or his detractors are correct, the bizarre actions of the Reagan administration are enough to demonstrate that it had pursued policies directly contrary to America's interests. President Reagan had asserted that he would never negotiate with terrorists, but he certainly did so, going beyond mere negotiations. He authorized providing arms directly to people who were using them against the United States. Moreover, the mere fact that the Iranians freed the prisoners exactly when Reagan took office could mean that they despised Carter *or* that there had been some illicit agreement to hold them until then. There can be no doubt what Republicans would have said if a President Clinton or a President Obama had done anything remotely similar.[18] Certainly, whatever went on between Reagan's campaign and the Iranian leaders provided the foundation for the Iran-Contra arrangement, whereby arms were secretly provided to Iran throughout Reagan's time in office.

To say that this was a major scandal is a huge understatement. Because of foreign involvement, when viewed objectively, it dwarfed Watergate under Nixon. Even without considering the charges of collusion, Iran-Contra itself would have justi-

---

17   See Gary Sick, *October Surprise: American Hostages in Iran and the Election of Ronald Reagan* (New York: Crown Books, 1991).

18   See Skidmore, *Unworkable Conservatism*, 28–29.

fied impeachment, which could well have followed had Reagan not been elderly, failing, and soon to be leaving the presidency. As Jane Mayer and Doyle McManus put it in their penetrating study of Reagan:

> The final judgment of the congressional committees was polite but unsparing. Even the president's staunchest defenders said they were profoundly disturbed by what they had learned. A bipartisan majority concluded that the president had, in fact, violated his oath of office. Congress had no stomach for the idea of impeaching Ronald Reagan in the last year of his tenure, but the committees gently charged him with an impeachable offense all the same.[19]

However reluctant the Republicans were to move against Reagan, it is clear that the party had not yet sunk to the depths we see today, as they continue to fawn over Trump. Republicans then were still capable of being shocked by political malfeasance and of doing something about it, but it was not long before they banded together to pursue power, regardless of what that required.

Legal proceedings can be a key indicator of the ethics of an administration. The number of indictments and convictions of Reagan administration officials and political supporters made Reagan's one of the most corrupt presidencies in American history. (To be sure, Trump's corruption is dwarfing the worst of Reagan's.) Reagan's Vice President and successor, George H. W. Bush, escaped any judgment, but his role in the Iran-Contra fiasco was, and still is, obscure. He professed to have been uninformed about the arms transfers to the Iranians until after the fact.

---

19   Jane Mayer and Doyle McManus, *Landslide: The Unmaking of the President 1984-1988* (Boston: Houghton-Mifflin, 1988), 390–391.

The Sins of Bush I

I n any event, his 1988 election made Bush the first sitting vice president to be elected president since Martin Van Buren was elected in 1836 to succeed Andrew Jackson. By the time of Bush's victory, Reagan had been unmasked as primarily a befuddled figure who was easily manipulated.

Bush managed to maintain his reputation as a decent man, even though he ran a thoroughly racist (but effective) campaign against the Democratic nominee, Massachusetts Governor Michael Dukakis. The "Willie Horton" campaign will forever be remembered as Bush's employment of the "Southern Strategy," only in this case, broadcasting it nationwide, not merely to the South.

His campaign manager, Lee Atwater, the architect of Bush's victorious and notoriously rough annihilation of Governor Dukakis, famously apologized on his deathbed for some of what he had done. He died of brain cancer in 1991:

> In 1988, fighting Dukakis, I said that I "would strip the bark off the little bastard" and "make Willie Horton his running mate." I am sorry for both statements: the first for its naked cruelty, the second because it makes me sound racist, which I am not. Mostly I am sorry for the way I thought of other people. Like a good general, I had treated everyone who wasn't with me as against me.[20]

Regardless, shortly before Bush left office, after having been defeated by Democrat Bill Clinton, he issued six pardons pertaining to Iran-Contra. One went to Elliott Abrams, who had been Assistant Secretary of State for Central America (Trump recycled him

---

20 For a broader discussion, see John Brady, "I'm Still Lee Atwater," *The Washington Post* (December 1, 1996), https://www.washingtonpost.com/wp-srv/style/longterm/books/bckgrnd/atwater.htm?noredirect=on (accessed February 18, 2019).

back into government in 2019), one to Reagan's former national security adviser, Robert McFarlane, and a third to former CIA official, Alan Fiers. All had entered guilty pleas. Another CIA official, Clair George, had been found guilty.

The most controversial pardons, however, were to CIA official, Duane ("Dewey") Clarridge, and Caspar Weinberger, who had been Reagan's Secretary of Defense. Their pardons were preemptive; they had not yet come to trial. Inevitably (especially considering that the president issuing them had once been director of the CIA), the more suspicious observers raised questions about whether these pardons were to prevent information detrimental to Bush from being revealed. Whatever the reasons for all this unusual exercise of clemency, Bush declared that the six, whether they had been right or wrong, had been acting out of patriotism.[21]

Republican Efforts to Topple a Democratic President

After the elections of Ronald Reagan and George Bush, Republican conservatives were shocked at the 1992 defeat of Bush for reelection and the victory of the upstart Bill Clinton of Arkansas. They had begun to assume that the presidency would be theirs, that the Senate would usually be theirs, even if it shifted occasionally to the Democrats, and that the House would remain in Democratic hands. After all, they had elected Nixon twice, and Carter's defeat of Nixon's unelected successor, Gerald Ford, could be dismissed as an aberration due to Watergate. All had returned to normal when Republican Reagan defeated Carter and then Mondale, and then his Republican Vice President Bush had defeated Dukakis, the Democrat. Clinton's

---

21 See Bush's statement on the pardons, "Proclamation 6518—Grant of Executive Clemency," *The American Presidency Project,* https://www.presidency.ucsb.edu/documents/proclamation-6518-grant-executive-clemency (accessed February 18, 2019).

Democratic victory came as a profound disruption of what they assumed would be the natural order, and they never accepted his legitimacy.[22] They rationalized his victory as a result of Ross Perot's third-party candidacy, which captured Republican votes.

The difficulty with this assumption is that there is no evidence demonstrating that Bush lost because of Perot. On the contrary, there is considerable reason to assume that Clinton would have won, regardless. Nate Silver, one of the more perceptive election analysts in the country, calls it the "Perot Myth." As his blog *FiveThirtyEight* puts it: Perot's was "one of the most successful third-part bids in U.S. history; Perot won 19 percent of the popular vote. But, no, Perot did not cost Bush the election." *FiveThirtyEight* collaborated with ESPN to produce a film by the title "The Perot Myth," which makes Perot's effect clear.[23]

Rationalizations aside, the Republican Party had been vigorous in its competition with Democrats, but the Clinton presidency saw the Republicans as moving rather quickly to the right, becoming even more cohesive, and setting aside comity in a way that was to lead to a rule or ruin, tribal dedication to not only defeat, but destroy.

Newt Gingrich, who was still a rather obscure representative from Georgia, concluded, among other things, that Republicans could win the House if the public became disgusted with Congress as an institution. Since Democrats had more members of Congress than Republicans did, creating disgust with officehold-

---

22   In fact, the respected party historian, Lewis Gould, makes a plausible case that for numerous reasons, Republicans by and large never accept the legitimacy of Democrats as officeholders, especially as presidents. Their reactions to Clinton and Obama certainly fit his analysis. See his *The Republicans: A History of the Grand Old Party* (New York: Oxford University Press, 2014).

23   FiveThirtyEight, "The Ross Perot Myth: Deep Voodoo, Chicken Feathers, and the 1992 Election," *2016 Election* (October 6, 2016), https://fivethirty eight.com/features/the-ross-perot-myth/ (accessed February 19, 2019).

ers would harm more Democrats than Republicans. Republicans took the majority in both the Senate and the House in January 1995. The newly elected Republicans in the House were convinced, no doubt correctly, that they owed much to Gingrich's efforts, electing him Speaker.

Jacob Weisberg wrote in *Newsweek* that "small herds" of responsible Republicans still "roamed around Washington" in the 1980s. They helped overturn Reagan's veto of a tax bill that would reduce "the fiscal harm of his 1981 tax cut," they helped pass bipartisan immigration reform in 1986, "in 1990 they were spotted with President George H. W. Bush at Andrews Air Force Base conspiring to reduce the deficit." Then, they became all but extinct as the party adopted its "zero-sum view of politics."[24]

It now is conventional wisdom that the Republicans impeached President Clinton because of an improper relationship with a twenty-two-year-old White House intern, Monica Lewinsky. The investigation into the Clintons, however, began with a land deal in Arkansas that had taken place some twenty years previously, in which they lost money. It uncovered no Clinton wrongdoing.

The investigation then expanded until it culminated in a scandal regarding a subject that had always assured lurid headlines in the United States: sex. Regardless, Lewinsky had never come to the attention of the public—or to Congress—until December 17, 1997, when lawyers for Paula Jones sought her testimony in the course of a lawsuit Ms. Jones had filed against Clinton. Even then, Lewinsky's name was far from a household word or the subject of impeachment activity.[25]

24   Jacob Weisberg, "Why Responsible Republicans are Almost Extinct," *Newsweek* (April 15, 2010), https://www.newsweek.com/why-responsible-republicans-are-almost-extinct-70321 (accessed February 19, 2019).

25   See, "A Chronology: Key Moments in the Clinton-Lewinsky Saga," *CNN: All*

Before anyone in the process had ever heard of Lewinsky, a fire-brand Republican/Libertarian from Georgia who was then a US representative, Bob Barr, had filed a resolution of impeachment against Clinton. He filed that resolution on November 5, 1997. Barr's resolution had eighteen co-sponsors, with no mention, of course, of sexual impropriety or of Ms. Lewinsky. It read, in part:

> considerable evidence has been developed from a broad array of credible sources that William Jefferson Clinton, President of the United States, has engaged in a systemic effort to obstruct, undermine, and compromise the legitimate and proper functions and processes of the executive branch.

Thus, Republicans were ripe for any anti-Clinton action and were only too happy to use the sexual scandal as an excuse when it emerged. Years later, after Barr was no longer in the House, he hoped to dust off his earlier resolution against Clinton and find someone to use it for him again, this time against the next Democratic President, Barack Obama.[26]

Although Republicans succeeded in impeaching only Clinton but not Obama, Barr's zealotry demonstrates that some elements in the Republican Party remained consistently willing to do anything to achieve their political ends. Too many times, their party followed those extremist elements' lead. Additionally, as an aside, all those involved—not only Republicans—treated Ms. Lewinsky in a cruel and shocking manner.

Politics, http://www.cnn.com/ALLPOLITICS/1998/resources/lewinsky/timeline/ (accessed March 7, 2019).

26 See David Weigel, "Bob Barr is Ready to Impeach Another President," *Slate* (January 29, 2014), https://slate.com/news-and-politics/2014/01/bob-barr-is-ready-to-impeach-another-president.html (accessed March 7, 2019).

The Sins of Bush II and Cheney, Continued by Trump

The administration of Republican George W. Bush and Vice President Richard Cheney took America into the massively destructive Iraq War. The rationale they presented for doing so was false. Bush and his officials knew it was false, as did their ally British Prime Minister, Tony Blair. This was made clear when a British intelligence worker, Katharine Gun, courageously leaked a top-secret memorandum, violating the UK's Official Secrets Act, at great personal risk.[27] Republicans have become so notorious for disregarding the truth to accomplish their ends that such duplicity should hardly be a surprise.

The venomous tactics directed against their opponents (and disregarding the truth), as might have been expected, did not halt. The Vice President became outraged at Ambassador Joseph Wilson—who had not accepted the administration's word without seeing it for himself, and who had been sent to Niger by the CIA to investigate whether Iraq had purchased nuclear materials in Africa. He discovered that, without question, Iraq had not done so. Nothing in the world is more carefully regulated than the radioactive materials required to create nuclear weapons. Any diversion of such materials to Iraq would have been impossible to hide. Because no official would act on Wilson's findings, he made them public in a *New York Times* op-ed, "What I didn't Find in Africa."[28] He did this at great personal risk, sacrificing his career and incurring the wrath of the Republican administration. This courageous man died on September 27, 2019. He should be remembered, not forgotten, and remembered, furthermore, as a

---

27 See Marcia and Thomas Mitchell, *The Spy Who Tried to Stop a War* (Sausalito, CA: PoliPoint Press, 2008); this was the book that inspired the gripping film "Official Secrets," with Keira Knightly superbly playing Katharine Gun.

28 Joseph C. Wilson, What I Didn't Find in Africa," *New York Times* (July 6, 2003), https://www.nytimes.com/2003/07/06/opinion/what-i-didn-t-find-in-africa.html?auth=login-email&login=email (accessed September

great patriot, whose first concern was his country.

The result of his article was public identification of Valerie Plame, Wilson's wife, as an undercover agent of the CIA. She had had a distinguished career, working abroad gathering intelligence, and was active in the efforts by the West to keep nuclear weapons from Iran. At the time that conservative journalist Robert Novak revealed her identity, she was undercover abroad. She had to be brought home immediately. Disclosure of her identity as a CIA operative not only put her at serious risk of kidnapping and assassination, but also led to the sudden disappearance—almost assuredly the murder—of many of her contacts. Without a doubt, it hampered the efforts with which she had been connected and considerably increased potential threats to the United States. This was of no apparent concern, it seems, to the Republican officials responsible for identifying her to America's enemies, nor to the conservative columnist who happily did their dirty work.[29]

Although a court has not ruled on a definitive identification of the source of the leak of Valerie Plame's identity, Richard Armitage of the State Department has been identified as the immediate source. He apparently said that it was unintentional: a slip. Regardless of who actually relayed the information to Novack, it is clear that it resulted from the anger of government officials at Ambassador Wilson, her husband, for not adhering to official, but untrue, explanations of Bush policy. That anger emanated from sources above the State Department.

One of these angry officials was I. Lewis "Scooter" Libby. Libby was Vice President Cheney's chief of staff and also held the title

29, 2019).

29   See Valerie Plame Wilson, Fair Game: My Life as a Spy, My Betrayal by the White house (New York, Simon and Schuster, 2007); see also Muriel Kane and Dave Edwards, "CBS Confirms Raw Story Scoop: Plame's Job Was to Keep Nukes from Iran" (October 20, 2007) https://www.rawstory.com/news/2007/CBS_confirms_2006_Raw_Story_scoop_1020.html (accessed March 14, 2019).

of assistant to President Bush. A federal court subsequently convicted Libby—*United States v. Libby*—of obstruction of justice,
perjury, and false statements. He was sentenced to jail and fined,
but President Bush commuted his jail sentence so that he did not
have to serve time behind bars. Bush did not commute his fine,
but years later, in a clear demonstration that he was unconcerned
about damage to the US by exposing an undercover CIA agent,
Donald Trump in April of 2018 gave Libby a full pardon.

There can be no doubt that officials in the State Department and
the Vice President's office were willing to sacrifice American interests for political reasons. This was consistent with previous
Republican actions, and in fact was duplicated, even multiplied,
by the Trump administration.

In Spring 2019, Trump, furious at ongoing investigations into his
corruption and the lack of security in his administration, sought
to divert attention from the damning evidence in the Mueller Report by insisting that the report completely exonerated
him—which clearly, it did not. Then, in May, Trump ordered his
new Attorney General, William Barr, to conduct an investigation
into the reasons for having an investigation related to Russian
interference with the 2016 election in the first place. As part of
the "investigation into the investigators," Trump declassified all
material relating to the probe and recklessly gave Barr full authority to release any information to the public at his discretion. One
should remember that Trump openly selected Barr as Attorney
General to serve as his henchman, rather than to pursue justice.
Barr evidently accepted that warped charge. In fact, by his actions, he has made it clear that he is only too ready and willing to
carry out Trump's wishes, regardless.

It is telling that the continued attacks on the Mueller Report
tend to ignore its findings. Without concerning themselves with
the damning results, many firebrand Republicans allege that
there were inadequate reasons for the investigation in the first

place; thus, no matter what the findings are, they are irrelevant. They also charge that the findings result from investigators who were—shudder—Democrats! Even if this were true, it is beside the point. The implicit assumption is that only Republicans can be relied upon to investigate. Democrats should never be permitted to do so. Common sense would direct attention to the essentials: the important thing is the truth of the findings, regardless of how they happened to be generated.

It has now been documented that the genesis of the investigation was related to Russian officials close to Vladimir Putin and that Trump had no concerns about releasing their identities. This dangerous action almost assuredly will inform Putin of the identities of Russian officials who chose to aid the Americans and expose them to torture and murder. This is a treacherous way to treat friends of America, making them "collateral damage" to Trump's frenzied lashing out at critics of his incompetence and his disloyalty to the country that placed him in its presidency.

This willful disregard of American security and of America's helpers abroad draws a direct line from the Office of the Vice President under Cheney to the Trump administration, including the current president himself. It becomes even more obvious when one considers Trump's pardon of Libby, and his profligate use of his pardon power to suit his personal political purposes. He even mused about whether he could pardon himself.

There can now be no doubt that there has been a trend of senior Republican officials continuing the tradition of ignoring American interests when politics suggests that it is to their advantage. The "outing" of an undercover agent should also be a cautionary note to future American agents that they may not be able to count on the government to protect their identities. This sordid practice documents a trend among Republican officials to let nothing stop their efforts to punish those who offend them or those who would weaken their grasp on power, even when it requires them to betray American interests.

Perhaps the most frightening example of this ill-will toward their own country when it is in the interest of Republican power-holders are the consistent actions of Senate majority leader, Mitch McConnell. When President Obama wanted to issue bipartisan statements warning the public and officials of Russian meddling in the elections of 2016, McConnell refused. In fact, he threatened to accuse the Obama administration of politically motivated meddling in the election if Obama issued his own warning. Not only did McConnell block all finance reform in July 2019, he blocked all proposals to shore up the safety of American elections—even the requirement for paper backups for ballots. He said they were partisan bills.

McConnell's excuse is to cite the traditional conservative resistance to federal involvement in elections, keeping them fully under the control of the states. Whatever the reason for state control originally, the idea that fifty separate entities can effectively fend off a cyber-attack upon the entire country is ludicrous.

Antebellum Southerners had similarly banded together to oppose enhancing the power of the national government in general, and on internal improvements in particular. Their true motive was the fear—quite justified, as it turned out—that a more powerful central government someday would pose an existential threat to slavery.

McConnell, similarly, clothes his resistance to involving the federal government in securing elections in constitutional terms. His real motive, as always, has nothing to do with the Constitution, or with American political norms and values. It is to provide security, not for the elections, but instead for conservative Republican dominance (Russian-enhanced or not) in those elections. Common sense should indicate, however, that his weapon is many-sided. His recalcitrance preserves not only the Russian ability to meddle, but also the ability of many other countries around the world to do so, a number of which might have aims considerably at odds with what the majority leader wishes.

There certainly is some partisanship involved, in that any tightening of security of American elections would make it more difficult for the Russians to involve themselves, and their extensive involvement thus far has been on behalf of Republicans. The Mueller Report verified these actions, and Republicans—from candidate Trump's open invitation to the Russians to meddle onward—have demonstrated an eagerness to accept such help.

There is a possibility—one can hope, a reality—that there is so much outraged public resistance to McConnell's blatant disloyalty that he could waver. Although he shrugs off criticism, usually with a chuckle, this time may be different. When an erratic opposition candidate challenged him in the primary, that candidate absurdly accused McConnell of being involved in drug trafficking, calling him "Cocaine Mitch." McConnell was delighted, and for a time allegedly answered his phone, "this is Cocaine Mitch."

When Dana Milbank of the *Washington Post* called him a Russian asset, though, McConnell was furious. Milbank began his piece by saying, "This doesn't mean that he is a spy, but neither is it a flip accusation" and proceeded to point out that Russia has attacked the US, but that "each time we try to raise our defenses to repel the attack, McConnell, the Senate majority leader, blocks us from defending ourselves." Milbank simply meant, as he put it, that McConnell was, "arguably more than any other American, doing Russian President Vladimir Putin's bidding."[30]

McConnell and the Republicans were predictably in high dudgeon. Much was semantic, saying that an "asset" required a per-

---

30   Dana Milbank, "Mitch McConnell is a Russian Asset," *Washington Post* (July 28, 2019).

son to be consciously carrying out Russian orders. Milbank had not said that McConnell was deliberately accepting Russian direction.

A few days later, *The New York Times* reported on the controversy. The front-page article suggested that the political fallout could be causing Republicans to reconsider their support for McConnell's position and that McConnell was fuming. The hashtag trending on Twitter, "#MoscowMitchMcTraitor," did not amuse the majority leader. McConnell said he would not be "intimidated into acting on election interference," and the article indicated that he "will probably not be answering his phone 'Moscow Mitch.'"[31]

It is interesting to note that Republican extremists have long accused Democrats of being "soft on communism" or even of quasi-treasonous activities. The accusations go all the way back to even earlier than the 1950s and Senator Joseph McCarthy. The accusations, however, were completely without foundation. The Republicans now find themselves subject to similar charges, but this time there is fire, as well as smoke.

Apart from Bush-Cheney malevolence, the reckless irrationality that began a war against Iraq (a power that was no threat to the United States and was unconnected to the events of 9/11), and general incompetence (such as led to the near loss of an American jewel, the City of New Orleans, following Katrina, a severe hurricane), that administration also demonstrated focused incompetence. Incompetence, unfortunately, is another trend that leaped from Bush-Cheney to Trump, who demonstrated open malevolence toward Puerto Rico, as well as incompetence, after Hurricane Maria. The island of natural-born American citizens continues to suffer as a result.

Although Bush and his cronies crowed about protecting Ameri-

---

31 Carl Hulse, "Pressure Mounts on Senate Leader to Secure Ballot," *New York Times* (July 31, 2019), 1.

cans against terrorism—accompanied, one should note, by loud applause from their Republican cheering section—common sense demonstrates that Bush-Cheney set the record for their absolute failure to protect the United States. After all, the worst terror attack the US mainland suffered in its history came on Bush's watch—hence, on that of the Republicans.

In view of today's heightened susceptibility to conspiracy speculation, it should astonish no one that extremists on both ends of the political spectrum fantasized, absurdly, that Bush and Cheney were behind the 9/11 attacks. Their list of documented political and civic sins is bad enough; sufficient, certainly, to warrant condemnation—in fact, a chorus of damnation—but to allege that they somehow were complicit in that disaster is not only unpatriotic, it is paranoid and stupid.

On the other hand, Bush, Cheney, and their officials were far from blameless. Clinton and his aides had been deeply concerned about terrorism and had marshaled government resources accordingly. They made the danger clear to their successors in the incoming administration. Most likely being conditioned, however, to disregard anything coming from Democrats as wrong at best, and as probably designed to sabotage Republicans, Bush and his officials paid no attention.

Kurt Eichenwald, a contributing editor at *Vanity Fair* and a former *New York Times* reporter, wrote a devastating op-ed in the *Times*, "The Deafness Before the Storm," a year after the attacks He described a clear warning that came barely a month before 9/11.[32] That alert came on August 6, 2001, in the form of the President's daily briefing. It "was perhaps the most famous presidential briefing in history," and came with, as Eichenwald put it, the most "infamous heading: 'Bin Laden Determined to Strike in U.S.'" It is

---

32 Kurt Eichenwald, "The Deafness Before the Storm," *The New York Times* (September 10, 2010).

possible, certainly, that it might have been impossible to avert the attacks even if the government had been on high alert, as it should have been, based on this and numerous other warnings that Eichenwald cited. We will never know, since there was no such alert.

Warnings were not limited to those that came from the Clinton administration, nor to those from Bush's own intelligence officials in the daily briefings. Richard Clarke had served in the Reagan administration and in that of the first President Bush. George H. W. Bush had appointed him to take a lead in countering terrorism and had appointed him to the National Security Council. President Clinton had kept him on, as had President George W. Bush. For all these presidents, he worked in high-level counterterrorism positions—sometimes the highest. Clarke indicates that he worked diligently to warn Bush and attorney general John Ashcroft of the threat, but they did not take him sufficiently seriously to direct resources to protect the country. Clarke wrote a penetrating memoir describing his efforts and Bush and his officials' reactions or lack thereof.[33]

It is questionable, however, whether the public is aware that the Bush administration ignored many strong warnings. After having been inundated by so much scandal, incompetence, and irrationality from Trump, it makes sense to wonder whether now they would even care.

Republican Efforts to Cripple the Next Democratic President, and to Justify the Worst from the Next Republican

During President Obama's time in office, there were comments from various Republicans, including notably, among others, Senator James Inhofe of Oklahoma and

---

33   Richard A. Clarke, *Against All Enemies: Inside America's War on Terror* (New York: The Free Press, 2004).

Representative Jason Chaffetz of California (neither the most able nor the most influential members) that Obama should be impeached, but nothing came of them. The attacks began even before he took office, emanating from the bombastic Donald Trump alleging the racist nonsense that Obama had been born in Kenya. Senate Republican leader Mitch McConnell openly boasted during Obama's first term that for Republicans, "the single most important thing we want to achieve is for President Obama to be a one-term president."

Glenn Kessler of the *Washington Post* examined the comment and concluded that it actually was benign; Kessler concluded that McConnell was only referring to achieving the Republican agenda.[34] Kessler's conclusion was absurd. The goal of Republicans, Democrats, and all office-holders should be the good of the country, not striving to gain political power. McConnell's subsequent conduct made it clear that he opposed measures simply because Obama favored them, just as Trump has done even more overtly after Obama was out of office.

It was during this time that the allegation emerged among the far right that to be born a citizen, an infant had to have citizen parents. That is nonsense and disregards the clear language of the Fourteenth Amendment that all persons "born in or naturalized in the United States and subject to their jurisdiction" are citizens, but the racist foundation of such an argument is so powerful that its adherents ignore the language of the Constitution and argue that it says what it does not say and that it does not say what it does say.

Even common sense is unnecessary here. The relevant clause of the Fourteenth Amendment is unequivocal. Such absurdity

---

34   Glenn Kessler, "When Did McConnell Say He Wanted to Make Obama 'a One-Term President?'" *The Washington Post* (September 25, 2012), https://www.washingtonpost.com/blogs/fact-checker/post/when-did-mcconnell-say-he-wanted-to-make-obama-a-one-term-president/2012/09/24/79fd5cd8-0696-11e2-afff-d6c7f20a83bf_blog.html?utm_term=.2a1d030ea915 (accessed April 2, 2019).

among the Republican fringe did not die with the Obama presidency. Many of the more irrational are convinced that Obama someday will be declared an alien and are already resuscitating the nonsense for use against presidential hopeful Senator Kamala Harris. They concede generally that she was born in the United States, but argue that she, again despite the clear language of the Fourteenth Amendment, cannot be a "natural born citizen," because her parents at the time of her birth were not citizens. They did not apply it, in 2016, to one of their own, Ted Cruz, who was born in Canada. Go figure.

The Republican approach—or at least the approach of far too many Republicans—is obvious. As soon as Obama took office, they did everything they could to obstruct him throughout both of his terms. They were not interested in discovering those areas in which Republicans and Democrats might agree sufficiently to work together for the good of the people. The people's good was of less concern to them than doing harm to an "enemy" president, especially since he was the first person of African descent to achieve the position.

For example, in March 2015, during the Obama administration, Senator Tom Cotton of Arkansas, an intemperate and reckless firebrand, persuaded forty-six of his Republican colleagues to join him in signing a letter to the Iranian leadership, opposing the nuclear agreement that President Obama—the sitting American president—was negotiating. The letter that the forty-seven Republicans signed lectured the Iranians, purporting to "educate" them regarding the US Constitution, and urging them to ignore the American president. The agreement was concluded, regardless, but as I wrote elsewhere, "dealing directly with a foreign power to undercut the foreign policy of a sitting president is not acceptable, and would have created outrage if done by Democrats against a Republican president."[35]

---

35   Skidmore, *Unworkable Conservatism*, 30.

Similarly, as part of the Republican effort to subvert President Obama and to oppose any agreement with Iran, then Speaker John Boehner "invited the head of government of a foreign nation to address a joint session of Congress in order to undercut President Obama's Iran policy, and deliberately withheld information of the invitation from the president. The foreign leader, Israel's Benyamin Netanyahu, accepted, unwisely, and came to the United States, where he delivered his address." The Reuters news service commented thusly: "House Speaker John Boehner's annoyance with President Barack Obama is turning into a grudge match against the Constitution." His invitation to Netanyahu, said Reuters, "had no precedent in American history. And for a simple reason. It's unconstitutional." Boehner admitted that he deliberately kept the information from the authorities constitutionally responsible for foreign policy, the State Department and the President, because, as he explained to Fox News, he wanted to make sure that "there was no interference."[36]

It now is clear that Republicans are comfortable with foreign meddling in American politics anytime it is to their advantage. They not only freely accept help in American elections from an unfriendly power, Russia, but also actively solicit such assistance anytime it might help them attain victory. They were blasé about Trump's admitted attempts to coerce Ukraine into meddling on his behalf in his re-election campaign, attempts that were so outrageous that as of this writing (late September 2019), they appear to have brought Trump to the brink of a richly deserved impeachment.

Although help from elsewhere abroad, specifically Netanyahu's Israel, has received less publicity (and comes from a power we view as friendly, not antagonistic), common sense would now suggest that receiving help from foreign powers to advance their foreign policy goals and electoral fortunes has become the new

---

36   *Ibid.*, 30–31.

normal for Republicans. Moreover, they do not care at all where that help originates.

As a follow up to all this, when Mr. Trump came to power, he railed against the agreement with Iran that had caused them to put a hold on their nuclear program. Saying the agreement was horrible, he unilaterally withdrew from it, breaking this country's formal promise to another. It did not matter that all authorities agreed the Iranians were abiding by its terms. In June 2019, with the US no longer abiding by the agreement, the Iranians announced that they were proceeding once again to enrich uranium. The Netanyahu government of Israel and the Trump government of the United States asserted that this demonstrated Iran's lack of "good faith," but it was curious that conservatives in both Israel and the US thought that the Iranians had an obligation to honor an agreement that the Trump administration had cancelled.

When Obama's presidency was in its final months, Senator McConnell succeeded in stealing a Supreme Court appointment by refusing to hold hearings on the President's nomination of Judge Merrick Garland to fill the vacancy left by Associate Justice Antonin Scalia's death. That was bad form and violated all tradition and rules of good conduct, but perhaps worse—trending more toward actual treason, in fact—was McConnell's role in suppressing information regarding Russian interference in favor of Donald Trump during the 2016 election.

As former vice president Joe Biden described it, the Obama administration wanted to issue a public warning about the interference and had sought Republican support for a bipartisan statement. Senator McConnell refused, although a letter did go to state election officials warning them to tighten their systems' security. The Obama administration could not send the intended warning without Republican support because they worried they

THE COMMON SENSE MANIFESTO

would then be accused of attempting to sway the election.[37] Undoubtedly, they would have been. Despite its liberal orientation, the conclusion from *Daily Kos* is not partisan: it is pure common sense: "Sen. McConnell," said the article, "needs to explain himself. So far, as usual, he has remained silent." What seemed very clear, however, was that McConnell "became a man so obsessed to blocking Obama and boosting his Republican agenda that he not only dismissed intelligence reports of ongoing hacks of America's election process, but blocked attempts to react to them by threatening that he would himself sabotage the effort."[38]

Ignoring the good of the country and placing party above all should certainly lead to a thorough electoral revolt, sweeping Republicans from office. It isn't as though they really did not believe the intelligence. House Republican leader Kevin McCarthy, for example, speaking to a private gathering of Republicans in June before the 2016 election, said, "there's [*sic*] two people I think Putin pays: Rohrabacher and Trump." (Dana Rohrabacher was a Republican representative from California, notorious for defending Russia in the House.) Then Speaker Paul Ryan intervened and, amid laughter, swore the group to secrecy. When the *Washington Post* reported the comment, McCarthy first denied that it happened; when informed that there was a tape, he said it had been merely a joke.[39] Of course it was.

---

37   See Edward-Isaac Dovere, "Biden: McConnell Stopped Obama from Calling Out Russians," *Politico* (January 23, 2018), https://www.politico.com/story/2018/01/23/mitch-mcconnell-russia-obama-joe-biden-359531 (accessed March 19, 2019).

38   Hunter, "Sen. Mitch McConnell Needs to Answer for his Role Covering up Election Attacks," *Daily Kos* (December 11, 2016), https://www.dailykos.com/stories/2016/12/11/1609840/-Sen-Mitch-McConnell-needs-to-answer-for-his-role-covering-up-Russian-election-attacks? (accessed March 19, 2019).

39   Matt Flegenheimer and Emmarie Huettemann, "Payoffs from Putin to Trump? McCarthy Says No, He Was Just Kidding," *The New York Times* (May 17, 2017), https://www.nytimes.com/2017/05/17/us/politics/kevin-mccarthy-donald-trump-vladimir-putin.html (accessed March 19, 2019).

Republican Conservatism and Right-Wing Extremism

In January 2019, Anthony DiMaggio wrote that it "makes sense to speak of American politics under Trump as falling victim to 'creeping fascism.' This classification is not new," he concedes, having drawn it from numerous "journalistic and historical works." He points out, though, that it is senseless to attempt to divide Trump's politics from "white supremacy and fascist ideology."[40] Unfortunately, says DiMaggio, "few intellectuals, scholars, journalists, or political officials have managed to connect the dots."[41] Trump may not call openly for "an exclusively white ethno-state," but he certainly has employed themes from "far-right ideology and fascism in his rhetoric and policies." Additionally, one would have to be deliberately obtuse not to discern a connection between gun policies of American "conservatives," and firearm violence that, despite the "lone-wolf" rhetoric seeking to minimize the ideological nature involved, reflects fascist terror. "Fascism," says DiMaggio, "has become a permanent feature of American political culture," and with Donald Trump as chief executive, "American fascists now have one of their own in office and can look to him for inspiration."[42]

Sadly, it not only is American fascists who can do so. The terrorist who slaughtered Muslims in New Zealand mosques in March 2019 looked to Trump as a symbol of white supremacy.[43] Moreover, right-wing violence around the world from Norway

40 Anthony DiMaggio, "The Shutdown as Fascist Creep: Profiling Right-Wing Extremism in America," *Counterpunch* (January 4, 2019), 1, https://www.counterpunch.org/2019/01/04/the-shutdown-as-fascist-creep-profiling-right-wing-extremism-in-america/ (accessed March 27, 2019).

41 *Ibid.,* 13.

42 *Ibid.,* 13–14.

43 Thomson Reuters, "White House Dismisses Praise of Trump by New Zealand Shooter," https://www.aol.com/article/news/2019/03/17/white-house-dismisses-praise-of-trump-by-new-zealand-shooter/23694289/ (accessed March 27, 2019).

and New Zealand to the many bombings and shootings in the US are related ideologically. "Attacks By White Extremists Are Growing. So Are Their Connections," was the headline of an article in the *New York Times* that went into detail regarding the relationships among the right-wing perpetuators of mass shootings around the world.[44] Despite efforts by the National Rifle Association and numerous conservatives to convince the public that those responsible for such outrageous tragedies are "lone wolves," extremists acting alone with no connection to others, that is false. The *Times* article quoted Dr. Heidi Beirich, an expert from the Southern Poverty Law Center's Intelligence Project, who pointed out that "it has never been the case that these people didn't think in a global way," they always sought to build and participate in "an international white movement." They think of themselves as internationalists, not as citizens of nation states, not as "Americans or Canadians, very much like the Christchurch killer didn't see himself as Australian; he saw himself as part of a white collective."[45]

In adopting fascist language and symbols, Trump has not imposed an extremist posture upon a hitherto benign political party. He merely seized upon elements that had been there for many years, waiting for a demagogue to employ them. This certainly is not to say that all Republicans have been right-wing extremists, but for some time, an affinity has existed between classic themes of the extreme right (more recently, dubbed the "alt right") and the large element of the Republican Party that calls themselves American conservatives. It is simple to verify this.

Law enforcement officials became aware decades ago that one of the greatest dangers threatening Americans came from white na-

---

44   Weiyi Cai and Simone Landon, "Attacks By White Extremists Are Growing. So Are Their Connections," *The New York Times* (April 3, 2019), https://www.nytimes.com/interactive/2019/04/03/world/white-extremist-terrorism-christchurch.html (accessed April 9, 2019).

45   *Ibid.*

tionalists and various neo-Nazi groups. This is especially true given the widespread availability of even the most lethal firearms to virtually anyone in the United States. Prudently, the Department of Homeland Security began to look carefully at such groups and study them seriously.

When they learned of such studies, however, American conservatives vehemently protested. Studies of threats from the extreme right, they shrieked, were attempts to suppress "conservatives." So powerful was their reaction that the Department of Homeland Security halted all such studies. Republican officeholders recognized immediately that studies of right-wing dangers absolutely required the study of the dangers of American conservatism itself.

Damning examples are easy to find. In 2016, Ron Nixon wrote in the *New York Times* that "Homeland Security Looked Past Antigovernment Movement."[46] In 2012, an article in *Wired* was titled, "DHS Crushed This Analyst For Warning About Far-Right Terror."[47] As far back as 2011, the *Washington Post* reported that "Homeland Security Department Curtails Home-Grown Terror Analysis."[48] All that led to the anguished cry in November of 2018 that "Law Enforcement Failed to See the threat of White Nationalism. Now They Don't Know How to Stop It."[49]

---

46   Ron Nixon, "Homeland Security Looked Past Antigovernmental Movement, Ex-Analyst Says," *New York Times* (January 8, 2016), https://www.aol.com/article/news/2019/03/17/white-house-dismisses-praise-of-trump-by-new-zealand-shooter/23694289/ (accessed March 27, 2019).

47   Spencer Ackerman, "DHS Crushed This Analyst For Warning About Far-Right Terror," *Wired* (August 7, 2012), https://www.wired.com/2012/08/dhs/ (accessed March 27, 2019).

48   R. Jeffrey Smith, "Homeland Security Department Curtails Home-Grown Terror Analysis," *The Washington Post* (June 7, 2011), https://www.washingtonpost.com/politics/homeland-security-department-curtails-home-grown-terror-analysis/2011/06/02/AGQEaDLH_story.html?noredirect=on&utm_term=.abfcf3e66cc2 (accessed March 27, 2019).

49   Janet Reitman "U.S. Law Enforcement Failed to See the Threat of White

The irony of the situation is what it says about the unintended candor of the conservatives who protested in the first place. In a twisted way, there is something humorous here. Despite their generally staid lifestyles as privileged members of the moneyed elite, Republican elected officials argued that targeting dangerous extremists—those who were often living in the woods while stockpiling assault weapons and the like—was to target "conservatives."

They were closer to being accurate than they seemed. The casual observer could have thought of this as paranoid nonsense, but the conservatives knew better. They knew very well that the most violent elements of society were their ideological kindred souls. As the discussion here makes clear, the violent potential of their ideology brought them closer to their alt-right relatives. Such closeness between overt violent extremists and their kindred in the alt-right has brought about a most terrifying result.

The Republicans have energized the most violent and least rational segment of the American electorate. Because the Electoral College disregarded nearly three million more votes for Hillary Clinton, they managed to elect to the presidency of the United States an ignorant and malevolent buffoon. Despite some early criticisms from a few Republicans, he quickly became "their guy," and Republicans lined up to give him their firm support as he slashes, burns, and rips.

At the same time, he also whines and complains that he is being mistreated. He, who obviously knows almost nothing about history or past presidents, says that he is being treated more unfairly than any other president in history.

A widespread uprising has yet to be experienced, but irrational violence is becoming increasingly common. Mass murders are so

---

Nationalism. Now They Don't Know How to Stop It," *The New York Times Magazine* (November 3, 2018), https://www.nytimes.com/2018/11/03/magazine/FBI-charlottesville-white-nationalism-far-right.html (accessed March 27, 2019).

frequent that they seem almost to have become normalized. On August 3, 2019—on a single day—there in fact were two such massacres by white nationalist terrorists, widely separated. The first was in El Paso, Texas, which was followed shortly by the other in Dayton, Ohio. Each caused multiple deaths. Even Trump conceded that "perhaps" more should be done (at least until later, when he backtracked after having spoken with an NRA official). His supporters, and perhaps others as well, say that it is unfair to hold Trump responsible. To anyone familiar with American politics and Trump's rhetoric, common sense should make it impossible to deny a definite connection.

Republican Affection for the Electoral College and their Rejection of Majority Rule, the Key Principle of Democracy[50]

The US Constitution specifies that state legislatures have the authority to select a state's electors, who then with electors from other states choose the President and Vice President. Initially, in most states, the legislature of the state did pick the electors for that state. Gradually, however, states adopted laws permitting their voters to choose their electors. Today, state laws and their own state constitutions provide for the popular vote of electors. In other words, the state's legislature has adopted laws empowering the people to choose the state's presidential and vice-presidential electors.

The US Constitution, however, has not changed in that respect. The state legislature still has the complete authority to determine how that state will choose its electors. All states permit the voters to make the selection, but the state legislature still has the power to change the procedure.

Even if the state's own constitution specifies that there must be

---

50   See also the additional discussion in Chapter VII.

a popular vote, a state legislature can decide to make the choice itself; even if the people already have cast their votes for electors, the state's legislature can interpose its will after the fact, and over-rule the vote of the people. Neither a state law providing for a popular vote, nor a state constitution requiring such a vote can prevent a state legislature from deciding on its own, at any time, to do the deed itself.

A state's own constitution cannot overrule the Constitution of the United States, nor can a state law prevent a legislature from enacting a contrary law. This will no doubt seem shocking to many readers, but this is precisely the power of a state's legislature. The actual language the Court employed is clear; there should be no misunderstanding. The relevant portion of its ruling in *Bush v. Gore* is as follows:

> The individual citizen has no federal constitutional right to vote for electors for the president of the United States unless and until the state legislature chooses a statewide election as the means to implement its power to appoint members of the electoral college.

"Moreover," continued the Court,

> the state legislature's power to select the manner for ap-pointing electors is plenary; it may, if it so chooses, se-lect the electors itself." Once having chosen a method for selecting electors, "the state, of course, after granting the franchise in the special context of Article II, can take back the power to appoint electors.[51]

Thus, regardless of any previous action or agreement, a state leg-islature can at any time in the process decide to act, and choose electors itself.

---

51   See the discussion and quotation in Skidmore, *Unworkable Conservatism*, 163.

One might question whether any group of Americans would act in such an extreme manner that violates the nation's long-established traditions. "If this sounds far-fetched, recall that GOP governments in North Carolina, Michigan, and Wisconsin have all pulled lame-duck attempts to limit the power of incoming Democratic governors, with varying degrees of success." Consider also that in 2000, members of the Florida state legislature were contemplating just such a scenario. However cynical it sounds, they "were effectively saying, 'Hey, if it turns out Gore wins in court, we're not going to accept that, and we're going to assert an authority to appoint electors directly.'" Beyond even that, Trump's former attorney, Michael Cohen, has suggested that Trump might refuse to accept the election results if he were to lose, and speculation has emerged regarding what might then happen.[52]

Bear in mind the repeated assertions from candidate Trump that the 2016 election was "rigged." He said, in widely broadcast words, that he would accept the results *only if he were the winner!* In an expression of chutzpah at the most extreme and also of delusion—Trump continues to condemn the election, implying that only the mighty Trump could have overcome and win even that "rigged" election. Given the workings of the Electoral College, one can agree that the election was indeed "rigged," but definitely in favor of the loser, Trump.

Common Sense Warnings About Donald Trump

Early in Trump's presidency, I wrote elsewhere that he was the most unusual president in the history of the United States—certainly not in a good sense. As I write this in his third year in office, he has changed only in his apparent deterioration. He gropes for words, he misuses words, he makes up

52 See, e.g., Daniel Block, "How Trump Could Lose the Election and Remain President," *Washington Monthly* (April/May/June 2019); quotations in this paragraph from this article.

words, he remains unfamiliar with the details of legislation, he continually reflects a lack of basic knowledge of American history, the presidency, and the processes of American government, he has a dramatically brief attention span, he is preoccupied with trivia to the point of obsession, he seems continually unable to control his impulses, and he uses the power of the highest office in the land to attack defenseless citizens, demonizing them, and urging the scrutiny of officials and others who fail to pay him the homage that he considers his due. As a private citizen and as a television entertainer "he attracted attention, if only as an eccentric." Now, as president of the United States, he has made "absolutely no revision in the direction of gravitas."[53]

All this was entirely consistent with the beginnings of his political efforts as a Republican. Leaping into full-fledged racism, well before he declared his own candidacy for the presidency, he fantasized loudly that Barack Obama had been born in Kenya, and therefore was ineligible to be president. Thus, Trump disregarded all the voluminous and completely persuasive evidence that made it unquestionable that Obama had been born in Hawaii. This reflects his total unconcern with being documented as a liar. He simply does not care; nor do his most fervent supporters.

Trump's supporters delight in angering liberals—or libtards, cucks, or snowflakes—by cheering on the clownish president when he refers to Hillary Clinton (who holds no office) with their chants of "lock her up," as he calls for attacks upon a free press and upon all who disagree—promising all the while to cover any legal expenses that violent actions might bring to them. After all, "there are good people on both sides." Trump's racist tropes exacerbate the fierce racism present at his rallies—and

---

53 See Max J. Skidmore, "The Early Days of the Trump Presidency: Policy Rhetoric, Vision, and Reality," in John Dixon and Max J. Skidmore, *Donald J. Trump's Presidency: International Perspectives* (Washington: Westphalia Press, 2018), 39–67.

supplies the racists more opportunities to anger liberals and all people of good will—when he refers to "the Squad," four, new, US representatives of color (three of whom were born in America), and they respond with "send them back."

Note that Trump's spokesmen try to clean up his "both sides" comment by saying that the "both sides" comment applied only to supporters of Confederate monuments. What that obscured, however, is that those who gathered in Charlottesville to protest the removal of those monuments, the monuments' supporters he was praising, were in fact the violent, neo-Nazi groups whom Trump somehow seemed to believe were the victims.

Trump's practices have already brought vast changes in the way that America's national government operates. Tactics once considered to be extreme had become ordinary years before Trump took office. Holding the government hostage by refusing to raise the debt ceiling had become a routine way for Republicans to seek to achieve victory on legislation. Similarly, Republicans normalized the filibuster in the Senate so that it became a common observation that in order to pass that body, a bill had to received 60 percent of the votes, rather than a simple majority. Trump made clear efforts to adopt government shutdowns as a way to achieve what he wanted but that Congress refused to provide. Following that, he attempted to establish the practice of issuing executive orders as a substitute for obtaining funds that Congress refused to appropriate.

Senate Republican majority leader Mitch McConnell became perhaps the greatest single force in disregarding accepted rules of procedure. Placing holds on nominations became his rule to thwart Democratic appointments so that both parties began to use the tactic. Under his Senate leadership, it became clear that he had led Republicans to become so extreme as never to permit a Democratic president to fill a vacancy on the Supreme Court; as mentioned previously, some of his colleagues even growled that if Hillary Clinton became president, they would never permit her to fill a Court vacancy—possibly holding a seat open for more than eight years. To reiterate, the ultimate in this regard was when Donald Trump sought to create a new presidential tool: closing the government if Congress did not give him whatever legislation he desired. Subsequently, he adopted yet another: when the Democratic House would not provide the level of funding he wanted for his pet obsession, the border wall, he simply declared a national emergency, hoping that would permit him to transfer funds already appropriated for other agencies and programs.

Somewhat related to his other bizarre tactics, and certainly related to his hostility to regulations, is Trump's reluctance to fill government positions. He announced many times that he intended to leave positions unfilled, asserting that they are not necessary. If this keeps agencies from doing their jobs, so much the better. This is consistent with the Republican proclivity to oppose government in general, except for its policing and military functions. Trump finds some governmental functions to be especially odious: those that call him to account, or restrict what he can do. For example, the Federal Election Commission (FEC) is an agency headed by six commissioners. No more than three can belong to the same party, to preserve its bipartisan nature and functioning. Because Trump has left half of the positions unfilled, the commission cannot convene a quorum, and therefore cannot function. That means that it has too few members to take any action against him, regardless of how much it may be warranted.

As DiMaggio has warned, along with many other thoughtful commentators, fascism has already permeated American politics.[54] In fact, it has lodged in one of America's two major political parties. Trump is its representative—with all that implies—occupying the highest political office in America. Those who do not

---

54   As early as 1980, Bertram Gross identified the phenomenon in *Friendly Fascism* (New York: M. Evans and Co), 1980.

recognize this are not paying attention, are willfully ignoring reality, are woefully uninformed, or refuse to face the truth. Never has the danger been greater, at least since the period immediately prior to the Civil War.

Common Sense Warns: Don't Trust Today's Republicans

Until Trump's 2016 campaign, Republican appeals were usually somewhat subtle. With Trump, they became overt. After the Electoral College ignored a sizeable popular-vote victory for Clinton and handed the victory to Trump, "pundits" and many Democratic analysts were highly critical of Clinton's campaign. They deemed her uniquely at fault for failing to appeal to white, working-class voters. She didn't speak of jobs, the critics said—even though studies demonstrated that she stressed jobs far more than Trump had. She showed no respect for white workers, the critics said, even though it was Trump who condemned all who were not materially successful as "losers," while he mocked the disabled, cast scorn upon women, and openly called for violence against his opponents (as well as against reporters).

Clinton's campaign undoubtedly could have been more effective. Nevertheless, in their eagerness to condemn her, critics displayed a startling ignorance of American political history. Roughly a half-century before then, Wallace demonstrated electoral strength among white working-class voters in states such as Wisconsin and Michigan. Republicans had been working themes similar to Trump's ever since; they simply tended to be less overt than Trump. Republicans had also demonized the Clintons for decades. No candidate for a first presidential term had ever been as well prepared as Clinton, nor had any candidate of any political party ever been so vilified by political enemies for so long.

THE COMMON SENSE MANIFESTO

One should remember that Hillary Clinton—the first woman chosen as the candidate by a major political party—won a substantial majority of the popular vote. It is only America's complex and irrational Electoral College, boosted by clever foreign meddling, that denied her victory and gave it instead to the least well-prepared candidate in American history. This is not to say that Trump's loss of the popular vote makes his presidency illegitimate. One could plausibly make that argument regarding voter suppression and Russian interference, but not because Trump substantially lost the popular vote; the Founders clearly designated the Electoral College to make the choice, not the voters. Whether such a system in modern, more democratic, times makes "common sense" should perhaps now be a topic that demands consideration.

Still, common sense should lead to massive, scornful, protest from the public when they hear that "the people chose President Trump." Senator McConnell and other Republicans chortle that "the people spoke" on behalf of their policies. It should be obvious to all that "the people" did no such thing.

Today, a long chain of Republican policies has led guns in every location with mass shootings sadly commonplace, even though the people favor gun control. We still have the world's most expensive healthcare, large numbers of people without health coverage, relatively poor outcomes from our costly healthcare, and yet there is strong public desire for good healthcare for all and preference for reform. Today, nearly everyone would recognize that corporations are not "people" and that spending money is not the same thing as free speech, yet Republican policies have led the courts to declare otherwise. Today, money floods into politics, corrupting the process, despite massive public disapproval, and most people recognize how wrong it is for minority interests to overpower majority concerns, yet these things persist. Today, all well-thinking people agree that it is wrong to seize infants and toddlers from their parents' arms, and yet this institutionalized cruelty remains government policy.

Keep in mind, also, that the Roberts decision in *NFIB* v. *Sebelius* that to the country's relief upheld the Affordable Care Act, or Obamacare, also contained two extraordinarily pernicious rulings. First, the mandate to states to expand Medicaid was ruled to be unconstitutional. Thus, some Republican states continue to lose benefits for their citizens and much-needed funds to their states simply because of an ideological commitment to reject programs that President Obama supported. This was an immediate blow to the equal treatment of American citizens. The other, more long-term threat was a stealth decision that potentially imperials all social legislation since the New Deal. Roberts undercut reliance upon the Constitution's commerce clause as the basis for national legislation, and that clause is the basis for most relevant post-New Deal laws.

These complaints could go on and on. The point is that our political system, dominated by conservative Republican policies and practices, has repudiated common sense. That, regrettably, is characteristic of conservative policies in general, however enthusiastically Republicans embrace them.

As an illustration of Republican success in normalizing the outrageous, consider an article in October, 2019, in the *New York Times*. If ever there were an action that any person, however politically naïve, should consider a serious danger to the country, it would be foreign meddling in politics and policies and in the country's elections. Trump, however, is so persuasive to the unperceptive and the slavish, and so dominant in the cultish atmosphere that he has created in the modern Republican Party, that America's newspaper of record found it necessary to explain why it is important not to have elections in the United States corrupted by foreign influence. Readers had apparently asked, in sufficient numbers, why we should be concerned, and the *Times* had to explain it to them.[55] The *Times* is to be complimented for its public service, in this, but the state of civic awareness must have been far more damaged by Trump bombast and Republican acquiescence than anyone could have imagined—especially considering that readers of the *Times* are no doubt more politically literate than the average citizen. America! Please restore your common sense!

Keep this record of the Republican Party in mind whenever considering any reform that would rely upon Republican good faith to function. Good faith no longer exists among Republican officeholders, who blindly follow an outrageous leader, flout the rules, disregard ethics, and do not hesitate to break their word or even to countenance unconstitutional, possibly treasonous, acts to seize or maintain power.

---

55   Katie Rogers, "'Get Over It'? Why Political Influence in Foreign Policy Matters: Readers Have Asked The New York Times Why Asking Another Nation for Help Ahead of an Election is Such a Serious Issue; Here Are Some Answers" *The New York Times,* (21 October 2019); https://www.nytimes.com/2019/10/21/us/politics/trump-inquiry-foreign-meddling.html; (accessed 25 October 2019).

CHAPTER II

Common Sense in Voting; Does the Majority Rule?

Common Sense in Casting Votes

C ommon sense would suggest that we act in ways that have a chance of achieving what we hope to achieve. If you were to cast a vote for president, for example, it is likely that you would be hoping to contribute the best outcome. Our political system at the state and national levels is based solidly upon a two-party structure, with single-member districts. Voters have an obligation to do whatever they can to help the better of the two candidates win—or, the other side of the coin, to do what they can to keep the other one out of office. Being "tired of voting for the least worst," then, is simply a slogan; in this instance, a dangerous one, and it does not improve politics to operate on slogans.

This may not be ideal. Of course it might be better if it were different. It is certainly desirable to work to change the system, but that is irrelevant to the casting of a vote in a given election.

System changing is as long-term effort and does not take place in the course of indicating a preference for a candidate. If one wishes to work for change, all well and good. In casting a vote however—certainly at the national level, and especially for president—there is only one valid consideration: determine which two candidates are the only ones who have a chance of winning, and then, of those two, determine which one would be better for the country, its people, and ultimately, the world.

When casting a vote for president, for example, forget which one is the more likeable. According to most accounts, George W.

Bush was very likeable, but that hardly translated into a beneficial presidency. Casting a vote based on whether one likes or dislikes a candidate is pure self-indulgence. Equally irrational is the frequent assertion that if a candidate doesn't behave in a certain way, that candidate or that party doesn't "deserve" to win. If a candidate does, or does not, concentrate a campaign on, say, teachers, blue-collar workers, billionaires, or some other group—or if the campaign pays too little or too much attention to a given state then that party or candidate does, or does not, "deserve" to win. Nonsense.

The presidency is the prime elected position in the American system. Achieving it confers the country's greatest honor on the victor (or at least it customarily has been assumed to confer such honor). No one, though, should become president because he or she is deemed to "deserve it." The honor is so great that no person sufficiently deserves to be so entitled. Similarly, no candidate or party should be condemned as "undeserving" because of the flaws of a campaign or other such trivia. The only candidate or party who "deserves" defeat is the one whose presidency would be less beneficial to the country than that of the opposition, not the one failing to meet some assumed standard.

In 2000, the mantra (no doubt cleverly, and stealthily, spread by the Republicans) was: George W. Bush is the "candidate I'd most like to have a beer with." Setting aside the fact that Bush doesn't drink, however counter-intuitive it may seem, whether one liked or disliked him should have been recognized as irrelevant. There was only valid consideration, and that was: would Bush be a better president than Gore?

The chances are overwhelming that, had Gore been elected, we would not, in response to 9-11, have invaded Iraq, a country that had absolutely nothing to do with the terrorist attacks. There even is a plausible argument that a Gore administration might have heeded the multiple warnings that there was to be an attack in the United States, and therefore possibly would have headed off 9-11 entirely.

In any event, there almost without a doubt would have been no Iraq War. That conclusion does not require the paranoid, and absurd, notion that Bush and Cheney were behind the 9-11 attacks. They were not. Bush was a reckless president, and certainly did not insist on solid intelligence before launching an especially tragic war. That war, by itself, demonstrated that there were no weapons of mass destruction and made it plain that the rationale the Bush administration offered was bogus.

Bush in fact was aware that his rationale was false, as was his ally British Prime Minister Tony Blair. This was made clear when Katharine Gun, a British intelligence worker, risked her career and her freedom by leaking a top-secret memorandum, violating the UK's Official Secrets Act.[1] This was simply another in a long chain of duplicity by Republican administrations. Nevertheless, Bush was no traitor, and was certainly not complicit with the attackers.

The war was an enormous disaster for the United States, the world, and especially the people of Iraq. Yes, Saddam Hussein was a tyrant, and personally "deserved" to be overthrown. No, that was not the rationale for the war. No, overthrowing him was not worth that brutal war. Regardless of what Hussein did or did not "deserve" on a personal basis, it is difficult to make the case that the people and the culture of Iraq are better now than they would have been had he continued in power, or that America and the world are better off.

Hussein suppressed religious fanaticism, one of the greatest destabilizing factors in the world today. Had Hussein remained in power, the status of women in Iraq would likely not have deteriorated as it has done. There almost assuredly would have been

---

1   See Chapter I, "The Sins of Bush II and Cheney," above, which refers to Gun and cites Marcia and Thomas Mitchell, *The Spy Who Tried to Stop a War*.

no ISIS. The rest of the world would likely have been far more favorably disposed toward the United States and its goals than they now are, and in all probability the vast turmoil that has characterized the Middle East would not have become so extreme.

Perhaps some people voted for Bush because they thought he would be a more pleasant drinking companion than Gore. If so, those hypothetical brews were disastrous beers.

In 2016, once the parties had nominated their candidates, there were only two who had any chance at all of winning: the Democrat Hillary Clinton and the Republican Donald Trump. That is the way the system works. Third parties receive praise in some quarters for "giving voters more choices," or for enabling voters "not to be captives of the two-party system." The praise is misplaced. Again, those are slogans with no substance.

One can argue that third parties have a legitimate place in the system, in that they offer a mechanism for introducing ideas into the political discussion that are too far out of the mainstream to be considered. Those ideas can be discussed and then discarded, or perhaps gain sufficient acceptance that they then can be incorporated into the mainstream and become part of the program of a major party.

That argument may be plausible for some races, but not at the presidential level; particularly not when there is a wide variance in the stances, character, or competence of the two candidates. When elections are close, there is no excuse for throwing a vote away. Most of the time, to be sure, third parties are too weak to have an effect. If they have an effect, however, it is almost assuredly going to be pernicious—as it definitely was in Florida in 2000. There and then, the presence of Ralph Nader on the ballot brought the country (and the world) the administration of Bush and Cheney, who proceeded to adopt the most reckless and dangerous policies up to that date in modern times.

In 2016, astonishingly, the third-party effect was far worse. The presence of Jill Stein on the ballot in Michigan, Wisconsin, and Pennsylvania arguably brought a bumbling, egomaniacal, amateur to power, someone who makes the second Bush look like a statesman. As is made clear in the following chapter, in every one of those states, Stein received considerably more votes than the slight difference between Hillary Clinton and Donald Trump. That made the Electoral College difference that threw the election to the least "deserving" candidate in every sense.

That effect, in fact, was explicitly encouraged by Russian interference, interference that now is amply documented by all of America's intelligence agencies and the Mueller Report. In an unprecedented—and certainly unanticipated move, the Trump campaign and the candidate welcomed that interference. Not only that, it had been openly and boastfully solicited by that candidate; this would have been immediately blasted as treasonous had a Democratic candidate ever been so foolish as to have done it. It surely was also effective. In a matter of a few hours at most, that interference began.

There are far better and less pernicious ways to introduce new ideas into American politics. Bernie Sanders in 2016 acted appropriately to introduce ideas into the system without causing voters to cast futile or dangerous votes: he worked within one of the two established parties, the Democratic Party. He did not follow the path trod by Ralph Nader, Gary Johnson, and Jill Stein, which would have contributed to disastrous electoral results.

Worse than merely throwing votes away, then, let it be reiterated: at the national level, third parties are spoilers. There can be no doubt that Ralph Nader's candidacy in 2000, especially in Florida, made possible the disastrous presidency of George W. Bush. Similarly, a quick look at the results in 2016 will reveal that the fringe candidacy of Jill Stein in the three narrow wins for Trump in the upper Midwest—Michigan, Wisconsin, and Pennsylvania—almost assuredly threw the election to Trump.

Additionally, the role that Russia played in the Trump victory now is amply documented, even though some commentators—either through naiveté or duplicity—continue to dismiss it by saying that there is no proof that Russia affected the counting of votes. Of course, though, that is not the issue. Russian influence was designed to influence the *casting* of votes, not the counting. That influence used massive social media accounts to boost the Trump candidacy, damage Hillary Clinton's candidacy, and work to divert support to the fringe candidacy of Jill Stein. As an NBC report put it, "Building support for Stein was one of a 'roster of themes' the Moscow-sanctioned internet trolls turned to repeatedly in their effort to disrupt the election." Analyses found huge numbers of tweets urging votes for Stein. An expert on Russia, Andrew Weiss, noted Russia's efforts on Stein's behalf and said that promoting "her candidacy is critical to our understanding of Russian interference in the 2016 election."[2] It is beyond comprehension that Stein voters recognized that they were contributing to Trump's election, but they were.

Nader and Stein, whatever their intentions, severely damaged the candidacies of Gore and Clinton. They deserve to be condemned for their contributions to the election of the brash younger Bush, and even worse, the election of Donald Trump, who makes even Bush look good by contrast.

Those who may be inclined to forgive Stein or to believe that she acted purely from praiseworthy motives have to overlook her arrogant self-righteousness and should also consider that she eager-

---

2   See Robert Windrem, "Russians Launched Pro-Jill Stein Social Media Blitz to Help Trump Win Election, Reports Say," *NBC News* (December 22, 2018), https://www.nbcnews.com/politics/national-security/russians-launched-pro-jill-stein-social-media-blitz-help-trump-n951166 (accessed June 30, 2019).

ly appeared on Russia's English-language propaganda channel, RT. She also just as eagerly accepted Putin's hospitality. It should be difficult to excuse the infamous, and widely-published, pictorial evidence of Putin's stroking of her ego, showing her at the same table with the Russian dictator (and, incidentally, also with the convicted former national security aide to Trump, Lt. Gen. Michael Flynn).[3] Stein's excuse is that she participated in Putin's conference to criticize him. That, to put it mildly, hardly seems possible—let alone plausible. There is no evidence that she criticized him, and Putin is not known to extend his hospitality to those who condemn his policies.

In the 2016 election, some voters said, "I just don't like Hillary." Others said, "I don't like either candidate. I'm tired of voting for the least worst. I want to send a message." Those words should be recognized as cringe-worthy and directly reflect propaganda both from the Republican Party and Russian trolls. Those voters were irresponsible. "Sending a message" may be appropriate at times, but national elections are not one of those times. Voting for the least worst is far better than voting for the worst—as now should be clear to any informed person capable of rational thought. "Likes" should not be a consideration, nor should "messages" be. To repeat, the only valid consideration should be: what, or who, will be better?

One other consideration did enter into the equation. There were those who argued that the "system" is so corrupt that it is necessary to elect a destroyer. Someone from outside, who can

---

3   For the photo in question, as well as a huge number of others, some innocuous and others that seem damning, see https://www.google.com/search?q=Picture+of+Jill+Stein+with+Putin&tbm=isch&source=iu&ictx=1&fir=3AdzpmWpK9bg3M%253A%252CTsnUMOuE17an yM%252C_&vet=1&usg=AI4_-kT0zeYXG8XbLcNmbOGkA7M 1tyFuXQ&sa=X&ved=2ahUKEwiRpZe4opbjAhVSLs0KHW0cD QUQ9QEwAHoECAcQBA#imgrc=3AdzpmWpK9bg3M (accessed July 2, 2019).

fearlessly "shake things up" and bring down the existing arrange-
ments so that something better emerges. This, too, was a meme
spread by Trump supporters, yet any student of history should be
aware that chaos breeds only chaos; destruction does not bring
better lives. The reckless irresponsibility of those who sincerely
believed that an unqualified, boastful narcissist, who understood
little and cared less, would be better for people's lives can hardly
be overstated.

One can imagine a well-meaning German in 1932 saying that
Hitler is so bad that if he becomes chancellor, it will bring all
good people to defeat him and make things better (actually I
suspect that there were well-meaning people who did say that).
What happened to such well-meaning Germans does not have to
be imagined. Naomi Klein has made this point crystal clear in her
studies of such idiocies.[4]

Common Sense, Majority Suppression,
and Discarding the Rules

Both parties have drawn district boundaries to benefit
their candidates. In recent times, though, the practice has
become so sophisticated that it is possible for a party that
has a narrow majority in the state, or even a minority of the state's
votes, to have complete dominance of a legislature or to elect
most of a state's representatives in the US House. North Carolina
presents an extreme case. Although Republicans won just barely
over 50% of the popular vote, because of the way in which they
had created districts, they succeeded in sending ten Republicans
to Washington, while Democrats elected only three. Two North
Carolina Republican leaders in an op-ed piece in *The Atlantic*
even argued that they should not be "demonized" for doing this.
They maintained that it was appropriate.

---

4   See especially Naomi Klein, *The Shock Doctrine: The Rise of Disaster Capital-
     ism* (Picador [Henry Holt], 2008).

Demonstrating the quip that the devil can quote scripture for his own purposes, they noted that Court decisions approved creating districts to ensure representation for racial minorities. This, they argued, gave them full legal right to create districts designed deliberately to disadvantage Democrats. They interpreted the language of the Voting Rights Act even to require this. Therefore, they should be judged, they thought, on the full "backstory," which they obviously believed made it all right. They should not be judged merely on their admission that they did "draw the maps to give a partisan advantage to 10 Republicans and three Democrats, because I do not believe that it is possible to draw a map with two Democrats and 11 Republicans."[5]

This illustrates the mindset among modern Republicans: they have the right to rule, regardless of the wishes of the voters. Because they have come to believe their own propaganda that Democrats cannot legitimately hold office, they can justify any action to hold on to power—regardless of votes, the law, or common sense.

The United States Supreme Court, on June 27, 2019, despite the extreme situation, declined to permit the federal judiciary to become involved. The five conservative justices joined to issue the majority opinion in *Rucho v. Common Cause*, by Chief Justice John Roberts. The Roberts opinion removed any federal restraint on partisan gerrymandering. This was especially alarming to Democrats, because as a result of the Republican landslide of 2010, they control more states than Democrats do. Fortunately, however, the Supreme Court of the State of North Carolina saw through the sophistry and struck down the gerrymander, requiring a speedy redistricting before the 2020 elections.

---

5   Ralph Hise and David Lewis, "We Drew Congressional Maps for Partisan Advantage. That Was the Point," *The Atlantic* (March 25, 2019), https://www.theatlantic.com/ideas/archive/2019/03/ralph-hise-and-david-lewis-nc-gerrymandering/585619/ (accessed August 9, 2019).

The Roberts ruling was reminiscent of President James Buchanan's position on secession. Buchanan—demonstrating why he was among the weakest and most unsatisfactory of presidents—on December 3, 1860, sent a message to Congress arguing that secession was illegal, but that the president had no power to affect it. Similarly, Roberts admitted in his opinion, that "excessive partisanship in districting leads to results that reasonably seem unjust." Nevertheless, he argued, the federal judiciary is powerless to deal with the issue. No "One Man One Vote" for this Court, which, sadly, has come a long way from *Baker v. Carr* (1962) and *Reynolds v. Sims* (1964).

This ruling is only the latest in a series of actions from the Court that reflect the modern Republican disdain for majorities and eager willingness to adopt "results that reasonably seem unjust"—or, one may say, that are flagrantly corrosive to democracy's functioning. To put it even more bluntly, regardless of rationalizations, the Court has become the action arm of Republican conservative extremists (who succeeded in stealing a Court seat and have threatened never to confirm a Democratic appointee if they can prevent it) and has, ruling by ruling, diminished the power of the people over their own government. Elite political minorities now have received authority from the Court to entrench themselves in a stranglehold over majorities throughout the country.

In 2000, there was *Bush v. Gore* that departed from Court practice and ruled on a state matter, overruling the state's own court. The decision halted the recounting of votes and handed the election to the Republican, George W. Bush. The decision was 5 to 4.

On January 21, 2010, the Court handed down its opinion in *Citizens United v. Federal Election Commission*. Accepting the obviously class-based and anti-democratic assertion that political spending is a form of free speech (rich people, then, by this definition can speak far more than others) and coupling it with the equally dangerous—and no less ludicrous—idea that corporations have the free-speech rights of "persons," the Court provided protection to the "rights" of corporations to support or oppose political candidates, so long as they do not give money directly to those candidates. In other words, corporations can legally influence elections in much the same way the Russians illegally influenced American elections in 2016. The decision was 5 to 4.

In 2013, the Court struck down, in *Shelby County v. Holder*, a key provision of the 1965 Voting Rights Act, in effect gutting the law. The decision, of course, was 5 to 4 and again was a Roberts decision on behalf of the Court's conservative majority, at odds with majority rule. Section 5 Act required states (or, in the case of some states, political subdivisions), primarily in the south, with stark histories of racial discrimination and suppression of votes by their minority citizens to obtain federal approval for any changes in voting requirements.

The 2019 *Rucho* decision was merely the most recent decision demonstrating for anyone with common sense to see that the Court had shamelessly become partisan; it now is the activist wing of a political party. Unfortunately, that party is the Republican Party: the party that in its current incarnation seeks to suppress the power of the people's votes.

This means that the federal judiciary has become sufficiently corrupted that it must be reformed. Reformation will require not merely a Democratic victory in 2020, but a huge Democratic wave that will sweep Republicans from office so decisively that they may be destroyed as a force in American politics. Whether or not this is likely, and however extreme it sounds, it is necessary for it to happen if America is to survive as a democratic republic.

CHAPTER III

Two Inside Views of a Bizarre Election, with Forthright Comments from the Outside[1]

After only two hours of sleep, I awoke early on the morning of December 9, 2016. The Electoral College a few hours before had rejected the popular-vote winner, who would have been (and who had been widely anticipated to be) the first female president. She also had been the most thoroughly prepared candidate for a first presidential term in America's history. The chosen winner, Donald J. Trump, was by far the least well-qualified candidate ever. Since that time, the dangers of putting in office one so ill-qualified with regard to preparation, ability, character, and competence has become increasingly obvious—if not to the most fervent members of his "base."

The defeated candidate, Hillary Rodham Clinton, had many distinctions. She had been first lady (and the only one ever subsequently to serve in high office), a US senator, and the US Secretary of State. She also had an additional, and unwanted, distinction. For more than a quarter century, she had been the target of a continuous slander campaign, making her arguably the most vilified political figure ever to run for election to any position—certainly, for president. The truth was irrelevant. No slur, regardless of how outrageous, was too absurd for her opponents to fling at her, or for many of her less perceptive opponents to believe (how could any sentient being, for example, even though spread by high Trump associates, take seriously the charge that she was a

---

1   An earlier version of this chapter appeared as an article, "Two Inside Views of a Most Bizarre Election—With a Forthright Analysis from Outside," *Poverty and Public Policy* 10, no. 1 (March 2018).

pedophile, who worked a ring of child abuse headquartered in a pizza shop in Washington, DC?).

The slurs worked. It was common to hear voters say that, whatever Trump's transgressions and however dangerous he might be, it was impossible to vote for Clinton, "because of all those scandals"—without being able to name one—or because, "I just don't like her." Even if she had been the perfect candidate, it would have been almost impossible for a marginally informed voter to penetrate the propaganda barriers sufficiently to recognize it.

I checked my phone and saw a message asking me to appear on a radio show at 10:00 that morning to discuss the bizarre election. Irritably, I turned over to go back to sleep, hoping to ignore the whole thing and to be able for a few hours to forget that tragic result. Guilt immediately intervened. I made myself get up and get ready, thinking I had a civic duty to accept, which I did.

The best and most thorough television coverage of the Trump campaign had come from Katy Tur of NBC News and MSBC. In addition to providing consistently superb reporting in general, she adapted with linguistic flair, and with considerable courage, to whatever she encountered—including public abuse from the candidate himself that at times put her in genuine physical danger.

After the election, and with amazing speed, she produced her impressive campaign memoir, *Unbelievable*, in which she deftly captured in full "the craziest campaign in American history."[2] At the same time, she succeeded in introducing herself seamlessly to her readers. She had been the child of news professionals, she determined early to become one herself, and she decided not only to report, but also to go into depth to inform the public.

---

2   Katy Tur, *Unbelievable: My Front Row Seat to the Craziest Campaign in American History* (New York: Harper Collins, 2017).

In this instance, she was compelled to act quickly, and give the public inside information about what had just happened.

The result should be destined to become a classic of American electoral politics. Despite dealing with only one side of the race, it ranks alongside Theodore White's *Making of the President* series of the campaigns of 1960, 1964, 1968, and 1972—although Tur's work is more in the spirit of Tim Crouse's great romp through the Nixon and McGovern campaigns of 1972, *The Boys on the Bus*.

She opened *Unbelievable* brilliantly, especially considering the electoral catastrophe. At risk of offending literary purists (and of course recognizing that Tur has made no pretense of producing a novel), I would place her beginning alongside Melville's "Call me Ishmael," but with the additional punch of Sinclair Lewis's, "Elmer Gantry was drunk." With reference to Election Day at 10:59 pm, her initial words, capturing much of the country's sentiment, were: "I'm about to throw up."

She had called it, and had anticipated the outcome, but had to come to grips with the decision of "an Electoral College of American voters. They've decided that this menacing, indecent, post-truth landscape is where they want to live for the next four years" (4).

She gets it, she said. You can lose a job for telling a joke, your town is boarded up, you reach someone in India when you call for technical support, bills go up but paychecks do not, and it seems that no one cares. What she does not get, she says, is "little old ladies in powder-pink MAKE AMERICA GREAT AGAIN hats calling me a liar. I don't get men in HILLARY SUCKS— BUT NOT LIKE MONICA, T-shirts. I don't get why protesting a broken political system also means you need to protest the very notion of objective truth" (5). She also does not get why Trump conducted such a war on the media that networks (not including Fox News) had come to require security details.

Katy Tur had lived in New York, London, and Paris on various assignments for the network that abruptly called her back to New York. Perhaps because she at the network and Trump as a candidate both were low on their respective totem poles, she became the reporter covering the Trump campaign.

When she first interviewed him, she noted that some people "have a presence that's bigger than their physical size, an ability to ripple the air." Trump was one of those, "and he's orange. There's no other way to describe him. He's the color of orange marmalade ..." (24). The first thing he asked was didn't she want a picture? She did not—she was a reporter in a news interview, not a fan—but she agreed in order not to offend him. He told her he had been to Iowa and New Hampshire many times and that people loved him. He said he had had "tremendous success," and no one else had received so many standing ovations. She had difficulty making sense out of his "word salad," but the interview continued for twenty-nine minutes (25-27). Then they shook hands—amicably, she thought—when suddenly he yelled that she would have to air the interview in full, because he knew how the network would edit to distort. If you do not, he told her, we have cameras here of our own and will release the entire interview. She did not understand the sudden hostility (27).

The network decided to air the interview in full, and despite her trepidations, her status as a newscaster took a sudden jump. She had arrived among the top rank of American newscasters (27-36).

Much of the book is impressionistic, almost stream-of-consciousness, but with embedded gems. "Some politicians have a gift for language. Trump is not one of those politicians. His sentences call to mind an aerial shot of a burning, derailed freight train. The syntax is mangled. The grammar is gone." She quotes from an article in *Politico* that "Trump isn't a simpleton, he just talks like one" (79).

As an aside here, it is startling to compare Trump's language today with clips on various television shows from twenty years or so past. In those days, although giving no evidence of deep thought, Trump spoke in full sentences that were coherent and normal. Now, he has changed. His vocabulary has shrunk remarkably. He seems to grope (no pun intended) for words, and he repeats himself constantly. Tur says that "every fourth word seems to be *very, great, beautiful,* or *tremendous*. He loves the word *winning.*" His specialty seems to be insults, but Tur notes that "his insults are even simpler. Our leaders are 'dumb,' 'stupid,' or 'weak.' Our deals are 'terrible.' His critics are 'losers' and 'haters.' The press is 'scum.' Women he doesn't find attractive are 'disgusting.'" She calls him the opposite of Obama, whose rhetoric "soars." Obama, she says, "is controlled and calculating," but "Trump is persistent and loud." Nevertheless, she says, "it works for him." No doubt it does, but it also suggests that there could be something seriously amiss.

Regardless, there is no doubt that Tur is correct when she says that, for Trump, everything good is "we," while if it's bad, it's "they." His supporters identify with him, despite his great wealth. "He talks just like us," they say. "He's the rich guy they would be if they were rich" (80).

Unfortunately for them, they won't be. Yet, inspired by Trump from whom they get nothing beyond rhetoric, they can dream.

Trump's rallies were something rarely seen in America and never before with a national audience. Violence seethed just below the surface, and sometimes with Trump's verbal support it broke through. Seeing her among the reporters, he said, "She's back there, little Katy." He not only informed the public about his Muslim ban, but also about his view of Katy Tur: "Third-rate reporter, remember that. Third rate. Third rate" (81). The crowd expressed its love for Trump as it became "a large animal, angry and unchained" (82). MSNBC had cleared her and wanted her and her crew to leave as quickly as they could. She understood why when a Trump staffer told her "These guys are going to walk you out." They were two Secret Service agents, concerned that she needed protection. Her mother called and told her she needed security. "Then it hits me. I'm a target" (83-84).

The media picture today is far different, she notes, from that during the days of FDR. During his presidency, monopolies or near monopolies controlled the airways. They were in a position to punish candidates, but with today's multiplicity of sources, such monopolies no longer exist. No single outlet today can rival the power or stature of the earlier media giants, but that has not softened Trump's reactions. He took every perceived slight personally, and responded with venom. He wanted Tur to apologize for her "dishonest" reporting. Her reporting was, she said, accurate, and "journalists do not apologize for accurate reporting." She said that tweeting that she should be fired, calling her a liar "in front of millions of people on national television, and receiving death threats from his followers shortly thereafter was not enough punishment. He wants penance. He wants groveling" (90-91). He appears to equate a mild response, or no response at all, with weakness, and "Trump cannot bear looking weak" (93). She takes issue with journalists who argue that the crowds really were not with Trump. "I can tell you," she says in response to his calls for violence, "the crowd loves it." In fact, "the scariest thing about being at a Trump rally is that you don't know who believes it and who doesn't" (96).

Television of course is widely recognized as a major force in American politics, but Tur points to the influence of cable news as a phenomenon that intensifies the overall influence of television. Both network news and cable news, she says, "breed intimacy, because both come right into your home," but network news comes only at prescribed times, and being confined to "particular windows," engenders "a lot less audience loyalty than you might imagine." For cable, on the other hand, that is not the case. "Cable is on all day. Viewers know you like they know their own family. When you're doing live shots every hour, your personality bleeds through. There is nowhere to hide ..." (200). They develop likes and dislikes. "Imagine how you'd feel," she says, if every night and all day this little blond-haired girl was shining a critical light on your beloved figure. Who is she to question his plans? Double-check his statements? Follow up on his promises? You would hate me. And people do." Trump "crashed through the guardrails of traditional politics," and all has changed (201-202).

Tur may have risen dramatically through the ranks, but she still faced what too many women still face in our society: being relegated to the sidelines when it matters. In her case, this was during the presidential debates. Whatever happened regarding debate coverage, though, the 2016 debates mattered little. Clinton clearly —overwhelmingly, in fact—was superior in knowledge and seriousness, but just as clearly that had little effect on the outcome. What has become lost in all this, Tur makes plain: sound reporting is important. Otherwise, the public receives information only from a candidate. However much there may be complaints about reporters filtering news, "no American voter accepts one-sided accounts in their personal life. We wouldn't trust our teenager's perspective on a fender-bender. We wouldn't trust a single co-worker's description of a crucial meeting. We wouldn't even wholly trust our best friend's version of a nasty breakup. We look for holes in the story" (233-234). We constantly seek additional information in order to develop a well-rounded view. "We should demand the same in politics. And yet so often we do not" (234). This is so obvious as to be painful, but nonetheless often goes unnoticed.

Consider, for example, the deterioration of public discourse as it pertains to the presidential candidacy of Donald Trump. During no other presidential race have such slogans proliferated as were almost ubiquitous on t-shirts and elsewhere. "Trump that Bitch," "KFC Hillary Special: 2 fat thighs, 2 small breasts, left wing," and others. Tur notes that these were not even the worst.

One of the virtues of America's political system, one that owes much to the peaceful change of administrations when John Adams in 1801 left quietly after his defeat by a political enemy, Thomas Jefferson, is that losers do not face prosecution or violence, and can regroup, should they wish, in hope of future victory. Violating this principle were bleats of "jail her," "off with her head," and the like, and the slogan on the shirt of a man in Melbourne, Florida, who "posed for pictures in front of the press pen" in a shirt reading: "I wish Hillary Married OJ." Tur was aghast. "Let me say that again," she wrote. "He posed for pictures in front of the national media in a shirt that unsubtly conveyed that he wished Hillary Clinton had been brutally stabbed to death in the 1990s."

A year previously, she said, she never would have believed that Americans would have "stooped so low or accept gratuitous name-calling—on either side, against either candidate." Now, however, "Trump is crude, and in his halo of crudeness other people get to be crude as well" (240). Because of the tenor of Trump's campaign, and the release of the *Access Hollywood* tape, another release on the same day—less lurid, but far more important—received little attention at the time. "A joint press release from the Department of Homeland Security and the Office of the Director of National Intelligence ... read in part: 'The U.S. Intelligence Community (USIC) is confident that the Russian Government directed the recent compromises of e-mails from US persons and institutions, including from US political organizations." The translation, she said, was clearly that, with regard to the hacked server of the Democratic National Committee and the stolen e-mails of the Clinton campaign chairman, "we think we got the guy. His name is Russia. And we think that Russia is stealing this information with one singular goal: 'to interfere

with the US election process'" (241). See below for more discussion on the Russian role, for Trump's openly expressed hope
that Russians or others would interfere, and for Tur's own role in
reporting Trump's statement, and for giving him the opportunity
to walk his comments back from the brink of treason, which he
refused to do. As in the case of his infamous taunt that he could
shoot someone on 5th Avenue and not lose a vote, not even this
served to deter his supporters.

Testing the definition of normal is something that has happened
on every day of the Trump presidency, and Tur documents that
it happened "every day on the campaign trail" as well. It isn't as if
the electorate did not have ample warning. Trump as a campaign-
er "calls for jailing his opponent. He openly admonishes sitting
generals. He singles out minority groups for blanket condemnation. He goes after the spouses of his rivals. He questions the
integrity of the election itself. He is endlessly hostile toward the
media" (257). Why should it be any surprise that as president he
has changed his behavior not at all?

One of the many unbelievable things about Trump was his success in elevating insignificant details to the political equivalent of
forest fires. In common with many others, Clinton had used a private e-mail server. "From that flicker of misconduct her Republican opponents had started a major political blaze, and Trump
had emerged as the arsonist in chief." Astonishingly—and these
are not Tur's words or implications—the director of the FBI became what had all the appearance of a Trump accomplice, creating what almost bordered on a political coup. While ostensibly
defending Clinton, saying that no reasonable prosecutor could
have brought charges against her, he savaged her as irresponsibly
careless, thus offsetting what should have been the impression
from his comment that there was no basis that any responsible
prosecutor could have used to prosecute. Later, he again intervened in the electoral process by sending a letter to Congress in

which he said that the FBI had located that might be "pertinent" to the Clinton e-mail question. "It was a short, carefully worded letter about a narrow legal matter, but it roared through the political world like a rocket." Trump shouted, nonsensically (reflecting his astonishing lack of knowledge of American history), that it was "bigger than Watergate" (269-270). NBC reported it as follows: "Breaking news tonight, a bombshell from the FBI, eleven days before the election" (272).

Of course, nothing came of those e-mails either—except that raising the issue at all, especially at such a critical time, was a huge blow to the Clinton candidacy. One wonders (and, again, this speculation does not come from Tur) if the rationale for such an enormous departure from precedent—or accepted behavior from a director of the FBI—may have resulted from an attempt to placate the circle of Giuliani-influenced agents in the Southern District of New York who were obsessively and rabidly anti-Clinton. If so, one can continue to wonder what those emotionally anti-Clinton agents who were so dedicated to a Trump victory may think now that Trump has viciously attacked and demeaned their beloved Bureau. Moreover, one can only marvel at the wrenching sense of disaster that James Comey, that former FBI director, so obviously feels regarding his role in Trump's victory.

Shortly before the actual election, Tur covered a talk by vice presidential candidate Mike Pence. She did not know whether Pence could hear a man shouting from the audience. Probably not, she said, "but I do, and I will never unhear him: not the man's message, and not the thousands of other voices that summarized 2016 by not shouting him down. 'Assassinate that bitch,' the man said. And the crowd said nothing. 'Assassinate that bitch,' and the crowd cheered on.'"

And Tur rushed to her word processor to write of her experiences in this sordid campaign. As painful as much of it is to read, her memoir is a major contribution. As bad as watching the campaign was—and the Trump presidency is—her memoir conveys a sense of how much worse it was actually to have been there at the creation.

If it was bad for Tur, consider how much more distressing it was for the defeated candidate, Hillary Clinton. She won a substantial victory in the popular vote and was positioned to become America's first woman president. Overturning it all was the functioning of the Electoral College, which changed her triumph into tragedy. It was certainly a tragedy for her, and without doubt for the country as well.

In her "Author's Note" to the memoir that Clinton produced,[3] she concedes that the experience was wrenching, but she considered it to be important to set the record straight, so that her grandchildren "and all future generations," can know what really happened. She knew that by producing her book she inevitably would face jeers that she was whining, or that her story was "self-serving," or that people simply want her to go away. She said that she recognized that "some people don't want to hear about these things"— especially, she said, from her, but regardless, she had a "responsibility to history." She needed to set the record straight (xii). Here it is impossible to resist repeating Senator McConnell's infamous words, "nevertheless, she persisted." It is fortunate that she did. Hillary Clinton's important, thoughtful—and yes, graceful— memoir does much to help correct the record. That, also, is the purpose of this chapter: not to justify or praise Clinton, but to counter the misrepresentations and misinterpretations that have driven much of the post-election commentary, and to consider just what effects the result portends for policy.

Not only did the cumbersome system that America has inherited for its presidential selection change the outcome, but much of

---

3   Hillary Rodham Clinton, *What Happened* (New York: Simon and Schuster, 2017).

the discussion regarding that outcome and its causes simply does not stand up to analysis. Certainly, the prevalent rhetoric from Republicans that "the people have chosen," to justify their draconian policies crumbles when one recognizes that the Trump administration was hardly "the people's choice"; rather, the choice was solely that of the Electoral College.

Nor is there any sense to the assertion that the Electoral College is necessary to offset the "bias" of a popular vote, because if the popular vote were to prevail, "California would choose everything." Nonsense. The Republican south has a far greater population than Democratic California. Just the two largest states of the old Confederacy in fact boast a combined 2017 population of about 47 million (about 27.9 million for Texas and somewhat more than 19 million for Florida), while the figure for California is about 39.4 million. Voting does not work that way in any event. Selecting by a popular vote would mean that Republican votes in California would be meaningful, as would Democratic votes in Wyoming; now, they are not. Every vote, Republican or Democratic, would count the same wherever cast. They all would be counted. Under the Electoral College (except in Nebraska and Maine, which divide their electoral votes among the parties) minority votes in a state do not affect the total count at all.

"Pundits" from both parties speak as if 2016 brought a Republican tsunami. It is correct that for a number of reasons—including Republican gerrymandering and Russian electoral interference directed at destroying Democrats—Republicans won powerfully at the very important state level. For the national government, though, in addition to winning a clear and significant percentage of the popular vote, the Democrats picked up seats in both houses of Congress. If that is a Republican wave election, it is an odd one.

Similarly, commentators tend to accept the rhetoric of a "coast vs. the heartland" explanation. The metaphor, whether important or trivial, in any case fails almost completely. For example, every east coast state south of Virginia—North and South Carolina, Georgia, and Florida—went red, or Republican, while in the "heartland," four substantial states: Minnesota, Illinois, Colorado, and New Mexico went blue, or Democratic. Moreover, the Republican victories in Wisconsin, Michigan, and Pennsylvania were extremely narrow. Rural vs. urban would be more meaningful, but even that is an oversimplification.

Another misconception was the character of Clinton's campaign. From both sides of the aisle, one could hear that she ignored the important issue of jobs, yet her speeches and position papers were full of discussions about how to increase employment, and improve working conditions. Also from both sides of the aisle were criticisms that she failed to show respect for workers, while in fact it was Trump who hurled insults indiscriminately at everyone. His constant comments about "losers" hardly resonated with the critics, while Clinton's comment about "deplorables" opened her up to the charge.

What she actually said, however, was considerably different. At no time did she say, or imply, that working people were "deplorable." Here is her exact statement (taken from *Politico*): "to just be grossly generalistic, you could put *half of Trump's supporters* into what I call the basket of deplorables. Right? The racist, sexist, homophobic, xenophobic, Islamaphobic—you name it. And unfortunately there are people like that" [emphasis supplied]. She followed with: "some [note, only "some"] of these folks— they are irredeemable, but thankfully they are not America," and "the other basket" contained friends "from Florida and Georgia and South Carolina and Texas," as well as from New York and California who support Trump because of legitimate fears and a sense that "the economy has let them down, nobody cares about them, nobody worries about what happens to their lives and their futures and they're just desperate for change." Angie Drobnic Holan in her *Politico* piece, "In Context: Hillary Clinton and the 'Basket of Deplorables'" (September 11, 2016, http://www.politifact.com/truth-o-meter/article/2016/sep/11/context-hillary-clinton-basket-deplorables/), supplied the omitted context by calling attention to these actual words from Clinton's comments.

What comes across from what Clinton actually said—as opposed to what her critics *said* she said—is that in no way was she a condescending, sneering, elitist candidate. Yet it is that distorted portrayal that has tended to dominate conversations about her campaign—certainly descriptions from Republicans, but also sometimes from the left as well. It is especially ironic that her opponents have succeeded in tarring her with the brush of disdain for "common people," when it notoriously is Republicans themselves who have worked so diligently to suppress the right of those very people to vote.

In a political and civic sense, the greatest insult to the people is discouraging them from voting, or even outright denying them this most fundamental right. In fact, not since the aftermath of reconstruction in the south has America seen such an enormous effort to strip the ability to vote from large segments of the country's people. *That* is the true display of elitist disdain for America's hard workers.

Clinton reminds us that *Vox* analyzed "all of my campaign events and found that I talked about jobs, workers, and the economy far more than anything else." *The Atlantic*, also, published an article titled, "The Dangerous Myth That Hillary Clinton Ignored the Working Class." In fact, it said that she "ran on the most comprehensively progressive economic platform of any presidential candidate in history." Moreover, in her convention speech, she talked more about jobs "than Trump did in his," as well as doing so in their first presidential debate that "was watched by eighty-four million people" (395-396).

Clinton began her memoir with the awkward situation of whether to attend the Trump inauguration. She did the correct thing, and was present. It would have been bad form for the defeated candidate and her husband, who formerly was president himself, not to be there.

Trump's inaugural was startling, and her description captured its nature. It was "dark and dystopian." In fact, "a howl straight from the white nationalist gut" (7). It was the culmination of years of disturbing trends within the Republican Party. Thus, the trend "didn't start with Trump." In 2007, a decade earlier, Al Gore wrote a book, *The Assault on Reason*. Two years before that, "In 2005, Stephen Colbert coined the word 'truthiness,' inspired by how Fox News was turning politics into an evidence-free zone of seething resentments." Earlier still, Karl Rove, notoriously, had "famously dismissed critics" as behind the time, living in the outmoded "reality-based community." It was only another step that brought a Trump administration with a spokesperson, Kellyanne Conway, who would defend outright lies as simply "alternative facts" (9). Clinton noted that former President George W. Bush himself—as was also widely reported—muttered after Trump's address: "that was some weird shit." She said she "couldn't have agreed more" (11).

As she was leaving, following Trump's address, Ryan Zinke, who would (rather briefly) become Trump's Secretary of the Interior, "brought his wife over to say hello." This was a surprise to Clinton, because during the campaign he had called Clinton "the Antichrist." She startled him by bringing it up, saying: "I'm not actually the Antichrist," whereupon "he mumbled something about not having meant it." She also chatted with Trump's daughter Tiffany and with Senator John Cornyn of Texas (12).

Despite the hurt, Clinton did not lose her sense of humor, even while hurling defiance at the winners. From Texas, she received a verse that helped to console her. The friend who sent it said that a friend of her father's had written it in the 1950s, after working for Adlai Stevenson, who lost twice to Dwight Eisenhower:

> The election is now over
> The result is now known.
> The will of the people
> Has clearly been shown.
> Let's all get together;
> Let bitterness pass.
> I'll hug your Elephant;
> And you kiss my Ass.

This seems to have reflected her own sentiments beautifully; a sentiment that was widely shared (recognizing, of course, that in contrast to the Stevenson-Eisenhower race, the verse this time was inaccurate regarding the will of the people) (25).

"If the inauguration on Friday was the worst of times," she wrote, "Saturday turned out to be the best of times." It was the day of the great Women's March on Washington, which she described as the "biggest single protest in American history." She decided not to attend, in order "to let new voices take the stage," but she watched in on television with delight (13).

The women's reaction of outrage to the Trump victory set in motion what is likely to be a sea change in women's rights, one that is very long overdue. Many women were chagrined that they had not seen the danger and had failed to vote. Clinton expressed astonishment. How, she asked, could Trump "attack women, immigrants, Muslims, Mexican Americans, prisoners of war, and people with disabilities—and, as a businessman, be accused of scamming countless small businesses, contractors, students, and seniors—and still be elected to the most important and powerful job in the world?" (15). But she was cheered as she watched the demonstration that far exceeded the modest attendance of the inaugural.

Clinton's book came out before that sea change was sufficiently in motion to be recognized, but there were disgusted reactions from many quarters with regard to the way male reporters dealt with her, as opposed to Trump. Two of those were the well-regarded Charlie Rose and the far less perceptive Mark Halperin. The worst, however, was the *Today Show*'s Matt Lauer, who moderated the "Commander in Chief Forum," for NBC. It took place in September, on the deck of the USS *Intrepid*, an aircraft carrier. She and Trump were each to receive 30 minutes and were not on stage at the same time. Lauer had promised her that the forum would be devoted to "national security and the complex global issues that face our nation" (217).

She said she was somewhat surprised that Trump had agreed, because he had "been tripped up on easy questions," saying that more countries should have nuclear weapons, including Saudi Arabia; that NATO was obsolete; and that he had little sympathy for prisoners of war, because he "prefers soldiers who don't get captured." He said he knew more about ISIS than the generals, and on and on.

Clinton lost the coin toss, and was the first to be questioned. Lauer's first question was about the most important characteristic that a Commander in Chief could possess, but as she began to answer, he "cut in to say, 'You're talking about judgment.' That wasn't what I was talking about, exactly," she remembered, but knew from the look on his face that he thought he had laid a trap. He began to talk about her email server, asking why that wasn't disqualifying. As she answered, he kept talking over her, firing more questions, all about emails, not letting her talk about policy. The disrespect he displayed was palpable. Then he turned to the audience. A Navy veteran whom he had selected asked Clinton how he could trust her when she "clearly corrupted our national security." Lauer next turned to another veteran to ask a question, and when she began to answer that one, the imperious NBC host again interrupted and ordered her to do so "As briefly as you can." Then, her time was over. "Later," she said, she "watched Lauer soft-pedal Trump's interview, beginning "what do you believe prepares you to make decisions that a Commander in Chief has to make?" and following up on nothing of substance.

It was embarrassing, and journalism poured deserved contempt on Lauer. Somewhat later, as the "Me Too" sea change began to gather momentum, it washed away all three of these figures. Lauer, along with Rose and Halperin, happily have vanished from the airwaves.

Firing was their fate. It came because they had clearly been guilty of sexual harassment that had nothing to do with their treatment of Clinton. Their punishment was laudable and severe penalty for such actions was long overdue, but each had been as guilty of journalistic sexism as of general sexual harassment itself.

During the presidential debates, in a particular display of crudeness, Trump brought "three women who had accused my husband of bad acts decades ago, plus a woman whose accused rapist I had been ordered by a judge to represent back in Arkansas. It was an awful stunt," Clinton wrote. As she pointed out, these old allegations "had been litigated years before," and Trump was not standing up for these women, but rather "using them" to "divert attention" from his own transgressions (138-139).

Later, as women across the country continued to increase their reactions against sexual harassment, there began to be more commentary about President Bill Clinton and Monica Lewinsky. Despite the passage of time, revisiting the incident aroused new emotion. One should remember that Monica Lewinski herself has consistently repeated that she felt victimized—but only by the later characterization of her as a predator. As a sad aside, one should note that the treatment of Ms. Lewinski from many sides has been a prime example of the cruelty with which the culture has treated women. She put it soundly when she asked how anyone would like to be judged through a lifetime by the most stupid act he or she had ever committed.

She stresses that she was not a victim of the affair, which, she maintains, was fully consensual and between adults. Even so, there were gratuitous comments that President Clinton "should have resigned because of the Lewinski affair."

What that would have accomplished would not have been a victory for women's rights, but a shattering of the presidency itself. If Republicans had succeeded in driving Clinton from office for non-criminal matters—a consensual affair—unrelated to his official duties, it is likely that no Democratic president ever again could survive with a Republican Congress, unless that Democratic president were completely passive. Remember, there were impeachment resolutions introduced against Bill Clinton before anyone had ever heard of Ms. Lewinski.

New York Senator Kirsten Gillibrand was one who commented that President Clinton should have resigned, and she was instrumental in the movement that has led to resignations from Congress. Such a movement, as indicated, was long overdue, and most of those—in entertainment, the media, and in political positions—who have lost their positions should have lost them long ago. Senator Gillibrand is a capable and effective senator.

Nevertheless, actions taken during times of excitement are not always wise. We should take care not to assume that all undesirable actions are equal. We should take care that we do not assume that because punishment for malefactors has been absent for so long, due process should be dispensed with. We also should take care that we do not create a situation in which political opponents can fabricate charges that can lead to severe outcomes without any basis in fact. We also should recognize that the calls for "zero tolerance" are not only irrational, but dangerous. Regardless of the subject, a zero-tolerance policy eliminates judgment, nuance, and due process. It always leads to irrationality and injustice. It is consistent with tyranny, not with a society dedicated to the rule of law.

It is time that women were heard, and it is well that they at last are being heard. That should not mean, though, that any charge is valid, nor does it mean that Democrats should leap into a circular firing squad and circumvent due process in response to allegations. This country saw at least a century and a half of black men murdered because white women levied baseless charges against them. Such charges can be rooted in politics just as much as they once reflected racism.

There often is a search for purity on the left. It was just a Sarandon/Stein-like rigidity and an ignorance of proportion that contributed to the Clinton loss and the Trump victory. Crimes should not go unpunished, but actions can be undesirable without being crimes, or without deserving the political equivalent of execution. A contrite legislator, for example, who has served well, worked diligently, and advanced the cause of women should not be sacrificed unless it is truly required—and deserved. What can one say about the comment, "it was unfair to him, but he had to go"? The comedian Bill Maher puts it well when he says that a flawed friend is better to have in office than a bitter and vicious enemy. "No person is irreplaceable," may technically be correct, but is more a cliché than a reasoned statement. You are not likely to hear it from one who recognizes the dangers from Trump policies and who also understands the political process.

Nevertheless, times are changing; perhaps, one can hope, they actually have changed. The change is long overdue. Unless there is a valid reason—such as the need to protect a child running toward a street, a need to protect others, or a need for self-defense, for example—no man, or person, has the right to put unwanted hands on anyone else. Women have been expected, even required, to tolerate the intolerable, and this must stop. Great change will bring some injustice, but the change is important, regardless.

One of the great strengths of Clinton's memoir is her discussion of policy. As she put it, "the policies you propose say a lot about your principles and priorities." You not only can evaluate a candidate's policy proposals on costs, effects, and whether it could pass Congress, she writes, but "you can also see it as a window into the candidate's heart: this is a person who cares about children and believes society has a responsibility to help care for the most vulnerable among us." She conceded that she may have undervalued how important a proposal's presentation to the public may be. The optics of a presentation may be more important than the details (224).

Another under-appreciated fact about American politics is the extent to which policy considerations are dismissed, overwhelmed by discussions of emails, emotional diatribes against selected groups, or friendly feelings toward a given candidate. Bush was "the guy you'd rather have a beer with;" you agree that Trump may be dangerous, but "you just don't like Hillary;" he's a billionaire, but "he does and says what I would do if I had that much money." Such considerations as these are pure self-indulgence. For the system to function well, a vote should be cast to achieve the best policies, not to make the voter feel better.

Clinton and Bernie Sanders contested vigorously for the nomination. Such a fiercely fought battle inevitably creates resentments. Clinton expresses annoyance at Sanders, but she did appreciate his energetic campaign and the "spirited contest of ideas" (226). Despite their disagreements, they fundamentally agreed on policy. She believes that lack of major policy disagreements led to criticisms of her character, and certainly such criticisms were strong from many of the Sanders supporters (228-229). Regardless, the Democratic Party should take pride in the quality of the two candidates it produced. In the long run it seems that the Party may well be stronger, and more effective, because of the ideas that came from both these bright and committed figures.

Clinton writes that she has given much thought to pushing "policy back into our politics" (234). (As an aside, and speaking from the discipline of political science, the field of study that should be most involved in policy, that discipline has rushed so enthusiastically toward its interpretation of "science" that it has almost completely abdicated the responsibility it once felt toward policy, which means it has abdicated what once was its core principle, the speaking of truth to power. Clinton should be praised for her concern to push policy back into politics, just as political scientists should be urged to do the same.)

Clinton has "a new appreciation for the galvanizing power of big, simple, ideas," she says. She credits Sanders for "proving again that it's important to set lofty goals that people can organize around and dream about, even if it takes generations to achieve them." Speaking from personal experience, she notes that this is what happened with healthcare. The effort went back fully a century. She and Bill had "tried to get it done in the 1990s," and did succeed in "creating CHIP, which provides coverage to millions of kids." (In another aside, this time an especially sad one, the current Republican Congress under Trump has let funding for CHIP end, and has done nothing substantial toward renewing it. Senator Hatch of Utah, who previously had supported the program, even made harsh comments about people expecting too much from the government and not wanting to take care of themselves. The issue was the health care of *children*, and the government's lack of money—and he was supporting tax reductions for the very wealthy, which, despite the assertions of ideologues, will reduce the amount of money coming in to the government.) Clinton discusses many of the broad initiatives that she supports, and had hoped to implement as president (234-241).

Her final comment in that section was that no matter what she will be doing, "I'll be chasing down new policy ideas that I think could make a difference. Not every election," she assures us, "will be so filled with venom, misinformation, resentments, and outside interference as this one was. Solutions are going to matter again in politics. Democrats must be ready when that day comes" (241). That is as important as any thought that came from this election.

It would be difficult to stress enough the dire effect that political propaganda in form of constant repetition about email had on the vote, even though the issue had almost no substance. Similarly, the vote was drastically affected by successful Republican attempts at suppression and by overt Russian propaganda. It would be one thing if the Russians had simply interfered on their own, but Trump overtly invited them to meddle in our internal affairs. "Russia, if you're listening," he said loudly before a large audience, "I hope you're able to find the thirty-thousand emails that are missing." These were messages deleted from Clinton's personal account. "I think you will probably be rewarded mightily by our press," he said.

Katy Tur was involved here as well. It was she who covered this bizarre statement from Trump. Clinton said that Tur followed up to see if it were a joke, "or if he really meant it." She asked if Trump "had 'any qualms' about asking a foreign government to break into Americans' emails. Instead of backing off, he doubled down. 'If Russia or China or any other country has those emails, I mean, to be honest with you, I'd love to see them,' he said. He also refused to tell Putin not to try to interfere in the election: 'I'm not going to tell Putin what to do; why should I tell Putin what to do?' This was no joke" (341).

There is also another issue, though, that should have received great scrutiny—especially considering what happened in Florida in the 2000 election—but has received very little consideration. Clinton pointed out that "a small but still significant number of left-wing voters may well have thrown the election to Trump. Jill Stein," Clinton said, "called me and my policies 'much scarier than Donald Trump' and praised his pro-Russian stance." Although this may sound shocking, it should not be. "Stein sat with Putin and Michael Flynn at the infamous Moscow dinner in 2015 celebrating the Kremlin's propaganda network RT, and later said she and Putin agreed 'on many issues'" (411-412). Just so.

Stein denied that she ever said Clinton was better or worse than Trump. She did, however, praise RT television, saying it gave more attention to American independent (or third party) candidates than American television did. That raises an issue that should be heavily emphasized in the education of all Americans, but goes largely unrecognized.

That issue is this: The American political system is based on two parties. One may object to that and hope that someday it will change, but so long as it is structured as it is, candidates must work with that system. Bernie Sanders, for example, worked diligently to secure the Democratic nomination; he did not run as an independent, and when he lost the nomination, he worked strongly for Hillary Clinton. Ralph Nader, in contrast, in 2000 ran as an independent. Doing so, he threw the almost equally divided state of Florida to the Republicans and brought about the Gore defeat and the George W. Bush win.

Stein, similarly, refused to work within the Democratic Party, and ran as an independent. What her candidacy could not acknowledge, is that on the 8th of November 2016, there were only two nominees who had any chance of winning: Clinton, the Democratic nominee, and Trump, the Republican nominee. All minor candidates had literally a zero chance. Casting a vote for one of them as a protest meant that, in effect, the vote supported the candidate not expected to win: Trump. The only way casting a vote for anyone but Trump or Clinton was rational would have been to say that the two candidates were equally bad. That was delusional. To calculate that Clinton would be as be as bad as Trump—or worse, that she would be more dangerous—was the height of folly.

There is one other possible calculation. As Clinton put it, "Maybe, like actress Susan Sarandon, Stein thinks electing Trump will hasten 'the revolution.' Who knows?" (412). That line of thought is ahistorical, and borders on the insane. Chaos does not bring utopia; it brings more chaos. The ultimate outcome is fierce repression and tyranny.

Clinton was not the only one who was aware of the importance of Stein's role, but it received hardly any publicity. The truth is that Stein must bear some responsibility for the Trump victory. As Clinton describes it, "she wouldn't be worth mentioning, except for the fact that she won thirty-one thousand votes in Wisconsin, where Trump's margin was smaller than twenty-three thousand. In Michigan, she won fifty-one thousand votes, while Trump's margin was just over ten thousand. In Pennsylvania, she won nearly fifty thousand votes, and Trump's margin was roughly forty-four thousand. So, in each state, there were more than enough Stein voters to swing the results, just like Ralph Nader did in Florida and New Hampshire in 2000" (412).

That is the role third parties play in a two-party system. Although there are rare exceptions at the local, or even state, level, there are none in presidential races. There are only two possible outcomes in a presidential race. Generally, minor parties receive so little support that they have no effect. If they have an effect, it will be to elect the party that is most detrimental to their ideals. Thus, when Stein praised RT for giving emphasis to "independent" parties, she (perhaps unknowingly, but in any case, foolishly) was giving it credit for affecting the outcome of America's election—an outcome that Trump, himself, in his comments to Katy Tur, clearly was hoping would be the case.

Clinton mentions, late in her memoir, that in the February 1991 issue of *Life* magazine, she had come across an article by "Lee Atwater, the Republican mastermind who'd helped elect Reagan and Bush with slash-and-burn campaigns that played to our country's worst impulses and ugliest fears. He was the man behind the infamous race-baiting 'Willie Horton' ad in 1988, the man who believed in winning at any cost. He was also mortally ill with brain cancer and not yet forty-years old." She said his piece "read like a death-bed conversion." He was having an "attack of conscience," and regretting his past as a "bare-knuckled political brawler." He wrote that his illness led him to see that what was missing in society was what was missing in himself: "A little heart, a lot of brotherhood" (434).

Like her husband, President Bill Clinton, Hillary Rodham Clinton is resilient. She said, recognizing that it might cause eye rolling, that she loves the country, and she praised its people. She wants to continue serving, although not by running again for office. She ended her memoir with the words she spoke when giving the commencement address at her alma mater, Wellesley College, asking, "What do we do now?" Her answer was: "Keep going" (464).

CHAPTER IV

Why Does Poverty Still Exist in the World's Richest Country?[1]

To a considerable extent, America's general population fails to have a clear understanding of the extent of poverty in the country or its severity. A number of factors combine to obscure the actual circumstances, including the growing ideological nature of the Republican Party—one of the pillars of the two-party system.

Conservative Republicans now routinely defer to religious fundamentalists. They seek to privatize everything possible. To defend their "conservative" preconceptions, they reject science and the very existence of objective fact. Apart from its coercive aspects (police, military, social control, and the fierce protection of "property"), they seek to weaken government, and reflect hostility to taxation.

Such a retreat from reality and from the resulting pressure to shrink government, as intended, has brought huge increases in income inequality, demonization of the "welfare state," marked declines in protective regulations, sharp enhancement of private commercial interests, and an atmosphere in which those with fewer means must fend for themselves unassisted. Wealth flows upward. Propaganda campaigns seek to convince the public that any policy conservatives oppose is "socialism," a term that they freely apply also to any situation of chaos or authoritarianism.

---

1   Much of this chapter reflects ideas from my article, "Considering Structural and Ideological Barriers to Anti-Poverty Programs in the United States: An Uninhibited, and Unconventional, Analysis," *Poverty and Public Policy* 10, no. 4 (December 2018).

Their current frightening example is to warn of becoming like Venezuela, which is not a socialist country. This, they predict darkly, would be the result if government seeks to "promote the general welfare," despite the Constitution's clear mandate. Any serious attempt by government to provide or ensure quality healthcare would be dangerous. Such an austere approach is certainly relevant to questions of poverty, but also has broad and general application to the circumstances of all Americans.

Much of this was evolutionary and often has aroused little notice. It is essential, however, in order to develop public support for sound policy, to publicize just how strenuously conservatives have worked to shape public opinion. Their campaign should be exposed over and over; it should be shouted from the rooftop. A recent work brilliantly (if figuratively) doing just that is Nancy MacLean's groundbreaking exposé *Democracy in Chains*.[2] Her subtitle sums it up her study superbly: "The Deep History of the Radical Right's Stealth Plan for America."

Many authors, including me, have covered the story of how the United States came rather late to formal programs of social welfare. Despite the passage of more than a century since former President Theodore Roosevelt's rousing call for a broad range of programs—first laying the groundwork in his famous speech in Osawatomie, Kansas in 1910, and then in 1912 during his third-party "Bull Moose Progressive" effort to regain the presidency—America has yet to achieve the levels of income and health maintenance achieved in the rest of the developed world. What Americans call Social Security emerged in Germany in the 1880s, and was not enacted into law in the United States until 1935. The United States had no legislation providing for disability benefits until 1956, when Republican President Dwight Eisenhower signed an amendment adding them to the Social Security Act.

---

2   Nancy MacLean, *Democracy in Chains: The Deep History of the Radical Right's Stealth Plan for America* (New York: Penguin Random House, 2018).

Universal healthcare still is not fully implemented, despite President Lyndon Johnson's addition of Medicare, healthcare for the aged, to the Social Security Act in 1965; and despite Barack Obama's legislation in 2010, the "Affordable Care Act" (or, under Republican terminology, calculated to demonize it, "Obamacare"). That act—created to expand coverage under private health insurance and under Medicaid (the program designed for those in poverty)—moved the United States in the direction of universal coverage without moving toward any true version of "socialism." Even its strongest supporters, however, admit freely that it falls far short of achieving coverage for all.

To make matters worse, we have a rapacious pharmaceutical industry, notorious for huge profits and astronomical pricing. Drugs that are made here and shipped abroad sell in the US for far more than anywhere else. Most of them have been developed with government support, yet Medicare—to take one notorious example, is forbidden by (Republican) law from negotiating drug prices with manufacturers.

Sadly, it could have been different. Anyone of a certain age remembers someone who died from polio, was permanently disabled by it, or was doomed to a horrible life in an "iron lung," which encased the entire body, leaving only the head outside. It breathed for the patients who could not breathe on their own, because of paralysis.

That, thankfully, ended when Dr. Jonas Salk developed the very effective Salk vaccine. He literally saved the world from a scourge that seemingly attacked from nowhere. Salk could easily have been a billionaire, and that was in the 1950s, at a time when the richest were multi-millionaires.

He refused to patent the vaccine, however, and would not even consider it. To do so, he thought, would be immoral. Such a necessary vaccine should not generate fortunes; it should belong to the people.[3] Too many holders of power today would seem to find such an attitude astonishing. To them it might appear quaint—a medical version of "tree-hugging"; it does not seem to fit their ideology. Certainly it would appear unrealistic, and perhaps even un-American.

There indeed have been impediments to full health coverage, and they continue to exist, but it is important to maintain perspective. The situation is more nuanced than the conventional wisdom has it. Theda Skocpol demonstrated in her landmark *Protecting Soldiers and Mothers* that by the end of the nineteenth century, the United States had extensive programs benefitting many of its elderly, disabled, and poverty-stricken citizens.[4] The explanation for the apparent contradiction is that the benefits were related to the ravages of the Civil War, and that war affected an enormous number of Americans of both sexes.

The military connection reflects one of the persistent realities of American politics: much that had appeared to be impossible could be achieved when justified by military considerations. Beginning in the early twentieth century, there were some federal programs for highway building. These generally were supported by considerations of national defense, but discussions in the 1930s buttressed later by what became the dynamics of the Cold War brought about what was perhaps the greatest public works program of all time, the Interstate Highway System. President Eisenhower signed into law the Federal Highway Act on June 29, 1956; the law is more widely known as the Interstate and Defense Highway Act.

---

3   See Max J. Skidmore, *Presidents, Pandemics, and Politics* (New York: Palgrave/Macmillan, 2016), 9.

4   Theda Skocpol, *Protecting Soldiers and Mothers: The Political Origins of Social Policy in the United States* (Cambridge: Harvard University Press, 1995).

That is not hyperbole. In designing and constructing the Interstate Highways, not only were they to facilitate ground transport for the military and its equipment, but as one historian of roads remarked, "superhighways can accommodate emergency landings and takeoffs of airplanes."[5]

Similarly, until the 1950s, there had been no widespread support for broad federal assistance to education: quite the contrary. Conservatives issued dire warnings of "federal control" of local schools. To be sure, education had previously had some support from the federal government. Perhaps the most notable was the Morrill Act that President Lincoln signed into law in 1862. That act created what became America's great land-grant colleges and universities, which considerably increased access to higher education, and there have been some targeted programs benefiting elementary and secondary education. Nevertheless, fears of "federal control" and resistance to taxation have always overwhelmed any support for broader assistance. The dynamics of the Cold War, especially the USSR's successful launch on October 4, 1957 of the first space satellite, *Sputnik*, made possible the National Defense Education Act that President Eisenhower signed into law on September 2, 1958. The act provided support for education at all levels, and emphasized science, mathematics, and foreign languages.

The factor that enabled the acceptance of these new programs was not transportation for its own sake. Possibly even less was it a concern for education. It was fear of a foreign military power. However, to be sure, Republicans these days have lost their fear of Russia. In fact, they seem absolutely nonchalant about Russian attacks on American institutions so long as the foreign meddling helps Republicans gain or maintain power. Regarding anti-poverty legislation, one might conclude—perhaps with cynicism—

---

5   Dan McNichol, *The Roads that Built America: The Incredible Story of the U.S. Interstate System* (New York: Barnes and Noble, 2003).

that it is unlikely to succeed in any major way unless it can be rationalized as needed for national defense.

Even that, however, with the advent of Trump, may have become obsolete as a consideration. The foremost concern, for Trump and his "base," at any rate, seems to have become retention of political power, regardless of threats from malign foreign influence. Tribal political considerations seem to have trumped all concern for national defense as American "conservatives" rally around their supreme leader, disregard evidence of foreign corruption of American elections, and dismiss any threat whatever from the source that for so long had been their obsession and their strongest fear: Russia. As Trump faces the danger of impeachment from his open attempts to solicit foreign aid in damaging his domestic political opponents, congressional Republicans as of mid-November 2019, have given little or no indication of concern. What once was an almost paranoid, and certainly hysterical, fear of Russian communism has morphed into support for Donald Trump's presidency and an apparent willingness to accept foreign influence rather than to risk the other American party, the Democratic Party, gaining office.

Structural Barriers

Structural barriers in the American system make the passage of nearly any legislation difficult. Bills must maneuver through a complex committee structure in two separate legislative chambers, and then secure executive approval, or legislative override. Financing requires additional legislation with its own challenges. Legislation relating to poverty faces the most formidable barriers of all, in that it must make its way through the complicated process, like any legislation, but additionally must overcome unique ideological and cultural barriers.

Ideological and Cultural Barriers

Misperceptions Regarding the Extent
of Poverty and its Effects

For a number of reasons, Americans who are not themselves poor are often uninformed or misinformed about
the degree to which poverty exists in the United States.
They are equally ignorant of its dire effects.

This first became apparent to well-read Americans in the middle of the last century, when Michael Harrington published his
scathing expose, *The Other America.*[6] In early 1963, Harrington's
book became the subject of a quite lengthy review by Dwight
MacDonald in *The New Yorker.* MacDonald's review was itself an
impressive work, and indirectly brought Harrington's powerful
condemnation to President John Kennedy's attention.[7]

Harrington directly challenged the conventional wisdom, a term
that itself was new.[8] The combined argument of *The Other Amer-*
ica and MacDonald's widely distributed review had considerable
influence. That influence became the subject of a fine analytical
article by Linda Keefe, in 2010.[9] She deftly traced the effect of
Harrington's work as MacDonald carefully presented and interpreted it. She also went into great depth regarding the effect on

---

6   Michael Harrington, *The Other America* (New York: Touchstone Books,
    1962).

7   Dwight MacDonald, "Our Invisible Poor," *The New Yorker* (January 16,
    1963), 82-132.

8   The brilliant economist and wordsmith, John Kenneth Galbraith, coined it
    in his own great work, *The Affluent Society,* of 1958; see my own retrospec-
    tive review of Harrington's work roughly a half-century after its publication:
    Max J. Skidmore, "Revisiting a Classic After Nearly a Half Century," *Poverty*
    and Public Policy, 1, no. 2 (July, 2009): Article 8.

9   Linda Keefe, "Dwight MacDonald and Poverty Discourse, 1960-1965: The
    Art and Power of a Seminal Book Review," *Poverty and Public Policy,* 2, no. 2
    (June 2010).

MacDonald's own career; the public had responded overwhelmingly to his perceptive work

Sadly, the attention to poverty that began under President John Kennedy and escalated considerably under President Lyndon Johnson with his War on Poverty quickly dwindled as their Republican successors, Nixon and Reagan, implemented their Southern Strategy. It dwindled even more rapidly as the Republican successors to Nixon and Reagan (exempting Ford) vied to go to even greater extremes than their predecessors in pursuing political power.

Recalling Harrington and MacDonald—and even merely reading Keefe on their work—makes it plain what has been lost. That was clear even before the current deterioration of American politics, but is more obviously tragic with Trump at the head of the government and his party. However apparent American poverty may be to those outside the US, it has again retreated to near invisibility within the country itself. As a UN report demonstrates, though, poverty remains an American phenomenon.

The *Washington Post* reported in late June of 2018 that "The UN says 18.5 million Americans are in 'extreme poverty.' Trump's team says just 250,000 are." The issue no doubt is complex. Conservatives argue that the higher figure ignores programs that assist the poor. Whatever the accuracy of the two figures, though, it is clear to those who study the issue (the *Post* cites a number of scholars) that the figure of one quarter million is absurdly low.[10]

Trump's ambassador to the UN at the time, Nikki Haley, called the report "misleading and politically motivated." The *Los Angeles*

---

10 *Washington Post Wonkblog*, "The UN Says 18.5 Million Americans are in 'Extreme Poverty.' Trump's Team Says Just 250,000 Are" (June 25, 2018), https://www.washingtonpost.com/news/wonk/wp/2018/06/25/trump-team-rebukes-u-n-saying-it-overestimates-extreme-poverty-in-america-by-18-million-people/?noredirect=on&utm_term=.db63626f9d78 (accessed July 9, 2019).

Times quoted the report's author and "the UN's special rappor-
teur on extreme poverty and human rights," Philip Alston, as con-
demning the Trump administration for "pursuing high tax breaks
for the rich and removing basic protections for the poor."[11] *The
Guardian* and other publications quoted Haley as saying that it is
"patently ridiculous for the United Nations to examine poverty
in America." *The Guardian* also noted that this furor came a mere
matter of days after the United States announced, through Haley,
that it would withdraw from the UN's human rights council, the
first country ever to do so.[12]

Whatever the merits of the report, there can be little genuine
doubt that poverty does, indeed, remain present in the United
States. It seems equally clear that the tendency with America's
government under Trump is to overlook its presence, deny its existence, deliberately attempt to divert attention, and generally not
to be concerned about whether it exists or not, so long as it does
not affect Trump's political fortunes.

Jeffersonian Heritage

Whatever the actual practices of the American political system,
certainly the heritage of Jeffersonianism, at least with regard to
the bulk of political rhetoric, reflects a widespread romantic attachment to what much of the public would consider (were they
to think about it and if they were sufficiently well-informed) to be
the ideas of Thomas Jefferson. Some people consciously adhere
to Jeffersonian ideas. Others have may have absorbed them with-

---

11   Jennie Jarvie, "Nikki Haley Calls UN Report on Poverty in US 'Mis-
     leading and Politically Motivated,'" *Los Angeles Times* (June 21 2018),
     https://www.latimes.com/world/la-fg-un-us-poverty-20180621-
     story.html (accessed July 9, 2019).

12   Ed Pilkington, "Nikki Haley Attacks Damning UN Report on US Poverty
     Under Trump," *The Guardian* (June 21, 2018), https://www.theguardian.
     com/world/2018/jun/21/nikki-haley-un-poverty-report-misleading-
     politically-motivated (accessed July 9, 2019).

out recognizing, or caring about, their origin. In both instances the acceptance of popular views of Jeffersonian ideas is unlikely to encourage nuance, or to permit understanding of the complexities of his thought.

Most prominently, Jefferson advocated localism, strictly limited government (especially at the national level), agrarianism, and a maximum of individual autonomy. At one level, the effect of such ideas can deserve praise. They can lead to efforts to be as self-sufficient as possible, and to support individual freedom for others as well as for oneself. At another level, the effect of such ideas can be pernicious. They can lead to such antipathy toward government that they bring opposition to any collective effort to assist those in need, a rejection of measures to prevent private power holders from imposing their will upon others, or hostility to all efforts to improve peoples' lives collectively. This means that it certainly is possible to use Jeffersonian rhetoric to oppose efforts to reduce income inequality or even to oppose social legislation in general or anti-poverty proposals in particular. Thus, it is possible to use Jefferson's ideas to support preferential or protective treatment of society's most powerful. This clearly is apparent in modern America. As I put it in *Unworkable Conservatism*: "The principles accepted by modern American 'conservatives' and libertarians emerged in the eighteenth century, crafted carefully to protect the people from the powerful. As they have evolved, or devolved, over the last half century or so, they now are carefully crafted to protect the powerful from the people."[13]

In any case, the use of such principles today is most unlikely to be based upon a clear understanding of the details of Jefferson's thought. Most prominently, as one example, it probably does not consider his preference for "ward republics." Jefferson formulated the idea not to strengthen the majority, but rather to enhance the

---

13   Skidmore, *Unworkable Conservatism*, 1.

ability of individuals actually to become governors, and to influence directly the forces that affect them.

However much the practice of slavery especially, and racism in general, sullied his record and make him vulnerable to the charge of hypocrisy, Jefferson's intellectual approach to authority and political equality condemned the "peculiar institution." He recognized slavery as absolutely unjust and evil. Regarding the evolution of anti-poverty legislation, however, Jefferson's legacy was pernicious (as was his emphasis on "states' rights") to American racial politics. The habit of speaking for the local, as opposed to the national (or even the state), as well as an assumption that the national government should limit itself to minimal action in the social realm, has always tended to put proposals for anti-poverty legislation at a disadvantage before they even were considered seriously. With the ascendency of southern strategies, the tender treatment of wealth, and pandering toward right-wing fundamentalist populists, the obstacles facing anti-poverty measures have become almost insurmountable.

Confusion Regarding Thought of "The Founders"

Although one often hears that the United States has departed from the ideas of "The Founders," and should return to their principles, those who are so adamant on the issue tend to extoll ideas that were common among the opponents of the Constitution, rather than those who supported it. Using the Founders as a guide would in any case appear to present difficulties, when one considers that the Founders as a group undoubtedly had their differences. Jefferson and Hamilton certainly were "Founders," and more often than not, their opinions were sharply different.

Certainly, Americans throughout their history have tended to honor Jeffersonian rhetoric: small government, strict construction of the Constitution, decentralization of power, limited taxation, and the like. Just as certainly, though, the country—all the while tend-ing to speak in Jeffersonian terms—erected a foundation built on the principles of Jefferson's antagonists, the Federalists.

To be sure, the Federalists as a party vanished within a few decades of the Republic's creation. Nevertheless, Federalist principles, ensconced in the judiciary, built the new Republic as it evolved. The great chief justice John Marshall, certainly "a Founder," speaking for the Court set forth judicial review, central power, and other Federalist ideas.

Outside the judiciary, even those in the Jeffersonian tradition often asserted presidential authority. President Thomas Jefferson, himself, regardless of his constitutional views, did what he thought was best for the country and negotiated the enormous Louisiana Purchase. President James Madison signed into law legislation creating a national bank. Andrew Jackson, the "Old Hero," who considered himself to be an old Jeffersonian, pioneered the use of the veto as a policy measure.

Regardless of what might be thought of as Hamiltonian practices, the use of Jeffersonian rhetoric and presuppositions through the years has been troublesome for advocates of legislation designed specifically to combat poverty. As noted above, any legislation aiming at the implementation of strong national domestic policy is handicapped to begin with. Its chances for success are best if put forward with justifications relating them to national defense. The need to provide such justification creates special hurdles for measures designed primarily to reduce poverty. President Franklin D. Roosevelt was extraordinarily perceptive when he proposed an "Economic Bill of Rights," in his State of the Union addresses in 1944 and 1945. He argued that economic security was part of national security.

Unfortunately, reasonable though the case certainly is, it has not been made sufficiently since then to be as effective as it needs to be to bring anti-poverty programs in the US to levels that prevail elsewhere in industrialized countries. Nevertheless, there are reasons for optimism. In reaction to the excesses, irrationalities, and overt cruelty of Trump's policies, there were elements of social reform in the great midterm victories in 2018 that led to the Democratic takeover of the House of Representatives and the restored speakership of Nancy Pelosi. However unlikely it still seems, that movement appears, in mid-2019, to have at least some potential to create a huge "blue tsunami" in the 2020 elections that would dwarf the Democratic gains of 2018. If it materializes, the resulting Democratic sweep could not only oust Republicans, but potentially even consign them to history's footnotes.

Fundamentalist Misrepresentations of America's Political Heritage

"Fundamentalism," as discussed here, refers to ideological rigidity and textual literalism. The argument is that it leads to a rejection of logic and even of fact. It is a mindset and is to be found not only in religion, but also in other forms of thought. It is as apparent in, for example, economics and constitutional interpretation as it is in all varieties of religion. The argument here suggests a relationship among fundamentalism's effects wherever one encounters them.

This is not a new argument; others have identified similar themes between religious and constitutional fundamentalism before. Smith and Tuttle, for instance, have produced a deeply thoughtful examination that deals with such similarities (and they consider dissimilarities as well). "Given the obvious similarities between these two interpretative approaches," they say, "it is perhaps not surprising that Cass Sunstein, Morton Horwitz, and others have pejoratively used the label 'fundamentalists' to describe originalists." Moreover, they note, it therefore "is not surprising that prominent conservative Protestant fundamentalists have praised originalism as the proper approach to constitutional interpretation in the course of criticizing the Supreme Court's nonoriginalist decisionmaking."[14]

The argument here, though, goes further than Smith and Tuttle do, and further than most others have done. This argument is that fundamentalism, wherever it is encountered, instills dogma. Its tendency is toward repression. It accommodates racism, opposes measures to enhance human freedom, and almost always leads to the subjugation of women—and women's subjugation itself is arguably the single greatest cause of poverty throughout the world.

Constitutional Fundamentalism

In 2018, there was considerable discussion of Trump's selection of Brett Kavanaugh to replace retiring Justice Kennedy on the US Supreme Court. Most Republicans who commented stressed the need for the new justice to be an "originalist," who would interpret the Constitution as authorizing only that which it specifically asserts.

Most of those commenting were less sophisticated than the late Justice Scalia, in that they asserted that "originalism" meant the Founder's "original intent." Scalia, however, was not so simpleminded as to believe that it is possible to discern original intent. What he meant by originalism was somewhat more practical: original understanding. That is, today's interpretations of the Constitution should be the same as the way the Founders interpreted it originally. However more practical this notion is, it remains more superficial than truly analytical.

The difficulty with any notion of originalism is that any complex writing, such as the Constitution—or scripture—is always subject to different interpretations. The Founders themselves had

---

14   Peter J. Smith and Robert J. Tuttle, "Biblical Literalism and Constitutional Originalism," *Notre Dame Law Review* 86, no. 2 (2013): 693-764.

widely differing interpretations of the Constitution's meanings. Thus, from the Constitution's very origins there were disagreements regarding meanings. Disagreements have always existed among people who are reasonable, well intentioned, and well informed. One may pick and choose among the Founders to support a wide-variety of interpretations, so any pretense of "originalism" is that that: a pretense to give justification to one's own interpretation. The great Chief Justice, John Marshall himself, wrote in a manner that seems to rule out originalism. He said that the Constitution was "intended to endure for ages to come, and, consequently, to be adapted to the various *crises* of human affairs."[15] Even Thomas Jefferson, well known for advocating a strict interpretation of the Constitution, recognized that it had to evolve with changing times.[16]

Conservatives, of course, dispute both of these interpretations. In any case, however, at its most fundamental, an originalist interpretation nearly always works to preserve the power of the privileged; hence, its popularity among conservatives, whatever difficulties it presents.

The related assertion (akin to biblical inerrancy in theology) that something must be specifically spelled out in the Constitution to be valid has itself been a source of debate throughout American political history. Witness the "Stewardship Theory" of Theodore Roosevelt: the president has the authority, even the duty, to take any action the public good requires, providing that the Constitution does not forbid it and that it is not forbidden by law. His successor, President William Howard Taft (who years after he left the presidency became the chief justice of the US Supreme Court), thought the Stewardship Theory was far too activist and

---

15 Quoted in Terrance Sandalow, "Constitutional Interpretation," *Michigan Law Review* 79, no. 5 (April 1981): 1033.

16 See Thomas Brennan, "Thomas Jefferson and the Living Constitution," *Journal of Politics* (July 2017).

dangerous. He believed that the Constitution and the laws limit presidents to what they specifically authorize. This argument deals with presidential power, but similar discussions have dealt with the power of the national government in general.

The absolutist argument, despite its strong support in libertarian and "conservative" quarters, is almost assuredly unworkable. The notion that a constitution can spell out fully every detail in governing a nation state is ridiculous. It was ridiculous in 1789, and is even more so today. In fact, one could argue that the absolutist argument itself is non-constitutional, in that the actual Constitution explicitly asserts that it does not include every detail. Those who assert constitutional fundamentalism themselves ignore the Ninth Amendment: "The enumeration in the Constitution of certain rights, shall not be construed to deny or disparage others retained by the people." In other words, the Constitution clearly contains principles that it does not explicitly spell out, and says so directly.

Yet it is common for a "constitutional conservative" to challenge an advocate of Social Security, for instance, to show anything in the Constitution that grants government the authority to create and maintain a system of Social Security. "Where does it authorize welfare?" is also common. Of course, these ignore the language of the Preamble, which asserts that among the purposes of the Constitution is the promotion "of the general welfare." Sometimes movement conservatives will dismiss the Preamble entirely, saying it is merely boilerplate, and not "really" a part of the Constitution. Saying that the Preamble is mere window dressing, though, could hardly be a literal reading of the Constitution. But defenders of social legislation do not have to rely entirely upon the Preamble. Article I, Section 8, uses the phrase again. In the very first sentence it grants Congress the "Power To lay and collect taxes, Duties, Imposts and Excises, to pay the Debt and provide for the common Defence and general Welfare of the

United States ..." In the last paragraph of that section, the Constitution further grants the Congress the power "To make all Laws which shall be necessary and proper for carrying into Execution the foregoing Powers, and all other Powers vested by this Constitution in the Government of the United States ..."

Regardless of whether it is appropriate, many Americans tend to assume that Jeffersonian rhetoric, or rhetoric that sounds Jeffersonian to them, is the rhetoric of "The Founders." Similarly, it bears repeating that many conservatives attribute to the Founders, not the arguments of the actual founding, but rather the arguments of those who opposed the Constitution. They argue, for example, that the purpose of the Constitution was to create a weak national government, when in reality the intention was to create a strong government at the center to replace one that had, in the minds of the Founders, too little power. That, along with a fairly common tendency to respond favorably to arguments based on constitutional fundamentalism, presents an obstacle to the passage and implementation of anti-poverty measures.

Economic Fundamentalism

Opponents of anti-poverty measures number among their prime concerns a preoccupation with cost. When cost is the prime criterion, any resulting program is likely to be entirely inadequate. As counter-intuitive as it sounds, the way to achieve good programs is to plan the program that best meets the needs, and only then plan for cost; at the national level, cost is a secondary consideration.

This will be resisted strongly. Every dollar the government spends, say economic fundamentalists, must come from taxing, selling assets, or borrowing (thus running at a deficit). Not putting costs first, they argue, is irresponsible and would be unsustainable.

The answer to this is simple. First, examine Medicare, Part D (the prescription drug benefit). Part D has its problems, but it has turned out to provide a useful benefit. Violating all the strictures of economic fundamentalism, the Republican administration of President George W. Bush shoved the program through Congress over the objections of Democrats, who argued that the program provided no financing mechanism. One should note that the program's major supporters were "conservatives," Republicans who presumably were devoted to economic fundamentalism, but who sacrificed such principles in order to gain political advantage. The Bush administration created a program without consideration of cost—and that program works.

True, Part D prohibits Medicare officials from negotiating drug prices with manufacturers, and thus adds to the absurdly high costs of American medicine. It also is true that this results in an enormous subsidy to Big Pharma. These are flaws. They could be remedied easily—and certainly should be. In fact, the major flaw in Part D is that it is a privatized approach that cannot serve the public as well or as efficiently as a public program can.

The key point is the good that Part D does. It provides a valuable benefit to the American people, an important benefit that helps them survive the unspeakably high costs of American medicine. It also, to repeat, was created with no thought of, or attention to, the expense. Had cost been a primary consideration, it is unlikely ever to have been passed.

Second, consider military expenditures. The very people who would argue that costs must be demonstrated to be "sustainable" when planning for social legislation never think to provide a rigid, set sum to the Department of Defense, and then say, "work within those limits." Rather, the practice tends to be, and has been at least since it began during the Second World War, to provide the military with that which they (and defense contractors' lobbyists) say they need, and worry about paying for it later, if at all.

The security of the American people is important enough to violate the principles of economic fundamentalism. The health security and economic security of the American people are equally important and should be considered accordingly.

Economic fundamentalists can never accept a key principle of American national government. At the state and local levels, this is not the case, but at the national level the Government of the United States controls its own currency. It pays its debts in dollars, borrows in dollars, and creates dollars as needed. It simply is not true that "every dollar has to come from taxation or borrowing (or selling assets)." The US government creates dollars all the time. As a result, as counterintuitive as it appears, at the national level, there is no direct relationship between government expenditures and the government's income.

Nevertheless, this is difficult to grasp, and somehow seems intuitively that it cannot be true. Dollars have to come from somewhere, is the sentiment. A family cannot create an IOU to pay its bills. When times are tight, families must tighten their belts. When times are tight, government, too, must tighten its belt, goes the conventional wisdom (President Obama, himself, once made a similar comment). Anything else is counterintuitive. Perhaps it is counterintuitive, but the conventional wisdom is wrong. "You cannot spend your way to prosperity," we hear. A national government with a strong economy, however, can— and most certainly does.

Still, the conventional wisdom creates another hurdle for anti-poverty measures. People detest having "their hard-earned money" going to others; often others who they believe are not worthy: others who do not want to work, who are of a different race, who are outsiders. Until people recognize that government could halt all welfare payments and it would not reduce their taxes, or that they could triple or quadruple all such payments and that would not directly increase their taxes, they will continue to believe that they are financing others of whom they disapprove. Of course. It adds to the misconception every time politicians speak of "the taxpayer's money."

Also adding to misconceptions are assertions that come from economic "pundits," as well as politicians, that are simply contrary to observed fact. Hardly any competent economist believes that reducing taxes increases general government revenue; experience from Reagan onward demonstrates that it does not. When Bush I and Clinton increased taxes, government revenue soared; enormous deficits followed Reagan's tax reductions, and the huge tax cuts under Bush II quickly substituted a great deficit for the surplus that Clinton left him. Witness, also, the financial disasters that resulted from slashing taxes in Louisiana and Kansas, under the misguided advice from supply-siders. Nevertheless, so seductive was the supply-side propaganda that spread after Reagan's tax cuts that many conservatives believed (or pretended to believe) that there was a free lunch: that the way to increase government revenues is to reduce taxes.

Similarly, pundits and conservative politicians offer austerity as the solution to economic downturns. All experience demonstrates that this is counterproductive and destructive.

We are told that raising the minimum wage creates unemployment. In July 2019, the CBO released a report on raising the minimum wage to $15 per hour. It concluded that such an increase would lift 1.3 million Americans out of poverty and increase wages for 27 million. The report said, though, that "the change *might* [emphasis added] cost jobs for 1.3 million workers." Said *Los Angeles Times* business columnist Michael Hiltzik, "that's the squishiest part of the agency's analysis." He noted that conservative analysts have seized upon the negative parts of the report, despite the "vastly broader gains" overall. Moreover, he quotes Heidi Shierholz of the "pro-labor Economic Policy Institute," as saying that "CBO's assessment of the literature has simply not caught up." Hiltzik points out that CBO itself stresses the imprecision of the job-loss figures, and that "most economic models of a minimum wage increase find little or no job loss effect."[17] Hiltzik is correct that CBO cautions about the unemployment rise. The report itself says, "there is considerable uncertainty about the responsiveness of employment to an increase in the minimum wage." It concedes that "many studies have found little or no effect of minimum wages on unemployment," but says others have found such effects. CBO's own figure resulted from a very imprecise range from no effect at all, up to several million; CBO analysts merely selected a middle figure, admitting that the report's estimate "of the effects of increases in the minimum wage on unemployment are uncertain." Yet it is this "uncertain effect" that conservatives stress to obscure the CBO's own conclusion that the overall effect of a minimum wage hike would be substantially beneficial.[18]

Despite the common refrain that raising the minimum wage creates unemployment, a quarter century of research beginning with the famous Card and Krueger study of 1994 indicates little or no such effect.[19] Card and Krueger had studied fast food jobs in the Philadelphia area, partly in Pennsylvania, partly in New Jersey. It was a perfect situation to study, because New Jersey had raised the minimum wage, while Pennsylvania had not. They found that the increase did not decrease the number of jobs.

---

17 Michael Hiltzik, "A Strong Endorsement of the $15 Minimum Wage from the Congressional Budget Office," *Los Angeles Times* (July 9, 2019), https://www.latimes.com/business/hiltzik/la-fi-hiltzik-cbo-minimum-wage-20190709-story.html (accessed July 13, 2019).

18 For the actual CBO report, see Congressional Budget Office, "The Effects on Employment and Family Income of Increasing the Federal Minimum Wage," July 2019, https://www.cbo.gov/system/files/2019-07/CBO-55410-MinimumWage2019.pdf (accessed on July 13, 2019); quotations from 5.

19 David Card and Alan Krueger, "Minimum Wages and Unemployment: A Case Study of the Fast Food Industry in New Jersey and Pennsylvania," *NBER Working Paper No. 4509* (October 1993); published in *American Economic Review* 84, no. 4 (September 1994): 772-793, https://www.nber.org/papers/w4509 (accessed July 13, 2019).

Conservatives, of course, have attacked these findings. Also, keep in mind that the economics profession as a whole is affected by its conventional wisdom, which makes it biased toward assuming that higher minimum wages adversely affect job numbers; that may well influence the studies that its journals accept for publication.

As the prominent liberal and Nobel Laureate in economics, Paul Krugman, put it in the *New York Times*:

> Until the Card-Krueger study, most economists, myself included, assumed that raising the minimum wage would have a clear negative effect on employment. But they found, if anything, a positive effect. Their result has been confirmed using data from many episodes. There's just no evidence that raising the minimum wage costs jobs, at least when the starting point is as low as it is in modern America.

Krugman, too, as any knowledgeable person would anticipate, has been the target of attacks from the usual suspects.

The *American Economic Review* supplies another striking example, equally revealing, possibly even more so. An enormously influential paper appeared in 2010, "Growth in a Time of Debt," by two prominent Harvard economists, Carmen Reinhart and Kenneth Rogoff.[20] Their examinations of the economies of numerous countries, they asserted, demonstrated that when debt levels reach a certain point, 90% of GDP, they generate a severely adverse effect on economic growth, reducing it, in fact, to negative rates. Former US representative Paul Ryan, then chair of the House Budget Committee, subsequently to be designated speaker of the House, and now retired—a noted austerian ideologue—used the article's conclusions as a foundation for his bud-

20   Carmen Reinhart and Kenneth Rogoff, "Growth in a Time of Debt," *American Economic Review* 100, no. 2 (May 2010).

get recommendations. Liberal economist Dean Baker pointed to the Reinhart and Rogoff effect as having caused enormous harm in Europe, where the austerian policies they encouraged pushed unemployment rates "over 10 percent for the euro zone as a whole and above 20 percent in Greece and Spain." Their ideas had "certainly taken the world by storm."[21] Then some two years later, the newly-minted "law of finance," as some commentators and policymakers had gone so far as to label it, suddenly not only was called into question, but in the eyes of reasonable observers had crumbled into nothing but unfounded dogma.

To be sure, Reinhart and Rogoff had not gone so far as had many of those who advocated austerity citing their study, nor would it be wrong to recognize that there can be some correlation, though not necessarily causation, between debt and growth. Discovering a "new law of finance," however, is another matter entirely.

Thomas Herndon, a doctoral student in economics at the University of Massachusetts—a mere student at an institution far from the august heights of Harvard, the lofty and comfortable location from which Reinhart and Rogoff confidently reported their findings—had received an assignment to select an influential economics article and provide a critique. Happily for the knowledge base, if not so for Reinhart and Rogoff, Herndon chose their study.

The result, Herndon discovered, was immediate frustration. He could not replicate their results; he could not make their figures work. Therefore, he went directly to Reinhart and Rogoff and sought their help. They graciously provided him with their data. Unfortunately, those data quickly revealed significant errors in the Reinhart and Rogoff study that had been so strongly influential. There was exclusion of important data, coding errors, and questionable weighting. Herndon and his professors, Michael

---

21   Quoted in Skidmore, *Unworkable Conservatism*, 89.

Ash and Robert Pollin, published a critical article in the *Cambridge Journal of Economics*, and concluded that Herndon's corrections revealed that the dreaded 90% figure had no special significance at all.

Reinhart and Rogoff conceded the errors, but continued to maintain that their conclusions were nevertheless accurate. Paul Krugman examined the controversy, and concluded that the important factor seemed to be whether countries "had their own currencies, and borrowed in those currencies." Such countries cannot run out of money, because they can create it as needed. Advanced economies can therefore carry large debt levels without generating crises. That is precisely one of the foremost conclusions of this chapter.

The key question here, Krugman asked perceptively, is how an academic study can become so widely accepted without anyone looking at it closely enough to see obvious errors. Common sense would seem to raise the question, also. The answer certainly is that it was such a convenient fit and so congenial to the conservative conventional wisdom that no one thought to examine it—or wanted to do so. Erskine Bowles, for example, said revealingly that the errors did not change his views because of his own "common sense." Here, one should note, is common sense used in a manner that this book warns against. His experience was, he said—revealing that he was unable to recognize that sovereign states with their own currencies are not businesses, households, or constituent units that do not control their own currencies— that debt is always an "enormous risk factor."[22]

Some time later, John Cassidy, a thoughtful and perceptive staff writer who deals with politics and economics for *The New York-*

---

22   See Ari Rabin-Havt and Media Matters, *Lies, Incorporated: The World of Post-Truth Politics* (New York: Anchor Books, 2016); see also Skidmore, *Unworkable Conservatism*, 90.

er, wrote, "The Reinhart and Rogoff Controversy: A Summing Up." Pointing out what should have been obvious, Cassidy noted the "enormous damage to Reinhart and Rogoff's credibility, and to the intellectual underpinnings of the austerity policies with which they are associated."[23]

Cassidy also pointed out further that the fiasco "has created another huge embarrassment for an economics profession that was still suffering from the fallout of the financial crisis and the laissez-faire policies that preceded it." As a journalist, Cassidy is less bound by disciplinary fastidiousness than academic social scientists (especially those other than economists) and was free to ask the embarrassing—and, again, the obvious—question: "After this new fiasco, how seriously should we take any economist's policy prescriptions, especially ones that are seized upon by politicians and agendas of their own?"

The question is apt. For our purposes, it is important to point out that it verifies just how irrational it is to be preoccupied with expenditures alone. More important is the overall *effect of those expenditures*; that is, the extent to which they meet the peoples' needs. Thus, the obsession that is so harmful to all social and anti-poverty considerations rests not firmly on fact, but actually on the unstable foundation of ideology.

Religious Fundamentalism

Religious fundamentalism might seem to be an unlikely topic to include in an examination of barriers to anti-poverty legislation. Religion and poverty, as themes, have had a complex relationship far earlier than Max Weber, and even far earlier than the emergence of Protestantism. The emphasis here is not on Calvinism; it is not on "The Protestant Ethic" that encouraged hard work as evidence that one might be among "the Elect." Such doctrine may have led

---

23 John Cassidy, "The Reinhart and Rogoff Controversy: A Summing Up," *The New Yorker* (April 26, 2013).

to an assumption that the poor did not work hard, and therefore were "undeserving." That, however, is not the major concern here.

Admittedly, in the American setting, as well as in the traditions inherited from England, the notion of the "deserving" and the "undeserving" poor has had considerable force. Such emphasis can be seen in contemporary politics with regard to the "Dreamers," those non-citizens who are in this country because their parents brought them as infants or children. On the one hand, there are those who argue that they should in some manner be accommodated, because they are here without "permission" through no fault of their own. Others charge that anyone here without documentation is a "criminal" and should be deported immediately. The law becomes sacred when considering immigrants, yet not when a president pardons those who engage law enforcement officials in standoffs. Nor is a law "sacred" when a political party goes to great lengths—as Republicans have done with the Affordable Care Act—not only to repeal it (which is within reasonably normal political practice), but also to sabotage it and attempt to ensure its failure (which is not). Trump, in his attacks on the ACA, in fact has committed an impeachable offense, in view of the Constitution's admonition that the president "shall take Care that the Laws be faithfully executed ..."

Nevertheless, as indicated, these issues are not the foremost concerns of this discussion. Regardless of the relevance of such issues, the concern with religion here relates to something different: that is, the practice often taught in fundamentalist-evangelical groups of "harmonization," along with excessive literalism. Vincent Crapanzano, an anthropologist, is one of the foremost scholars examining the effects of such literalism throughout American culture. His vital study is *Serving the Word*, but it is his subtitle that is especially appropriate: *Literalism in America from the Pulpit to the Bench.*[24]

---

24 Vincent Crapanzano, *Serving the Word: Literalism in America from the Pulpit*

Another anthropological scholar, Susan Friend Harding, a cultural anthropologist, similarly has studied "fundamentalist language and politics," which is the subtitle of her serious study, *The Book of Jerry Falwell.* [25] Her work should be required reading for anyone seeking to understand the Trump phenomenon, and how it is that Trump seems to be virtually immune to the effects of his own conduct. Trump noted this himself during the campaign, when he remarked that he could shoot someone on 5th Avenue and not lose a vote. That seemed at the time to be mere exaggeration, somewhat humorous, but in retrospect, if interviews with his supporters are representative, it appears to be literally correct. Jerry Falwell, Jr., for instance, when asked by Joe Heim of the *Washington* Post if there were anything Trump could say or do that would cause him, Falwell, to withdraw his support, he responded simply, "no."[26] What follows is an explanation of how this can be.

Harding discusses the practice of "harmonization" (for outsiders, she introduces it to them as a practice that no doubt comes as a surprise, because under more extreme interpretations, it seems to be a complete denial of logic or of linguistic meaning). Harmonization presupposes adhering to biblical literalism and scriptural inerrancy, despite the many contradictions within scripture.

To be sure, the question of inerrancy is a complex one, even among fundamentalist-evangelicals, and different groups have different interpretations of just what it means. It is most simple,

---

to the Bench (New York: The New Press, 2001).

25   Susan Friend Harding, *The Book of Jerry Falwell: Fundamentalist Language and Politics* (Princeton: Princeton University Press, 2000).

26   Joe Heim, "Jerry Falwell, Jr., Can't Imagine Trump 'Doing Anything That's Not Good for the Country," *Washington Post Magazine* (January 1, 2019), https://www.washingtonpost.com/lifestyle/magazine/jerry-falwell-jr-cant-imagine-trump-doing-anything-thats-not-good-for-the-country/2018/12/21/6affc4c4-f19e-11e8-80d0-f7e1948d55f4_story.html?utm_term=.b30153bfb61e (accessed July 14, 2019).

and most dogmatic, among the more extreme groups who generally argue that every word in the Bible must be literally true, because each word is God's, and cannot be in conflict with any other word it contains.

Believers are taught to develop the ability to consider contradictions, rationalize them, and then "harmonize" away the conflict. At that point, they have come to accept the whole as literally true, however logically inconsistent, and however impossible it seems to the imperfect human mind for two completely opposite notions each to be true (because "logic" is a human construct and may not encompass an understanding of God's will).[27]

Here is an illustration of how harmonization works in practice. Some time ago, a Baptist pastor responded to a question I asked him about the two versions of creation early in Genesis. Even among fundamentalist-evangelicals, many interpreters would assume that the two versions represent two different descriptions of the same event from two different sources, and that taken together, the present a whole truth. For the most literally minded, though, each must be correct precisely as written. In one version, God created Adam, subsequently created other animals, and ultimately created Eve, all for Adam's companionship. In the other, God created whales and other animals, after which, for creation to be complete, He created Adam. The question was, which version is correct? The answer was, both. The follow-up question, then, was which came first, Adam, or other animals? The answer was that they both came first. That was God's word, and therefore could not be in error or contradictory. What seems to be a contradiction was simply the inability of the human mind to comprehend God's truth.

---

27   See Max J. Skidmore, "Review of: *The Book of Jerry Falwell*," in *The European Legacy*, 7:3 (2002), 414-416; reprinted in Joey Skidmore, *The Review as Art and Communication* (Newcastle Upon Tyne, UK: Cambridge Scholars Press, 2013), 87-89.

Whether this is appropriate for religion is irrelevant. What is relevant is that people adhering to fundamentalist-evangelical traditions and modes of their most extreme thought have become enormously influential in American society. It seems not to be an overreach to suspect that bringing their habits of thought—learned from their religion—into political, economic, and social matters arms them against rational argument and logic when considering matters other than religion. This, if so, presents an obvious danger. It clearly is detrimental not only to the passage of social legislation—witness, for instance, the literally irrational reaction to the science of climate change—but also to the entire political process and to the dismissal of cruelty as the foundation of various policies as irrelevant.

Consider the thoughtful comments recently in *Religion Dispatches* by Hollis Phelps, of Mercer University in Georgia. Casting tact aside, Phelps titled his essay: "Maybe It's Time to Admit that the 'Grotesque Caricature' of White Evangelicals is The Reality."[28] He was led to write his essay because of a gathering of evangelical leaders at Wheaton College, in Illinois. They were concerned about damage in the "age of Trump" to the image of evangelicals by being considered (as Senator John McCain described them as early as 2008) "agents of intolerance." Although recognizing that "evangelicalism is and will remain a complex socio-political movement propped up by a religious rhetoric that emphasizes individual piety," and pointing out that many trenchant critics of Trump come from the ranks of evangelicals, he said that it should be impossible to overlook the overwhelming support that evangelicals as a group have given to Trump, ultra-right-wing policies, and extremist candidates. Modern-day evangelicalism, he says, "does not create a new problem for evangelicals and their image; it's simply casting a very bright light on what has always been

---

28   Hollis Phelps, "Maybe It's Time to Admit That the 'Grotesque Caricature' of White Evangelicals Is The Reality," *Religion Dispatches* (April 19, 2018).

there, at least for the past forty years or so." If their support for Trump seems more calculated than sincere, he remarks, "that's because it is."

Perceptively, he noted that "the line between religion and politics is flimsy at best, if not entirely non-existent." It simply is not true that "evangelicalism, in its current manifestation," is a religion corrupted by politics. Rather, it is a "social movement that works through a specific type of politics." It was there for Trump and his allies to exacerbate, but they did not create it. "Perhaps it's time," he said, for concerned evangelical leader to recognize that evangelicalism's public image "isn't a 'grotesque caricature,' but the thing itself."

It can be nothing other than ominous that undoubtedly large numbers of active citizens, in clear defiance of reason find that "contradiction actually strengthens faith." Harding describes the many character flaws that the senior Falwell exhibited through-out his career. "He could humiliate, deceive, and steal," she said. As an aside, it would appear from the many charges being di-rected toward Jerry Falwell, Jr., in autumn of 2019 that he has inherited many of his father's character flaws. Writing almost two decades before the political rise of Donald Trump, Hard-ing could write of the senior Falwell in terms that are eerily pre-scient, and that with the substitution of "president" for "preach-er," and "Trump's base," for "believers," provide an apt descrip-tion of the contemporary White House, and the entire Trump phenomenon: The preacher is a Godly man; evidence that he has sinned, that he is unscrupulous, that he is hypocritical mere-ly forces believers to harmonize "contradictions and infelicities according to interpretive conventions that presume, and thus re-veal, God's design. Their Bible, their preacher, is thus constantly creating new truth" (p. xi). "What makes Falwell's scandalous actions productive is that they also bound people to him" (p.

100). He engages in a "process, both languaged and enacted, in which a preacher's ... wrongdoing is productive, not a side effect; is necessary, not incidental" (p. 103).[29]

The relevance to contemporary policy, certainly including anti-poverty policy, is painfully obvious. Personal flaws of the leader, cultish or not, strengthen that leader against criticism, and demonstrate godliness. Looking at the political implications, rather than maintaining focus on religion, demonstrates that such teachings are cleverly designed to render leaders—religious, political, cultish, or all combined—beyond rational analysis, providing them with powerful armor against any attack.

Roger Williams was America's first true political philosopher, the founder of Rhode Island, and a deeply religious man. Centuries ago, back in the 1600s, he advocated complete separation of church and state, warning of the corrupting influence on both the church and the state when they are not fully separate. He implemented that separation in his colony of Rhode Island.[30] Hearing statements from both Falwells, Franklin Graham, and others brings forth a vivid reminder of Williams's wisdom. Corruption ensues when religious figures are seduced by power (consider, too, how leaders of fundamentalist evangelical churches have asserted that Christianity demands rejection of gun control and acceptance of conceal and carry; Jesus would be astonished). Remember: the principles that had been carefully crafted to protect the people from the powerful now have become distorted to protect the powerful from the people.

---

29   In Skidmore, "Review," 2002.

30   In addition to Williams's own works, see Max J. Skidmore, "What Might Roger Williams Say About Church-State Relations in the Elections of 2012?" in Douglas Brattebo et al., *The Presidential Election of 2012* (Akron, OH: The University of Akron Press, 2015); see also John Barry's superb study, *Roger Williams and the Creation of the American Soul: Church State, and the Birth of Liberty* (New York: Viking, 2012).

In Praise of Universalism: Political
Weaknesses of Targeted Programs

One of the foremost reasons for the popularity of Social Security and Medicare is that they are virtually universal programs. They are not targeted toward the poor, or "the other." Everyone, for all practical purposes, qualifies upon reaching the requisite age. No one is forced to demonstrate poverty to participate. There thus is no stigma attached and such programs have huge constituencies.

Programs targeted to the poor, on the contrary, tend to suffer politically. Among other things, the poor are not organized, have little to no political power, tend not to be considered sympathetically, and when they are the subject of legislation directed at assisting them, by definition they become "the other." Therefore, their programs are fair game for budget-cutters and for those who resent assisting those whom they deem to be "undeserving."

Social Security was not aimed at the poor and is not technically an anti-poverty program. Nevertheless, no program in American history has had greater success in reducing poverty. Medicare,[31] similarly, has greatly reduced poverty among the aged, and also had the accompanying effect of being one of the greatest tools against racial segregation in the South. Southern hospitals were rigidly segregated, but Medicare required them to cease segregation and discrimination as a condition of eligibility for the vital funding that began to flow to them from Medicare. And—the hospitals did so. There are other examples that suggest the effectiveness of universal programs, as opposed to those that specifically target the poor.

---

31   One might argue that Medicare, confined largely to the aged as it is, is not truly universal. The principle of universality, nevertheless, is virtually there, because Medicare applies to almost everyone (to everyone covered by Social Security), because they pay into it in expectation of future benefits, just as they do to Social Security.

If, therefore, there is a single recommendation here (apart from a sound and general education for democracy), it is that there should be massive programs to eliminate poverty in the United States. Such programs should be broad, aimed at all of us as citizens of a great country, and not directed specifically toward any groups, the poor or any other. The programs should be open to all. Their benefits also should be understood to be part of human rights, and designed so as to avoid any stigma attached to participation. They should be designed for maximum effect, not for minimum cost. It then is up to the government, to the society, to make them work, and make them sustainable.

All poverty is damaging to human development, and—to put it emotionally—to the human spirit. Whatever excuses may be offered, it is shameful for poverty to exist in a society as affluent as that of the United States.

★ CHAPTER V

Modern Political Economy and Public Policy[1]

T here is vast misunderstanding among the public regarding the functioning of America's political economy. This misunderstanding extends to the formulation and implementation of its public policy, and those who are misled include many otherwise sound thinkers. No one should find this surprising. A chorus of misinformation permeates public comments from people who present themselves as being well informed. "When times are tough," so a popular mantra goes, "families have to tighten their belts. Government has to tighten its belt too." As mentioned earlier, even so sophisticated a thinker as President Obama said something similar to that, which only demonstrates the power of conventional wisdom to shape understanding, even when—as in this case—it is completely wrong. As I have written elsewhere, prevailing public opinion (or, as the late John Kenneth Galbraith so graphically termed it, "the conventional wisdom") can be so powerful as to function effectively as a censor, not only of expression, but even of thought itself.[2]

Moreover, once any opinion becomes widely accepted—especially one congenial to conservative interests—it often persists, despite compelling evidence to the contrary. Consider the widespread belief that raising the minimum wage creates unem-

---

1   An earlier version of this chapter appeared as "Modern Political Economy and Public Policy," *World Affairs*, 182, no. 2 (June 2019): 187-204; there is some overlap between this and the previous chapter, but the points bear repeating.

2   See Max J. Skidmore, "Censorship: Who Needs It? How the Conventional Wisdom Restricts Information's Free Flow," *Journal of Popular Culture* 35, no. 3 (Winter 2001): 143-156.

ployment. The vast body of research from the famous Card and Krueger study onward indicates that it does not. That study from the early 1990s examined fast food jobs in the Philadelphia metropolitan area, which crosses the state line from Pennsylvania into New Jersey. Since one state, New Jersey, increased the minimum wage and Pennsylvania did not, it was well situated for a study of the effects of minimum-wage increases.[3]

Another example, an especially striking one that perhaps is even more revealing, deserves mention again. It arose from a highly influential study published in 2010 in the *American Economic Review*, "Growth in a Time of Debt." The authors were two prominent Harvard economists, Carmen Reinhart and Kenneth Rogoff. They asserted that their examinations of the economies of numerous countries made it clear that debt levels greatly damaged economic growth, even reducing it to negative rates, when debt levels reached the deadly level (not their term) of 90% of GDP.

This immediately became conventional wisdom, relied upon by austerians from former Representative Ryan and other Americans to European leaders. Within two years, however, reasonable observers recognized that, rather than being a "new law," the dreaded 90% figure had become meaningless, having been exposed as erroneous by a doctoral student at the University of Massachusetts. It had been based on erroneous calculations—calculations that should have been obvious all along.

Paul Krugman had concluded that the significant factor was whether countries "had their own currencies, and borrowed in those currencies." Because sovereign countries that have their own currencies can create money as needed, they can "carry large debt levels without generating crises."[4]

---

3   See the more detailed discussion in the previous chapter.

4   See *ibid.* for more detailed discussion.

There could hardly be a greater demonstration of the need for caution in policy planning than the fact that the 90% figure still finds its way into budgetary considerations, and that an academic study could become virtually dogma, without obvious errors being immediately detected. Undoubtedly, it happened because it was a "convenient untruth" (with apologies to Al Gore). Erskine Bowles, for example, continued to accept it, because he said it was common sense (again, that is hardly the common sense that this book recommends). He clearly failed to distinguish between sovereign states that issue and control their own currencies and entities that do not.

Although it may seem counterintuitive, it is irrational to be preoccupied with costs when crafting policy. What is important is to prioritize the overall *effects* of the expenditures, *not* what their level will be, nor to how much the program will cost. The fundamental question should be: to what extent do the expenditures meet public needs; how will they affect the people? The obsession to "pay as you go" may appear reasonable, but at the national level in reality, it is based on the crumbling foundation of ideology, not on sound finance. The comment above from Bowles demonstrates that he does not appreciate the distinct difference between private finance—say, as applicable to a corporation— and that of a sovereign nation with control of its own currency. In that, he certainly is not alone. Nearly all discussion of Medicare, for example (including Medicare for All), tends to treat it as a cost issue. Overwhelmingly, it is a matter not of economics but of health—the health of the public—and should be treated accordingly.

There are substantial differences between "family economics" and government financing at all levels. At the national level, however, the differences are so profound as to be entirely of a different order. Cities, counties, and states can overspend and run out of money. For many reasons, they must live within their budgets.

THE COMMON SENSE MANIFESTO

They depend on taxation for funds to operate, at least partly, but they also borrow, as when they issue bonds. Additionally, they receive huge amounts from the federal government. Certainly, they are limited in what they can spend by the amount of dollars available to them from taxation, plus funds from all other sources, including the US government, and from borrowing.

That restriction on overspending literally does not, and cannot, apply to America's national government, despite what budget hawks consistently warn. Cities, counties, states, and US territories cannot create dollars to pay their bills (witness the economic distress of Puerto Rico and the horrible consequences that it suffered, and continues to suffer, from Hurricane Maria—that took place *more than two years ago* as of this writing—as the Trump administration neglects its people, mentioning them, if at all, only to condemn).

At the national level, however, regardless of fevered comment from budget hawks, no economic circumstance, regardless of deficit or debt, could make the United States "become Greece," or make its economy duplicate that of a country in the Euro zone. Bluntly put, it simply is not possible.

The United States creates dollars and uses dollars to pay its bills. Thus, since it controls the sovereign currency, it can always generate any number of dollars it needs. In fact—and this is so counterintuitive that it is difficult to make people understand, but will be explained below—at the national level, there is no necessary relationship at all between government spending and government income.

The Need for Regulation

The common, unsophisticated, American attitude toward "government" can make many people accept as plausible the most irrational of propositions. For example, there was no wave of vocal opposition to one of Mr. Trump's policies, loudly stated when he assumed the presidency: his requirement that for every new regulation, two previous regulations should be eliminated.

The obvious assumption here, however silly, is commonly advocated by Republicans: the fewer regulations there are, the better. Regulation, itself, goes the assumption, is bad. The functions regulations perform are irrelevant. The only important factor is the *number* of regulations, not their effect. This is the typically simpleminded Trump approach. Any observer who thought through the issue should have recognized that adopting a bad regulation while eliminating two good ones is poisonous policy. Bad regulations should of course be eliminated, regardless of whether a new one is considered. Unquestionably, there can be legitimate disagreement regarding the desirability of any given regulation—that is up to the political process to determine— but to assume that regulation *per se* is undesirable is beyond absurd. Do people really want to risk e-coli or arsenic in their food, corrosive agents in their cosmetics, cribs that smother infants, airbags that explode causing injury or death, or, one might ask, sleazy strip clubs in the midst of ultra-affluent, gated, residential neighborhoods? If not, then they should recognize the necessity of regulation.

The United States relies heavily on regulation, rather than on the practice of government ownership that prevails in socialist countries. Regulation is essential in order to provide the checks and balances that the Founders so revered. Privately-owned corporations must be regulated to ensure that their pursuit of profit is not permitted to cause unlimited pollution, destruction of competition, elimination of personal freedom, and the like. An old, and sound, principle of political philosophy is that no person should be the judge in his or her own case.[5] Regarding corpora-

---

5 *Nemo iudex in causa sua* ("no man should be a judge in his own case"), most

tions (whether legally "persons" or not), because of the vast power they exercise, permitting them to be judges in cases affecting them is even more dangerous than permitting individuals to be sole judges in their own cases. The obvious, and essential, answer is regulation.

Minimal Government

President Theodore Roosevelt (the "Republican Roosevelt," as John Morton Blum famously described him in his landmark study[6]) had no objection to wealth or to bigness. Nevertheless, he recognized the obvious truth that economic resources generate power. He therefore insisted that "malefactors of great wealth" must not be permitted to use their wealth to the detriment of the public good. Hence, the vital importance of regulation. TR was well aware that, without regulation, human beings—and most especially those with great potential power—could not be trusted to act appropriately, or in any way unselfishly. Government in a democratic republic is the one agency powerful enough to counter private corporate interests, and the only one that has a real potential to be responsive to the public will. Thus, power in government is essential.

TR was correct in decrying selfishness early in the 1900s. He was correct then, and human nature certainly has not now improved in the twenty-first century, so he continues to be correct now.

Governmental regulation is a necessary part of the American political system. It is essential to protect the environment, to provide personal privacy, to ensure civil rights and civil liberties, to safeguard individual freedom, and to ensure that the economic system is compatible with political democracy. No well-mean-

---

famously expressed in Locke's Second Treatise.

6   John Morton Blum, *The Republican Roosevelt* (Cambridge: Harvard University Press, 1954).

ing, reasonable, and well-informed person could believe that it would be acceptable to have a society in which any agent, private or public, had the unlimited freedom to spread toxic wastes (including nuclear) into the air, soil, and water, to harass individuals or groups or to destroy their lives, to prevent citizens in general from voting or from participating in civic affairs, to restrict their abilities to choose and practice their religions, to select their politics or criticize political leaders, or to have an economy that rewards only the elite, and forces all others to live at no more than subsistence levels. A free society that protects all thus requires regulation, and that requires—to use language from a key Founder, Hamilton—an energetic government.

It may sound heretical to American ears, but (despite Paine and even more so, Thoreau) the best government does not govern the least. Even less does it govern not at all. A program designed with the foremost priority of operating at the lowest cost, rather than operating to provide the best service, would be a poor program. A program designed to operate with the highest priority given to the strongest police function—one that puts elimination of waste, fraud, and the like ahead of providing benefits to the people—would be a harsh program. Voting requirements designed primarily to make it the most difficult to vote, rather than making it the easiest, will be the least democratic and thus will subvert democracy itself. A democratic system will ensure that the maximum number of people can vote and that voting is easy, simple, and accessible. The purpose of voting in a democracy is to obtain votes from the largest number of people. Of course, the system should be designed to discourage fraud, eliminating it if possible, but harsh penalties for voting in individual cases can never be justified. The purpose of voting is to hear from the most people. If the system operates otherwise, if it puts any goal above providing easy and convenient access to the ballot, the result will be to suppress the people; that clearly is the result whenever any "anti-fraud" measure discourages qualified citizens from voting.

The government that governs least, then, is like the program designed for efficiency first, rather than for policy purposes. It is like the program designed primarily to make sure that every participant follows the rules, rather than the one designed to hear from, and to benefit, the greatest number. Such a government, the one that governs least, is a government almost assuredly designed to function badly.

Program Planning Should Ignore Costs

Could anything be more counterintuitive than to ignore costs when planning a program? Regardless, the more program planning involves costs, the less satisfactory any resulting program is likely to be. Considering costs during program planning inevitably causes inferior programs, or worse, prevents programs even from going beyond the consideration stage. To achieve the best programs, it is essential *to plan for the best programs* and that means to ignore the bean counters.

This is not the first statement of this principle, a principle that is valid, however much it may be counterintuitive. An excellent example may be seen in the recent and most thoughtful work co-authored by David Blumenthal, a physician and health administrator, and James A. Morone, a political scientist. In *The Heart of Power*, they studied the manner in which various presidents dealt with health policy and questions of healthcare. They asserted, correctly, that "many American presidents have dealt with health care issues, but none with LBJ's passion."[7] He did it in such a way as to provide healthcare that several of his predecessors wanted, but that none had achieved. Moreover, his Medicare program went far beyond healthcare. It delivered a powerful blow against racial segregation in a south that was still reeling from

---

7   David Blumenthal and James A. Morone, *The Heart of Power: Health and Politics in the Oval Office* (Berkeley: University of California Press, 2010), 165.

his Civil Rights Act. It was Medicare that desegregated hospitals throughout the old Confederacy. Lyndon Johnson achieved what he did because of passion and skill, and because, over and over again, as Blumenthal and Morone stress, he "muzzled his economists." He forbade his staff from dealing with numbers, and directed them to ignore long-term costs. "The net effect was to say:" they wrote, "Let's do expanded coverage now, and worry about how to afford it later."[8]

Stephanie Kelton, a brilliant economist and the leading exponent of Modern Monetary Theory, recently (along with co-authors Andres Bernal and Greg Carlock) put the same principle in blunt terms when dealing with a different (and even more vital) subject: the proposal for a "green New Deal."[9] Their piece in *Huffington Post* dealt with efforts to combat climate change, but made it clear that the point is valid across the board. "Anything that is technically feasible is financially affordable. And it won't be a drag on the economy—unlike the climate crisis itself, which will cause billions of dollars' worth of damage to the economy .... We must give up our obsession with trying to 'pay' for everything with new revenue or spending cuts." To be sure, taxes can be important. They can "shape incentives and help change behaviors within the private sector. Taxes should be raised to break up concentrations of wealth and income, and to punish polluters." This can be useful "not because we need 'to pay for it' but to end polluters' harmful behavior."

Lest this seems impracticable, leading to the unsustainable, there are two notable examples that clearly demonstrate the contrary, that Kelton and her co-authors are correct when they say that

8   *Ibid.*, 204.
9   Stephanie Kelton, Andres Bernal, and Greg Carlock, "We Can Pay For a Green New Deal," *Huffington Post* (November 30, 2018), https://www. huffpost.com/entry/opinion-green-new-deal-cost_n_5c0042b2e4b 027f1097bda5b

anything that is technically feasible is financially affordable. As the second example indicates, certain segments of American government actually have operated this way for decades.

First, as suggested in the previous chapter, let us examine Medicare Part D, the prescription drug benefit that became law under the George W. Bush administration. Democrats had supported drug benefit programs previously; President Clinton, for example, had proposed it in 2000. It was not adopted until President Bush signed it into law in December 2003. Democrats at that time opposed the Bush plan, because Bush pushed his measure through Congress with no provision for financing. It passed only because Republicans had control of both the House and the Senate, and the Bush administration used procedural maneuvers to coerce Republican budget hawks and overpower the minority Democrats.

It was an awkward plan and clearly designed to provide a windfall to Big Pharma. It also incorporated the irrational and strange "doughnut hole," which halted all benefits temporarily for beneficiaries after they had received a certain amount of benefits. These flaws, however, can be corrected. In fact, the Affordable Care Act (the infamous—but quite beneficial—"Obamacare" that Republicans love to hate) is actually closing that doughnut hole. One may consider the flaws to be a form of "collateral damage," because after a clumsy beginning, the program began to work well and in any case now provides a huge and very valuable benefit to millions of beneficiaries. The flawed program is filling a gap that badly needed filling. The Democrats were correct that it was an enormously expensive benefit that had no funding mechanism attached. In retrospect, though, they were wrong to have opposed it. To be sure, a better program could easily have been designed—a fully public program would have been far better in all respects, but to have insisted on funding would likely have caused the program to fail, despite majority party support. The benefits Part D provides make it worth accepting flaws that can be corrected. Moreover, there is no doubt that they economy can "afford" it, as the discussion below demonstrates.

The second example, also as suggested in the previous chapter, comes from military expenditures since the Second World War. Certainly, there have been complaints regarding waste of money, and certainly a budget hawk now and then protests. In general, though, "normal" budgeting has not been applied. Never does Congress allocate a certain level of spending and order the Pentagon always to work rigidly within those limits. Instead, Congress more or less funds whatever the military requests, with some occasional reductions. The result has been astronomical deficits, especially since the Reagan administration. Regardless of President Reagan's assertion as a candidate that he would "balance the budget," his policies generated the highest deficits in history up to that time—and not once (despite hypocritically calling for a balanced budget constitutional amendment, which, fortunately for the country was never seriously considered) were any of the budgets he submitted to Congress ever balanced.

Thus, those who argue that it is essential to "pay as you go" and that no other way is sustainable completely ignore military funding; in fact, they completely ignore the realities of national government finance. Vice President Cheney is not an authority most liberals would be comfortable citing, but when he said something to the effect that "President Reagan demonstrated that deficits don't matter," to some extent, he was correct (the caveat being, of course, that the productive capacity of the economy must be sufficient to accommodate the deficit). Never mind that this violates all dogma of American political parties—especially conservative, and most especially conservative Republican, dogma.

In the previous chapter, I set forth an argument that is relevant here. My point was to argue against "economic fundamentalism." I believe that consideration sufficiently important to be repeated in this discussion: "When cost is the prime criterion, any resulting program is likely to be entirely inadequate. As counterintuitive as it sounds, the way to achieve good programs is to plan the program that best meets the needs, and only then plan for cost; cost is a secondary consideration." The economic fundamentalists would protest vigorously, believing, as they do along with most others, that every dollar the government spends comes from taxing, borrowing, or the sale of assets. They would say that planners must put costs first, or they are irresponsible, and their plans cannot be sustained. The answer to this is to "concentrate on outcomes, all things considered." There are times, however, when even the economic fundamentalists deem certain expenditures more important than their principles, such as those for national security. "The security of the American people, in other words, is deemed important enough to violate the principles of economic fundamentalism. Certainly, one should think, the health security and economic security of the people are equally important and thus should be considered accordingly."[10]

Programs Whenever Possible Should be Universal

Programs targeted at the poor, or any deprived group, tend to have difficulties that universal programs almost never have to face. Programs for all automatically have an enormous constituency. Those aimed solely at redressing deprivation specific to some group are unlikely to have strong, organized support. Any group consisting of the poor, the deprived, or otherwise made up of those requiring remedial measures, tends by definition to be relatively powerless. Certainly, such a group is unlikely to be organized or to have significant political power.

---

10 See Chapter IV.

Thus, programs designed for them are almost assuredly destined to fall behind inflation, to be vulnerable to benefit reductions, and even to be in danger of elimination.

Social Security and Medicare are consistently popular; they benefit virtually everyone. No one has to demonstrate "need," or to undergo humiliating procedures that surrender all pretense of privacy and dismantle any semblance of dignity in order to secure benefits. Thus, there is no stigma associated with using benefits from Medicare, or receiving payments from Social Security. Everyone is part of the group; no one is cast out as "the other."

The moral here is that insofar as possible, all programs should be open to all, and should welcome all. Benefits should be considered to be a part of human rights. Their goal should be maximum benefit, and not minimum cost. Social Security, for example, was not designed specifically for the poor; it was designed for all, and continues to function as intended. Regardless, it clearly is the largest anti-poverty program in the country's history. The point is that a program can be designed to provide broad benefits and at the same time significantly improve the status of a specific group, all while maintaining broad popular support.

It's *NOT* "the taxpayers' money"

I t is tempting to assume that when government spends, it is spending "the taxpayer's money." Politicians piously profess to safeguard what they always identify as that "taxpayers' money," especially those conservatives who vote repeatedly to reduce taxes on the wealthy—asserting all the while that the sharp tax cuts will be "revenue neutral" and will "pay for themselves." When the inevitable happens and the cuts generate budget deficits, they then have an excuse to call for reductions in Social Security, Medicare, and various "entitlements" that work to enrich the lives of ordinary citizens, as opposed to the very wealthy. A simple glance at history will demonstrate that this is a regular pattern with Republicans since the Reagan presidency. Reagan pioneered it, George W. Bush followed it, and it now is happening under the Trump White House.

Government spending does not require money from the taxpayers. If the national government has the power to create as many dollars as it wishes—and it does—then receiving a flood of taxpayer funds does not increase its capacity to do so; nor, conversely, does a lack of taxpayer funds reduce its ability to generate dollars as it needs them. Every time the US government spends, it creates money. When it receives money in taxes, it takes money out of the system, thus effectively destroying it.

Kelton and her colleagues put it this way:

> As a monopoly supplier of U.S. currency with full financial sovereignty, the federal government is *not* like a household or even a business. When Congress authorizes spending, it sets off a sequence of actions. Federal agencies, such as the Department of Defense or Department of Energy, enter into contracts and begin spending. As the checks go out, the government's bank—the Federal Reserve—clears the payments by crediting the seller's bank account with digital dollars. In other words, Congress can pass any budget it chooses, and our government already pays for everything by creating new money.

This is precisely how we paid for the first New Deal. The government didn't go out and collect money—by taxing and borrowing—because the economy had collapsed and no one had any money (except the oligarchs). The government hired millions of people across various New Deal programs and paid them with a massive infusion of new spending that Congress authorized in the budget. FDR didn't need to "find the money," he needed to find the votes. We can do the same for a Green New Deal.

She and her colleagues are correct. We could, and should do the same for the Green New Deal. We could, and also should, go beyond that.

We should do the same for what FDR called for in his State of the Union message of 1944, an "economic bill of rights"; one that provided as a right, universal programs of healthcare, education (including higher education and training in trades), well-paying jobs for all who want to work, decent housing, and the like.

To add to FDR's list, we could, and should, resuscitate America's postal system, and do as many other countries do: charge it with providing basic banking services, especially to those with very little income, and perhaps charge it with regulating broadcast and other electronic communication media. Not everyone today can get a bank account, and middle-class people generally have no idea how difficult it can be in a modern economy to function without one. Such a system would permit lower-income groups to participate in the economy to a degree not currently possible and would supersede the ineffable and inexcusable payday loan industry.[11]

In view of today's pressing needs, when an unbelievably heavy burden is placed on both personal finances and the economy in general by student loan debt—greater, in the aggregate, even than the amount owed on credit cards—we could easily, and should, buy up and pay off student loans. If lenders profit, so be it; heavier taxes on the wealthy could and should redress that imbalance. There could also be subsidies to those who have already paid off their loans to prevent their outrage at others receiving a benefit not then available to them. Purchasing student debt would ease pressure on the economy and directly benefit millions, while at the same time providing an economic stimulus.

---

11   See Chapter VIII.

But, what about inflation? Kelton and her colleagues explain that "despite lawmakers' stated fears, larger public deficits are not inherently inflationary. As long as government spending doesn't cap out the full productive capacity of the economy ... it won't spin prices out of control."

Social insurance programs, such as Social Security and much of Medicare, may be seen as an exception because they were created to stand alone and to tie their benefits specifically to trust fund income. At the instant they receive dollars from payroll taxes, destroying them, they simultaneously add new ones to the trust funds, creating new ones, as though they merely flowed from taxpayers into trust funds. This is not necessary to successful systems, but it does have a useful purpose in creating a sense of ownership of the benefits for which a beneficiary has paid and in providing restraints on politicians who might wish to harm or even eliminate the programs. FDR himself argued for trust funds as a tool to keep some "damned politician from getting his hands on the money," or words to that effect. Such restraints have obviously become less effective as the Republican Party has become more ideological, and as opponents of social insurance have convinced some of the public that the highly successful programs are "unsustainable" without drastic revisions—always in the form of benefit cuts or program elimination.

Language is vital, and the manner in which the people use language matters. Consistently describing government payments as "the taxpayer's money" serves to create resentment among taxpayers, who then quite understandably assume they are bearing the costs of benefits to others, many of whom they may dislike. Equally damaging is the devious description of any lowering of taxes as "tax relief," thus implying that the taxed are suffering under a monstrous burden from which they need "relief." A comparison of US taxation with that in other advanced countries demonstrates that Americans pay at a relatively low level, even when all state, local, and payroll taxes are added to the national income tax.

Halting all benefits would not automatically eliminate taxes, nor would doubling, tripling, or any measure of benefit increase automatically raise them. This certainly would not eliminate all economic resentment, much of which is based directly on racial or religious prejudice, but it could make those prejudices more obvious—and, one may hope, make them socially unacceptable.

Conservative policies, as defined by Americans who call themselves conservative, have demonstrated time after time that they are extremely difficult, and often impossible, to implement. When implemented, they satisfy no one, least of all their adherents. That is why I wrote *Unworkable Conservatism* (cited above). Some of us are old enough to remember that even during the administration of the patron saint of modern American conservatism, Ronald Reagan, the pleas of his disappointed supporters, who could not bring themselves to criticize Saint Ronald directly, was that his advisers should "let Reagan be Reagan."

The chaos of the Trump administration demonstrates that change certainly is needed. The 2018 election results suggest that change may be on the way, as does the sudden energy in the movement to impeach resulting from Trump's open practice of putting his personal good above principle, country, or morality. If it comes, and if the changes are in the direction suggested here, the political economy of the United States, and its public policies, will at last be re-engineered to benefit the whole people of the United States, not the most powerful of economic elites, nor the fiercest of its ideologues.

CHAPTER VI

Crafting Public Policy in a Modern Political Economy[1]

W e have come to a clear realization of the fact that true individual freedom cannot exist without economic security and independence. "Necessitous men are not free men." People who are hungry and out of a job are the stuff of which dictatorships are made.

In our day these economic truths have become accepted as self-evident. We have accepted, so to speak, a second Bill of Rights under which a new basis of security and prosperity can be established for all—regardless of station, race, or creed.

Among these are:

- The right to a useful and remunerative job in the industries or shops or farms or mines of the nation;

- The right to earn enough to provide adequate food and clothing and recreation;

- The right of every farmer to raise and sell his

---

1   A preliminary version of this chapter was given as a paper at the American Political Science Association's Caucus on Poverty, Inequality, and Public Policy's panel on New Approaches to Poverty, Annual Meeting, Washington, DC, 2019. It is the culmination of the two previous chapters, Chapters IV and V. It also continues the argument of *Unworkable Conservatism*.

products at a return which will give him and his family a decent living;

- The right of every businessman, large and small, to trade in an atmosphere of freedom from unfair competition and domination by monopolies at home or abroad;

- The right of every family to a decent home;

- The right to adequate medical care and the opportunity to achieve and enjoy good health;

- The right to adequate protection from the economic fears of old age, sickness, accident, and unemployment;

- The right to a good education.

All of these rights spell security. And after this war is won we must be prepared to move forward, in the implementation of these rights, to new goals of human happiness and well-being.

America's own rightful place in the world depends in large part upon how fully these and similar rights have been carried into practice for our citizens.

President Franklin D. Roosevelt,
State of the Union Message, 1944[2]

---

2   FDR repeated his call for an Economic Bill of Rights in his next and final

Introduction: Previous Work

Chapters IV and V deal with the structure and function of American politics, and with the changes that have resulted in what I am calling a modern political economy. This chapter examines ways in which policies must be crafted to deal with the circumstances those chapters discuss. It samples the kinds of policies that have become essential, examines the most likely approaches that may lead to legislation, and stresses the changes that are necessary to produce more humane policies and a government and society that work for the whole: for the people, not merely the elites.

These three chapters together form a unit that continues the argument in my 2017 book, *Unworkable Conservatism*, describing the assumptions of American "conservatism" that violate common sense, are unhistorical, are based on ideology rather than experience or reason, and continue to produce difficulties for the American people. It presents a common sense, not ideological, approach to politics. Above all, it dispels the assumption that such things as healthcare for all, environmental protections, and the like—seen in the US as "radical," while matters of common sense in virtually all other developed countries—are too far out of the "mainstream" in America to be feasible.

Beyond the structural impediments to progressive change, these chapters examine ideological, cultural, and historical barriers. Some of these, for various reasons, have their greatest effects on the possibilities for implementation of social programs. Among these are misconceptions regarding the extent of poverty in the United States and its effects.

---

state-of-the-Union address in 1945; for a scholarly treatment demonstrating its continuing relevance, see Cass Sunstein's brilliant study, *The Second Bill of Rights: FDR's Unfinished Revolution and Why We Need It More Than Ever*, New York: Basic Books, 2004. Nearly two decades after Sunstein's book, the urgent need continues to increase.

America's Jeffersonian heritage engenders a widespread romanticism that, at least rhetorically, favors localism, agrarianism, decentralism, individual autonomy, and strictly limited government, especially at the national level. For many who hold Jeffersonian ideas, their attachment to them may be implicit or explicit. Regardless, in most instances it incorporates little or none of the nuance of Jefferson's thought. For instance, the individual well-being that permeated Jefferson's notions of "ward republics" is lost when individual autonomy takes the form of laissez-faire government policies that, under modern conditions, leave the individual at the mercy of oppressive corporate economic forces. These include the most expensive healthcare in the world, which is far less widely available than in any other developed country. One might also consider the enormously expensive system of higher education that makes it almost mandatory for students to go deeply into debt to achieve what they need to thrive in today's economy.

These chapters also point to the confusion typical in public discourse regarding the thought of "The Founders." Self-described constitutional conservatives often complain loudly that the United States no longer operates according to the ideas of the Founders. Many members of the public are misled into agreeing, not recognizing two important flaws in the criticism. First, the notion that it would be possible—let alone practical—to function without some adaptation for nearly two and a half centuries as the country evolved from a tiny pre-industrial group of fractious states into an enormous and complex nation-state—in fact, a superpower—is beyond silly. Second, the ideas conservatives tend to describe as those of the Founders are grossly oversimplified and misrepresented. They tend often—rather than representing the ideas of "The Founders"—to be the ideas of the early opponents of the Constitution; a group largely opposed in principle to an activist national government.

The Founders, among themselves, differed considerably in their opinions and were hardly unanimous. One widely shared opinion among them, though, was *not* that we needed a Constitution to ensure a weak central government. Rather, there was general agreement that the Articles of Confederation were fatally flawed in that there was almost no power at the center. The purpose of the Constitution was to create a strong national government.

Compare, for example, the ideas of Jefferson with those of Hamilton. The two men disagreed considerably, yet each was a prominent Founder. Hamilton, in fact, who today's conservatives mostly ignore, was far more influential in drafting the Constitution and in securing its ratification than was Jefferson, who actually had no direct role at all; he was in France during the Convention and did not return to America until the new government was in place. Yet his views of strict construction and governmental powers tend to be far more congenial to those on the right today, at least rhetorically, despite his actions as president. As an executive, he was far more an activist than his principles would have suggested or than today's constitutional conservatives would wish.

The practices that America adopted as it developed have tended to align more closely with Hamilton's ideas than with Jefferson's. American political rhetoric, though, has frequently reflected a romantic Jeffersonianism. This has often been troublesome for those who seek to secure progressive programs that require governmental activism. They often have had the most success when they can connect their proposals with some national emergency or national defense. An example was the National Defense Education Act that Republican President Dwight Eisenhower signed in 1958, providing long-sought and much-delayed federal aid to education.

The fact that the Republican Party today tends to coalesce around Donald Trump and completely disregard the principles that are supposed to be their hallmark, while accepting personal and political conduct from him that they admit they would reject from a Democrat, is beyond disturbing. It is useful, however, to demonstrate that without question, their prime motivation tends to be a tribal lust for power rather than commitment to any principle. The evidence is that, at some level, they recognize that their "conservative" principles are not likely to be implemented and would not work well if they were. The ease with which they sacrifice them at the altar of Trump is clear evidence of this.

Another barrier to progressive legislation that these chapters examine—and that requires intense scrutiny—is fundamentalism, defined as textual literalism and ideological rigidity. Fundamentalism is notable in religion, of course, but also in economics, constitutional interpretation, and most forms of thought. It tends to lead to a rejection—or at best a suspicion—of reason, science, and logic. It is apparent in today's political discourse, even on such settled scientific issues as climate change. Regarding political issues, it can lead intelligent officials to accept irrational and overly ideological measures that defy thought.

An example of several of the tendencies mentioned above may be seen in a personal letter I received some years ago in response to an article I wrote in the *Kansas City Star* supporting Social Security, calling for its expansion. I have reproduced the excerpts as received, with no changes to spelling or punctuation:

Dear Prof. Skidmore:

Your column of February 7 in the Kansas City Star reinforces the widely-held belief that UMKC is blatantly liberal. I hope you do not promote the philosophy of your column to your classes, as inexperienced students are not inclined to question pronouncements of the academic leaders as readily as more-seasoned individuals may do.

.... Social Security ... was established in a period when personal responsibility, loyalty, and respect for the law were governing characteristics of the vast majority of the populace. These and other desirable traits (one's word is one's bond; a handshake is a contract; I am responsible for my actions) have been eroded today to allow many to claim victimhood, where politicians no longer represent their electorate, and corporate leaders do not act to benefit their investors or their customers. Today's personal philosophies tend more to "How much can I get" or "How can I take advantage of this". Discourtesy, even rudeness, dictates the daily lives of many, from minor transgressions on the freeways to major criminality in corporate offices. Daily evidence of lawsuits, governmental inquiries and porkbarrel legislation results in monumental expenditures of time and tax monies, with no general benefit as a consequence.

Rather than expanding governments' bureaucracy and influence into citizens' lives, our need is to reestablish individual responsibility and invigorate personal savings habits, resulting in each wagearner creating his own retirement security. You, among all others, have the wonderful opportunity to create this mindset among your students. You have a captive audience, new every sixteen weeks, to whom you can expouse philosophies that can result in lower deficits, lower taxes, lower stresses, and a generally more enjoyable lifestyle, where each of us may trust promises made to be promises kept. As we have seen, promises made by governmental agencies are valid only for that session of the legislature. Your published suggestion only opens us all to more bureaucracy and opportunity for more disappointment.

Sincerely

I stress that this consistently anti-government, but highly varied, array of allegations and assumptions came before Trump was on the national political landscape. My response follows:

Dear Mr. _____ :

I appreciate your having gone to the trouble (more than once) of sending me your views. You clearly feel strongly that you are right. Since you urge me to incorporate your opinion into my lectures, you doubtless are confident of your own wisdom. I am not. I shall provide you with some reasons why I am not confident that your position is a wise one.

Simply assuming that everyone should fend for himself, regardless, is hardly sufficient foundation for a humane society. It is easy for some of us who are comfortable to assume that others who are not, are that way because in some manner they are undeserving. Christianity teaches me otherwise; it teaches me that all are worthy in God's sight, and that we all have obligations to others—not simply to ourselves. I infer from this that we would all be well advised—to paraphrase some advice that sounds almost quaint in the selfish climate of today—that it would be well if we would "ask what [we] can do for our country." That means for the other people in our country. I understand how you think, because I grew up as a very strong conservative in Southwest Missouri (one-time president of the College Republicans). I was surely at least as conservative as you are. Then, however, well into my adult years, I grew up, and recognized that over-simplification is simple-mindedness.

It is unrealistic (one could say heartless) to insist that personal responsibility is the only acceptable answer when economic conditions are as they are in modern America. The minimum wage is insufficient to provide for a family and put away enough for health needs and for retirement. The average worker (not the minimum-wage worker) simply does not make enough to provide for a decent post-employment life. The average college graduates are saddled with enormous student loans that are burdensome for years, and make it impossible to put enough aside to care for themselves. A health crisis is sufficient to wipe out the savings of even the affluent, and to plunge one into irretrievable debt.

Some people may believe that this is as it should be. I happen to believe that we can do better. Social Security is one thing that helps. Good public education is another. A more rational and efficient system of health-care delivery would be yet another. I refuse to look at a world and say, "it's harsh, but that's tough." I prefer to look at it and say, "I want to exercise personal responsibility, yes, but I also want to make things better." I also am willing to help pay to make things better. Teaching students that they have obligations only to themselves is not something that I could in good conscience do.

Sincerely,
Max J. Skidmore

Adapting to a Modern Political Economy

Adapting to a modern political economy requires that we operate on several principles that run counter to conventional wisdom. The term "Political Economy" has an old-fashioned air about it, but the disciplines of political science and economics are so closely related, and politics and the economy are so entwined, that it would be well to re-institute political economy as a discrete and widely-accepted field of study.

In suggesting that scholars turn their attention to Modern Political Economy, I argued that, whenever possible, America's national policies should be universal, not targeted toward specific groups. This is especially the case with policies aimed at alleviating poverty. I argued, further, that policies should be crafted to achieve their goals, *not* to fit within budgetary restraints, that far from being the best, the least government performs poorly, and that a miserly approach to spending is *not* a "wise use of the taxpayers' dollars."

With regard to those "taxpayer dollars," the national government of the United States controls its own currency, paying its bills in dollars. It issues dollars as needed (or desired), in whatever amounts it chooses, and thus is under no realistic restraint to "find the money" or to "pay-as-you-go." Taxes are useful for purposes of regulation and for control of income inequality, but are not relevant to expenditures. Neither spending dollars nor receiving them from taxpayers affects the government's ability to create dollars as it chooses.

As economist Stephanie Kelton puts it, to the horror of mainstream economists—but to the delight of many on Wall Street—"Anything that is technically feasible is financially affordable." To the inevitable protest that "printing money" leads to inflation, she points out that this need not be true. There is no need to fear inflation, so long as spending does not exceed the productive capacity of the economy.[3] Despite conventional wis-

---

[3] For an admirably concise, but nonetheless clear and thorough explanation of her thought and that of colleagues applicable to a potent political issue of today, see, Stephanie Kelton, Andres Bernal, and Greg Carlock, "We Can Pay for a Green New Deal," *Huffington Post* (November 30, 2018), https://www.huffpost.com/entry/opinion-green-new-deal-cost_n_5c0042b2e4b027f1097bda5b (accessed January 28, 2019).

dom, and regardless of the nearly-universal jargon of politicians, when government spends, it is not using "the taxpayers' money."

★

This chapter, as a culmination of the two previous ones, uses their principles. It offers speculations about possible ways to work around the structural, cultural, and political obstacles that progressive policies, however commonsensical they are, face in America. It assumes that this country is exceptional, in that probably more than in most developed countries, the United States has erected a host of obstacles that proposed social legislation—and much other needed legislation as well—must overcome.

Accordingly, the current discussion builds upon the foundational framework set forth in the previous articles: assume that proposals generally should be for universal programs, should plan for the highest quality, not for economy, and should educate the public that paying for them will not require "the taxpayers' dollars." It also, as previously indicated, incorporates the theme of my 2017 book, *Unworkable Conservatism*,[4] and urges that we discard the fear of big government: instead of *less government*, we should work toward *better government*.

That book's theme is that the typical American small-government conservatism itself presents two insurmountable obstacles. First, it is very difficult, and often impossible, to implement. Second, if it were implemented, it would satisfy no one, especially its advocates. They will argue that the fault in whatever plan was implemented is that it didn't go far enough or that it wasn't given a chance. It is relevant here to note the considerable publicity regarding the death, in August 2019, of David Koch, one of the infamous "Koch Brothers," the enormously wealthy

---

4   Max J. Skidmore, *Unworkable Conservatism* (Washington: Westphalia Press, 2017).

153

libertarian activists who poured huge amounts of money into American politics to foster "conservative" principles. The gist of much of the coverage was that the overall result had disappointed the Kochs.

As a resident of Kansas, for example, I could only marvel at former Governor Brownback's excuse for the state's sharp drop in revenues after he slashed taxes: he protested that the drastic cuts—after having been in effect for much of his tenure had not had time to work. Even more astonishing was the excuse of Arthur Laffer, Brownback's adviser and fellow ideologue, that the tax cuts were not sufficiently large.

Forgetting the "law of holes," conservative ideologues seem always to believe that the way to get out of one is to dig deeper. I am old enough to remember the great disappointment (now mercifully forgotten by conservatives) expressed by Reagan's fervent—but frustrated—supporters who pleaded with his aides: "Let Reagan be Reagan!"

The central theme of this current chapter, therefore, is a question: what means might be best be employed, built upon these principles, to implement these assumptions that I have just set forth, to make it possible to work around the numerous obstacles to success? Obviously, at this most preliminary of stages, this discussion must be speculative. Accordingly, I offer the ideas here as a thought piece, one pursuing possibilities, rather than offering carefully-crafted, and detailed, plans.

A simple beginning would be a commonsense approach that recognizes the superiority of government as the provider of governmental services. Above all, do not privatize and do not attempt to improve services by cutting them. Do not attempt to make government work better by shrinking it. Pay attention to the convenience of citizens and make government services readily available and accessible geographically—reverse the Republican approach of constantly reducing the numbers of post offices and Social Security offices, for instance.

Generally—under almost all circumstances, in fact—government should cease delegating authority to profit-making, private organizations to do what government itself can do better. That means, for example, not using collection agencies to collect unpaid taxes. Eliminating them at the national level was a step forward, but deferring to Turbo Tax and Tax Cut, in lieu of widely-publicizing the availability of free electronic filing, still places a burden on taxpayers. It is a burden that exists only because of heavy lobbying activities.

All of this also would entail no private prisons. Private organizations, especially profit-making ones, when so employed inappropriately exercise governmental powers. They tend to abuse citizens with impunity and have a record of shockingly poor performance, vastly inferior to government agencies—which themselves are bad enough and in need of reform.

Yet another example is Part C of Medicare, the so-called "Medicare Advantage." This is, and was planned to be, a step toward privatization. It has the superficial appeal of offering some additional incentives (membership in a health club or fitness center, for example) to beneficiaries, but it works to do so only by providing a substantial subsidy to the private health maintenance organizations (HMOs) that provide the services. To make a profit while providing more services than traditional Medicare, private companies simply cannot operate with costs as low as those of traditional Medicare. The belief that profit-making companies can offer health coverage more efficiently than government can—however consistent it is with the prejudices of the "constitutional conservatives"—is simply wrong. It also violates not only all official figures, but common sense as well. Unfortunately, a Trump executive order in late 2019 is designed to move steadily toward

Part C, with the covert (but clear) intend to privatize Medicare. As conservatives recognize, this is a significant step toward eliminating a huge, and enormously popular, government program without—they hope—arousing opposition.

The effect of Medicare Advantage, of course, is to increase, not decrease, healthcare costs—at the same time creating a privileged group of beneficiaries. In no way could or did it achieve the hoped-for increases in efficiency. The experiment demonstrates that seeking greater efficiency cannot rely on privatization if the aim is to achieve real results. This should have come as no surprise. Study after study makes it clear that Medicare, Medicaid, and other government health programs (those for veterans, for example) provide far more healthcare for every dollar spent than private profit-making plans do. Moreover, Advantage plans also come with the hidden defect of exposing beneficiaries to the danger of some of the worst practices of poorly-regulated private insurance: denied claims and services, a danger that does not exist for regular Medicare beneficiaries. Thus, the recommendation here is to incorporate the added benefits of Advantage plans into standard Medicare, make it fully comprehensive, and make it (or a fully nationalized and non-means-tested Medicaid) available to all.

An example of the kind of privatized Medicare Advantage flaws that most beneficiaries would not anticipate until they encounter them can be drawn from personal experience. I will accept the risk of criticism for becoming personal, because I believe it is important, and personal experience is valuable. Such flaws are typical of American private health care delivery.

I retired recently, nearly three months ago from this writing, shifting from my university's health coverage for its faculty and staff to a university-sponsored and subsidized Medicare Advantage plan for its retirees. As such plans go, it is an excellent one. It is advertised as accepted by any physician in the U.S. who accepts Medicare. My wife and I had been patients for a quarter century or so at a local practice. The first time I attempted went in for care after retiring, I encountered a shock.

"We don't accept this," said the receptionist. I said to her at it had been advertised as accepted by any doctor who accepts Medicare. We do accept Medicare, she said, but pointed out that this is not standard Medicare. I told her that I was aware of that, and she said that they would see me, and would bill Medicare, but they would not accept Medicare's reimbursement rates as payment in full. They would bill Medicare, she said, but I would have to pay the difference between what Medicare pays, and what they bill their patients who have standard Medicare. Moreover, I would have to sign a form (she had a stack of them) agreeing to pay what remained of their standard charges. She said that my quarter-century history as a patient did not matter. So far as "Family Care" was concerned, my insurance was worthless.

They would accept Medicare reimbursement rates as payment in full from anyone with standard Medicare, but would not accept the same amount as payment in full for me. Moreover, they would not provide service at all unless I accepted full responsibility for all additional charges, regardless of how great the difference was. I told her I considered that to be unethical, and left to find another family practice for my wife and me.

Therein lay another shock. I complained to my new insurance company, and they agreed with me that the family care practice in this regard was unethical. They were sympathetic and tried to be helpful. For example, they immediately emailed me an extensive list of doctors in the area that were accepting new patients. The first one I called, said that we could be accepted, but the first opening was eleven months later! (Another was a pediatrician, not exactly appropriate for us.)

The earliest I could actually get in to any new family practice of all the doctors on the list was nine months away. I made appointments for us, and my wife and I now have a mere six more months to wait before we have a new family doctor. In the meantime, we have to be confined to walk-in clinics. Next month I turn 86 and my wife is also in her 80s; fortunately, we are vigorous and in excellent health (for example, I am happy to affirm that I do not regularly need any prescription medication, and generally go years before I have need of an antibiotic).

For others of our age, though, this "normal" working of America's health-care delivery system could be a death sentence, or alternatively, could boost them speedily upon the road to bankruptcy, despite having "full coverage." Remember that the next time someone says government medicine is unacceptable because there are long waits in other countries to see doctors, or to obtain services.

We have through the years occasionally used systems in other countries, have always been able to get service within an hour; usually much quicker. Here, despite our expensive, top-of-the line, Medicare Advantage plan, we in effect not only have no choice, but at least for now, have no health care coverage at all for any serious situation.

Only in America ...

Examples of Possible Approaches

Despite the current dire political climate overall, there are some favorable indications. These come largely, but not entirely, from Democrats. A list of a few examples, selected at random and far from comprehensive, follows.

- Although the chances for a positive outcome for numerous reasons at best are dubious, reports of the May 2019 meeting of Speaker Nancy Pelosi and Senate Minority Leader Chuck Schumer with Donald Trump gave some reason for hope. The tone of the meeting appears to have been polite, perhaps even cordial, and the apparent outcome was a tentative agreement on a $2 trillion infrastructure improvement.

Technically, of course, this is not an agreement to provide what is necessary, regardless of cost. Also, there was discussion of ways in which to "find some way to pay for it," a need that actually does not exist. Nevertheless, the amount discussed was so enormous that it almost fits the criterion of planning without regard to cost. The mere fact that this president could have such a conversation with Democrats, that they were receptive, and that all participants seem to have been comfortable speaking favorably of astronomical sums suggests that there may be some possibility for movement toward a vital renewing of the country's aging, inadequate, and, in some instances, crumbling infrastructure. No one suffers more from the country's inadequate infrastructure than those who are the least affluent.

This, by the way, remains a somewhat hopeful sign, notwithstanding the subsequent—and obviously calculated in advance—fit of pique that Mr. Trump demonstrated by saying that he no longer could negotiate with Democrats and that he would not agree to any legislation unless they halted all investigations into perceived misconduct of his administration. One would think that, to most reasonable observers, his threat would appear to be another public instance, widely and deliberately publicized by the White House, to be added to the Mueller Report's recitation of attempted obstructions of justice. To be sure, given the magnitude of the misconduct of the Trump administration, all the various reasons for concern are now being melded together in one overwhelming issue: impeachment. It came suddenly, but in retrospect seems to have been inevitable given Trump's single consistently-applied principle: the pursuit of self-interest regardless of other concerns, including those of the country

- Another idea that resonates strongly with the public is Medicare for All. Social Security Works, an organization devoted to protecting and expanding Social Security, endorses the idea. Medicare, after all, is contributory social insurance and is authorized by the Social Security Act. Rep. Pramila Jayapal has introduced a Medicare For All bill that would provide full universal coverage as a human right and is the most generous legislative proposal yet.

As an aside, attention to language is always essential, although rarely recognized, as such. Progressives should stop their unconscious habit of repeating Republican phrases. Chris Matthews of "Hardball" on MSNBC, for example, no doubt without thinking about his word choices, tends to refer to universal health coverage as "government medicine," which it is not and would not be and which makes it unpalatable to many. Similarly, referring to reductions in taxes as "tax relief" carries the connotation of an America burdened by oppressive taxes, which, by world standards, it most certainly is not.

Among presidential contenders, Senator Bernie Sanders has made Medicare For All a centerpiece of his platform. His proposal includes the necessary expansion of Medicare to include long-term care, maternity benefits (not currently necessary in a plan largely limited to the elderly), vision care, dental and auditory care, no co-pays, and the like. There has been opposition because it would eliminate private insurance. This would not be necessary to the plan, however, and in any case, the purpose of a health plan is to provide healthcare, not to maintain jobs. There could be a parallel plan to compensate for the jobs it replaced, and the plan itself would create additional jobs.

Both the Jayapal and Sanders proposals would avoid one un-healthy side effect that could emerge from some Medicare For All discussions. Neither plan is a stealth effort to shift Medicare to a privatized plan, which would eliminate some of the features that make Medicare desirable.

- Another approach would be to make Medicaid, as opposed to Medicare, fully national and expand it to be available to everyone. Medicaid already has a much more extensive range of benefits than Medicare. There has been some talk of a Medicaid-based system, but most of the conversation revolves around one based on Medicare. Medicaid, currently, is a federal-state program, and has many variations from state to state. It also is a system designed for the poor and probably therefore suffers from such an identification. Nevertheless, it currently is the only program that provides long-term care, and many middle-class Americans—especially the elderly—have come to rely upon it for their disabilities, after depleting all of their financial resources.

For a more cautious approach, other schemes, such as those that rely on private organizations, might appeal to some as a better fit for the American political culture. This would not be "privatization," however, because to be satisfactory it would have to require that the private organizations be non-profit; their "non-profit" organization would have to be genuine and not a mere accounting device. Most universal health plans around the world are not "socialized medicine" in that they rely on private organizations. The difference is that the organizations are required to honor commitments (no armies of claims adjusters, as in American private insurance, to find ways to deny claims), and they must operate in a genuinely non-profit manner. The profit motive is one of the most striking differences between much of America's healthcare delivery system and those elsewhere. It also bears the blame for the huge costs of America's system, for its failure to cover the entire population, and for many of the system's failures of quality.

A word about Senator Sanders is appropriate here, because of his standing as a potential presidential candidate. He has been a voice for reason and common sense for decades, and also has solid and highly successful administrative experience. Before Vermont sent him to the US Senate, I wrote that, as mayor of Burlington, he had dealt with serious longstanding municipal issues. When he took office, there was almost no affordable housing, the city's beaches were polluted, its streets were full of potholes while sidewalks were crumbling, snow removal was uncertain at best, and for years "a local Democratic machine operated in collaboration with Republicans to resist change." He persuaded voters to accept his "Progressive Coalition" and demonstrated that he was a pragmatic leader, not an ideologue. During his tenure, snow removal not only became reliable, but also included the sidewalks. He arranged for a new and efficient sewer system that kept most pollution away from Lake Champlain; it even treated storm runoff. He brought new parks and bicycle lanes, and his administration brought a housing boom, both luxury and low-income. "Sanders reached outside the traditional framework of 'public or private.' At his urging, Burlington created non-profit corporations to deal with many of the seemingly-insoluble problems," bringing housing for the elderly and accommodations for the homeless. He brought programs of micro-loans for small business and created a "Community Land Trust" to build houses for sale and rent, selling them at below market value, "but requiring that, when sold, they be re-sold to the Corporation at a profit rate lower than normal appreciation."[5]

---

5   See Max J. Skidmore, *Moose Crossing: Portland to Portland on the Theodore Roosevelt International Highway* (Lanham, MD: Hamilton Books, 2007), 38.

He therefore has an innovative and practical background, which led him to propose Medicare for all. Although American conservatives generally balk at the idea, their disapproval simply demonstrates how much they are driven by ideology, how little they are concerned with the general welfare, and how little they recognize the United States as an outlier in world a world that has adopted common-sense solutions, while Americans suffer from astronomical health costs and less satisfactory healthcare quality than frequently prevails elsewhere. Those countries all pay far less for their healthcare, and tend to have far better results overall than the United States. Some form of universal health coverage is certainly needed for the United States, and Senator Sanders has put forth the nucleus of a comprehensive plan. Many of the other Democratic contenders have signed on to his proposal, including Senators Booker, Gillibrand (before she withdrew as a candidate), Harris, and Warren.

- With regard to Warren, it is interesting that she, too, along with Sanders, has impressive and innovative executive experience. When she was still a Harvard professor, she became aware of the enormous disadvantages consumers faced in the American marketplace. To provide some balance for the consumer faced with overwhelming corporate power, she formulated what ultimately came to be the Consumer Financial Protection Bureau (CFPB). She first published an article describing her idea in *Democracy*,[6] and then lobbied Congress to make it a reality. As described in the *New York Times,* the new bureau was "uniquely empowered to police the kinds of loans and financial schemes that led to the Great Recession." It was a new entity with the kinds of authority that were sorely needed, but that conservatives in general and Republicans in

---

6   Elizabeth Warren, "Unsafe at Any Rate," *Democracy: A Journal of Ideas*, 5 (Summer 2007), https://democracyjournal.org/magazine/5/unsafe-at-any-rate/ (accessed September 23, 2019).

particular despised. President Obama chose her to get it up and running, and "she spent a year recruiting investigators and enforcers for an office they saw as an exhilarating cause." For political reasons, she did not receive appointment as permanent director—if she had, she likely would have continued there, never running for the Senate, and never contending for the presidency—but the bureau that she had crafted was a striking success nonetheless. In the brief period before the Trump administration undercut its ability to function adequately, it caused $12 billion to be recovered for consumers.[7] It is ironic that the two most progressive candidates contending for the presidency, Warren and Sanders, have each proven to be highly skilled executives.

- Nearly all Democratic senators have gone on record as defying the Koch- and Peterson-driven efforts to create a conventional wisdom that Social Security is "unsustainable" without drastic cuts. Rather, they have called for substantial expansion. A growing number of experts on Social Security through the years have joined the call; I did so in my 2008 book, *Securing America's Future*.[8] In 2017, I joined Dr. David Kingsley to suggest, once again, an expanded plan. Our article, "Social Security for the Future," provided greater specificity than my earlier, more general, suggestions.[9]

As if to warn that vigilance for right-wing propaganda must not be relaxed, on June 13, 2019, *The New York Times*—once again—contained an extensive, scare-mongering article warn-

---

7   Alexander Burns, "In Losing Post, Warren Found a Path to 2020," *New York Times* (September 22, 2019), 1.

8   Max J. Skidmore, *Securing America's Future: A Bold Plan to Preserve and Expand Social Security* (Lanham, MD: Rowman and Littlefield, 2008).

9   Max J. Skidmore and David Kingsley, "Social Security for the Future: A Fiscally Sound Proposal to Expand Benefits and Add Progressivity to the System's Funding (With Additional Suggestions for Closure of Coverage Gaps)," *Poverty and Public Policy*, 9:2 (June 15, 2017).

ing of Social Security's demise unless the system is "reformed" (a euphemism for benefit cuts). It contained no recognition of the need for any complex, long-lasting system occasionally to require minor adjustments to deal with changing conditions. One clue to the nature of the source material for the article was the author's reference to Social Security's "so-called" trust funds.[10] Note that if the trust funds do not really exist, it makes no difference whether they draw down their assets or not, but the stated concern is that "next year," for the first time since 1982, "the program must start drawing down its assets to pay retirees all of the benefits they have been promised."

That, of course, merely reflects the plans of those who restructured the system in 1983. Those plans were to build up trust funds larger than needed to pay current benefits in order to be sufficiently large to accommodate the baby boomer retirements when they came. When the boomer retirement began and progressed, funds would be drawn back down; that is what is happening. There is no reason to maintain such huge funds after the boomers die off—as, inevitably, they will. The funds, in other words, were intended to shrink, but as they do so, they provide material for hysterical and misleading messages of alarm, generally Peterson-inspired, Koch-inspired, or both.

Another theme of the *Times* article assumes that demographics threaten the system. "Roughly 10,000 baby boomers are retiring each day," it says. "And life expectancy is increasing." All this means, according to the author, that a "slow-moving crisis is approaching for Social Security." Well, no.

The retirements were anticipated, and the 1983 adjustments took them into consideration. Moreover, recent and widely

---

10   Jeff Sommer, "Social Security is Staring at its First Real Shortfall in Decades," *New York Times* (June 13, 2019), Business Section.

publicized information from the CDC indicates that the life expectancy of Americans—far from increasing—has been *declining* since 2015: that of women remains the same, while that of men has been dropping.

Did Jeff Sommer, the author of the *Times* article not know this? He should have, because of the considerably publicity, including in his own newspaper. Did he know, but ignore, it? Probably not, giving him credit for journalist integrity. The most likely answer is that he was saying things that conservatives had introduced, in a skillful and stealthy manner, into the public discourse decades ago, and had absorbed them, to be repeated without examination whenever the subject of Social Security was under consideration.

Certainly, adjustments to Social Security may be necessary. Going beyond conventional wisdom, however, common sense could suggest that the projections are not prophecies. It could well be that the shortfalls will not materialize as projected, and that the "Low Cost, Alternative I" projections of Social Security's Trustees could indeed be more accurate than the "Intermediate," projections. The low-cost projections routinely call for no shortfalls whatever over the entire 75-year period the projections cover. Nearly all reporting completely ignores that the low-cost projections even exist.

The *Times* article could have been written any time in the last quarter century. In fact, articles containing the same or similar allegations actually have appeared many times in that period, including in the *New York Times* itself, which has published follow-up pieces including those by the same author as the one on June 13. There literally is nothing substantive in the recent flurry of concern that the *Times* has not repeated in similar articles, over and over, through the years. Note, too, that these articles, especially the one under scrutiny (June 13) were classified as "news" articles—although essentially devoid of

news—and were not in the opinion section—although largely opinion. This clearly verifies Paul Krugman's observation
(also in *The New York Times*) regarding Senator Elizabeth
Warren that there is a vast difference between serious political
and economic thought, and "Serious conventional wisdom."
"What Warren gets," he writes, "is that serious analysis is a lot
more favorable to a progressive agenda than Serious conventional wisdom, which is obsessed with keeping taxes low and
restraining spending."[11] Note that Krugman is not an advocate of Modern Monetary Theory. One might add that the
obsession from all quarters with the Trustees' Intermediate
Projections is another example of what Krugman terms the
Serious conventional wisdom. Stephen Colbert in his previous incarnation as a right-wing blowhard once captured the
idea superbly: "Reality has a well-known liberal bias."

- Democratic Presidential contender Andrew Yang has proposed what he calls a "Freedom Dividend"; a plan that would
  provide $1,000 a month to all Americans 18 years of age or
  older, with stipulations preventing borrowing or lending
  from the Dividend, and providing that only a constitutional
  amendment could change the program.[12] Although a universal basic income (UBI) sounds extreme, his website cites figures from varied points on the political spectrum who have
  either endorsed the general notion of UBI, or who have suggested that it be studied as a way to combat poverty, boost
  the economy, and counter the anticipated effects of technological unemployment. Related proposals began as early as
  Thomas Paine. In modern times, they include such diverse
  figures as Martin Luther King, Jr., Richard Nixon, Stephen
  Hawking, Elon Musk, Nicole Sallak-Anderson, and Mark

---

11   Paul Krugman, "Liberal Wonks Have a Plan for That," *The New York Times*
     (June 14, 2019), A23.

12   The Campaign of Andrew Yang, *The Freedom Dividend*, https://www.
     yang2020.com/policies/the-freedom-dividend/ (accessed May 23, 2019).

Zuckerberg. Others have discussed guaranteed annual incomes, or similar schemes. These include Milton Friedman, Barack Obama, Bill Gates, and Warren Buffett.[13]

There have been experiments with UBI, generally modest, in several places around the world, including some local jurisdictions in the US. Finland has recently ended a temporary plan, which probably was the most widely-publicized here. Such experiments not only have generated useful information for advocates, but have also led to increases in approval for some sort of UBI.

For example, Annie Nova recently reported on CNBC[14] that UBI supporters in the US believe that the country is moving closer to adoption. She noted a sharp upswing in support, which was a mere 12% ten years ago, but in 2018 had risen to 48%, according to a "recent Northeastern University/Gallup survey of more than 3000 U. S. adults." The most common proposal is one "in which the federal government sends out regular checks to everyone, regardless of their earnings or employment." The idea stems from deep concern regarding the enormous income inequality in the US. Nova quoted as a supporter "Guy Standing, co-founder of the Basic Income Earth Network." Recently addressing the World Economic Forum in Davos, Switzerland, he not only spoke favorably of UBI, but also disputed the common allegation that a basic income would encourage laziness and discourage work. Such claims, he said, are cynical, and he condemned them as "an insult to the human condition." The tendency, he said, is rather for UBI to increase, not reduce, work. He argued fur-

---

13   *Ibid.*

14   Annie Nova, "Universal Basic Income: U.S, Support Grows as Finland Ends its Trial," *CNBC Personal Finance* (May 1, 2018), https://www.cnbc.com /2018/05/01/nearly-half-of-americans-believe-a-universal-basic-income-could-be-the-answer-to-automation-.html (accessed May 23, 2019).

ther that UBI results in improvements in both physical and mental health of recipients. People with a UBI have more freedom to pursue "employment for reasons more meaningful than just a need to put food on the table." Nova said that 65 percent of Democrats and 54 percent of all people between the ages of 18 and 35 "want to see a universal basic income," while "just 28 percent of Republicans" do. She quoted the editor-in-chief of Gallup, Frank Newport, as saying that "anything that sounds like welfare gets a more negative reaction from Republicans."

Nevertheless, some conservatives do react favorably, seeing a need for some such program in today's technological economy. Standing made some points that certainly could have conservative appeal. "You can't have a free market economy if people are constantly insecure," he noted, pointing out that one cannot expect people to be rational when they lack security.[15] This was a more contemporary way of making the point that Franklin D. Roosevelt made when he proposed his "Economic Bill of Rights," excerpted as this chapter's heading. The idea had been around in some form for centuries, and therefore was not original with FDR, but he forcefully accepted it. He first made his support overt, specific, and public in his 1944 State of the Union message: "necessitous men are not free men." FDR made it clear that economic rights are required for national security, reversing the libertarian assertion that "economic freedom" means freedom to earn and spend money without limit. Properly conceived, "economic freedom" means the freedom to participate in the economy in a meaningful manner, a freedom guaranteed by a secure income.

Despite the counter arguments, the most serious objection to UBI might seem to be the possibility of destroying or reducing

---

15   *Ibid.*

incentive to work. Whether this would materialize or would not materialize, though, in a real sense is at its core irrelevant. Although the economy halfway through 2019 might suggest otherwise, in the long-run, one of the most serious challenges to the existing system may be technological unemployment. That is, the techniques of computer-controlled automatic systems with artificial intelligence have such potential that most jobs as we think of them could cease to exist. The argument is that, before long, it may be possible to function with relatively few jobs—certainly with too few to maintain a high level of employment. If that does happen (and by no means is this development a certainty[16]) We would have to reconsider just what employment means, what leisure activities mean, and how the essentials of "earning a living" might be reformulated for the bulk of the workforce. UBI might be a key factor in such a reconsideration.

• In 2014, then Governor Bill Haslam of Tennessee, a Republican, brought forth his plan, the "Tennessee Promise," which made all community colleges free of tuition for high school graduates. Some other states have programs that amount to full tuition scholarships for select students. Some states, too, have sought to reduce the expense of achieving higher education by experimenting with plans authorizing some community colleges to offer baccalaureate degrees.

Senator Elizabeth Warren has proposed a much more ambitious plan among her whirlwind of policy proposals. Her proposals include the broadest range of policies of any of the contenders for the Democratic nomination. They characteristically are well thought-out and carefully structured. She has become known for her well-received reply to questions about serious issues: "I have a plan for that."

16   See, e.g., Paul Krugman, "Falling Down the Robot Rabbit Hole," *The New York Times* (18 October 2019), p. A27.

Her carefully crafted policies long predated her election to the Senate, and were responsible—along with her genius for clear and persuasive explanation—for her entry into, and meteoric rise in, politics. Before running for the Senate, she proposed CFPB Consumer Financial Protection Bureau to establish some protection for people against the often overwhelming and generally unfair financial pressures that permeate America's economic system. Ultimately securing support from President Obama, the CFPB made it into law. Warren was made assistant to the president, and administered the bureau in its early existence, although she did not become its regular director. That appointment went to Richard Cordray, freeing Warren then to pursue her political career as a US senator and then presidential hopeful. The Bureau was extraordinarily valuable to Americans, until Trump succeeded in emasculating it by appointing a director who undercut its mission.

As for Warren's plan to make higher education more affordable, her "Free College Plan" is one of her more prominent and important proposals. One of the greatest drags on the American economy is the amount of student loan debt. The total amount now owed has been widely publicized as being roughly $1.5 trillion, considerably exceeding the amount Americans owe on credit cards. The amount seems staggering, until one puts it in perspective. The amount lost to the Treasury from the recent Republican tax cut, which went overwhelmingly to the ultra wealthy, is also roughly $1.5 trillion. Debt forgiveness of such a sum would be perceived as enormous, while conservatives tend not to bat an eye at the same amount of tax reduction for the already rich.

Senator Warren's plan would provide $50,000 of student-loan forgiveness to those making under $100,000 per year and incorporate some forgiveness on a sliding scale for those making up to $250,000. Her plan would require federal-state cooperation to provide free tuition at public colleges, community colleges, and trade schools. It would provide $50 billion to historically black institutions.

This is an excellent and characteristically well-thought-out proposal. To be consistent with the principles here, though, the loan forgiveness would need to be complete and apply to every student-loan debtor, regardless of financial circumstances. Senator Bernie Sanders, in fact, has proposed just such a plan: one that forgives all student debt, regardless of the circumstances. His plan would be a powerful corrective that would begin to reduce the unconscionable, and dangerous, level of wealth inequality that is so striking in the United States.

Why is it considered acceptable to spend billions or more to rescue organizations that are "too big to permit to fail," and why has it become conservative policy to spend equivalent amounts to ease the lives of the already ultra comfortable, the super wealthy, but it would be considered unacceptably "radical" to ease the lives of those whom the system burdens excessively?

Certainly, those who are affluent would receive a windfall that many would believe unwarranted, and wealthy lenders would profit. This, however, could be considered "collateral damage." It also could be taken care of by taxing it away. Certainly, too, those who worked through the years and managed to pay off their loans would have grounds for complaint (although a benefit to some would not create a hardship for others). To avoid such criticism, there could—and probably should—be compensatory credits for those who were forced to struggle and succeeded in paying off their loans. Both the loan forgiveness and the compensatory benefit would be a huge boost to the economy and would remove the great drag that exists from accumulated student debt.

Another advantage would be to remedy an injustice. Currently, it is far easier to discharge other debts—even those resulting from profligacy, such as those resulting from burdensome luxury purchases, losses from gambling, or any other foolish and unnecessary expenditure (such as mismanaging casinos to the point of bankruptcy or the purchase of gold toilets)—than it is to receive relief through filing bankruptcy from student loans. This injustice demonstrates a stark antagonism toward students; an antagonism reflected in a system that requires them to have advanced credentials, yet charges exorbitantly to get them, forcing much of the younger generation, their parents, and their grandparents into debt and then making it extremely—and uniquely—difficult, and often impossible, to pay off.

• Former Representative Beto O'Rourke, Washington Governor Jay Inslee (before each withdrew as a candidate), and Senator Elizabeth Warren have all proposed plans to deal with climate change. Subsequently, on June 4, 2019, former Vice President Joe Biden released his own plan that the *New York Times* called "an ambitious plan ... proposing $1.7 trillion in spending and a tax or fee on planet-warming pollution with the aim of eliminating the nation's net carbon emissions by 2050."[17] Governor Inslee has now dropped out of the presidential race to run for re-election as governor. He did a marvelous service, however, for the Democratic Party, the country, and the planet by concentrating so firmly on climate change. After his candidacy, however brief, one can hope that the concern with climate will remain at the top of the party's list of urgent action items.

The subject superficially may appear to have little to do with social programs, but an increasingly warm earth and its increasingly violent climate affects all living creatures adverse-

---

17   Coral Davenport and Katie Glueck, "Climate Change Takes Center Stage as Biden and Warren Release Plans," *New York Times* (June 5, 2019), A1.

ly, and anything that is harmful to human beings in general is almost assuredly most harmful to those who have the fewest resources to cope with adversity.

O'Rourke would have directed agencies of the US government to adopt policies that do as little harm to the environment as possible. He would again have joined other countries in the Paris Climate agreement to work toward sharply reduced emission of greenhouse gases. He would have employed measures to encourage the reduction of carbon emissions and called for spending $5 trillion on research policies to assure the use of clean energy. Inslee proposes that all American automobiles and most trucks be electrical by 2030 and that electrical production be emission-free. All these proposals come at a time when the EPA, under a hostile administration, has re-written regulations on air pollution to make them more favorable to burning coal and other fossil fuels.

Both these environmental proposals are related to the vastly more ambitious "Green New Deal" that Representative Alexandria Ocasio-Cortez (AOC) has proposed along with other Democrats. Her plan is not fully formulated, and she is not a presidential contender;: even if should she wish to be, she is too young. Senator Warren has proposed a "Green Apollo" program of investment in clean energy technology, and a "Green Marshall Plan" that would encourage other countries to purchase the resulting clean technologies from the US. This innovative proposal, too, is related to the Green New Deal.

All such plans have been derided as unrealistic and extreme. However counter-intuitive it may seem, however, they are neither unrealistic nor extreme. On the contrary, the current situation literally is similar to the plight of someone in a burning house. One must find a way to get out without delay (having once had a house burn down around me, I can speak to this from personal experience). Waiting—or worse, ignoring the situation—is unacceptable. However formulated, a Green New Deal would require comprehensive national efforts to deal with human effects on climate, just as FDR's New Deal geared up to deal with a severe economic crisis or the Manhattan Project concentrated America's economic strength to pursue nuclear weapons. Ideally, a Green New Deal would go beyond the New Deal, incorporating social measures, just as FDR proposed in his call for an "Economic Bill of Rights." Refer above to the epigraph on this point.

Incorporating environmental principles with social measures would be by far the most beneficial approach, and as Kelton demonstrates,[18] it is easily affordable. As she also stresses, to fail to accomplish this would be the foolish, and impossibly expensive approach—in every sense.

- As mentioned above, Democratic congressional leaders met with Donald Trump in an apparently affable session and informally agreed to support a $2 trillion infrastructure renewal plan. That lasted a matter of hours, until the mercurial Mr. Trump declared he would not cooperate with Democrats on anything until they called off investigations into his numerous questionable activities, including such things as enriching himself from his presidential activities, threatening to use—and actually using—the pardon for political purposes, and most unspeakably, his open invitation to the Russians: please interfere in the 2016 election to help destroy Hillary Clinton. Later, similarly, was his subsequent attempt to coerce Ukraine to provide him with information detrimental to the presidential campaign of a potential rival, former Vice President Joe Biden who hopes to get the Democratic presidential nomination. He has shown obsessive consistency where possible political rivals are concerned.

---

18   See Kelton et al., "We Can Pay for a Green New Deal."

The infrastructure agreement, though, however transitory, was a hopeful sign. If even a Donald Trump can agree (however briefly his agreement existed), it offers some hope that almost anyone else likely to hold his office might champion the cause.

Anyone who drives or merely rides on our pothole-pocked roads should be aware of the pressing need for improvement, and that is only one of the more obvious needs. There are serious shortcomings that cut through society, the economy, and the varied landscapes of the United States. Nearly everything American that could be considered part of the infrastructure presents deterioration, ranging from those that merely are of concern to those that potentially and literally are lethal.

As parents, we must recognize that our infrastructure is related to environmental concerns. We want our children, grandchildren, and other descendants not only to be safe, but also to be healthy, with clean air to breathe, clean water to drink, and food to eat without pathogens and dangerous chemicals. For a clean environment and adequate infrastructure, we must have clean politics, because government action and regulation are essential, and they certainly will run counter to some powerful interests.

- Most of the Democratic candidates have expressed recognition of the situation, but Minnesota Senator Amy Klobuchar has presented the most detailed plan to-date (June 2019). She identifies a pressing need for rural broadband, airport and school construction, excellent mass transit, and road and bridge upgrades. Her proposed public works package would be a comprehensive $1 trillion improvement to the country's essential physical foundation.

- Family leave and childcare are related issues that Democrats have stressed in their proposals. Before she withdrew from the race, Senator Kirsten Gillibrand pointed out that only the United States among advanced industrial countries fails to provide paid family leave. She advocated a plan for caregivers and new parents, who would receive 12 weeks of leave at two-thirds of their salaries. Others, including Republicans, have also proposed paid family leaves. Senator Elizabeth Warren advocates universal childcare, to be provided by a network of childcare centers. The services would be free to those earning up to twice the poverty level, and the fees for others would be on a sliding scale, correlated with income. Senator Warren points out that childcare in many locations is currently either unavailable or prohibitively expensive, often costing more than college tuition. Senator Cory Booker is proposing "baby bonds," a plan to help reduce income inequality among families. He would open a savings account for all newborns, with $1000. For children in low-income families, there would be additional annual payments up to $2,000. The Treasury Department would keep the accounts while they earn interest, and there could be no withdrawals until the child turned 18, at which point the funds could be used for worthwhile purposes, such as education or home purchases.

Progressives have an obligation to identify the most beneficial programs, and to give them their wholehearted support. Unfortunately, in many instances, they fall into the trap that the right constantly sets. They often argue among themselves about many of these proposals. They spend more effort trying to demonstrate that they cannot work than in putting in the thought and effort that will make them work—and work well.

Possibilities Beyond These Approaches

The suggestions for a universal basic income, free public college and university education, relief from oppressive debt from student loans, and baby bonds can be adapted, and melded together into a coherent program to lift up the less affluent, reduce huge fortunes, and otherwise reduce the enormous income inequality. As much as any other single factor, the great income inequality today has resulted from tax policies that began with Reagan. Since his presidency, the tendency has been to comfort the comfortable while afflicting the afflicted. Just as the mantra for some time has become "corporations have only one obligation: to enrich investors," not to exercise social responsibility, so, too, has the purpose of tax policy been to unleash the forces of acquisition.

To remedy these ills, we need to restructure the tax system. It needs to fall lightly, if at all, on those of lower income, and fall progressively heavier on those at the higher levels. Moreover, the higher rates should be quite high marginally for those of ultra wealth. Additionally, as Senator Warren suggests, there should be a wealth tax for those of extreme wealth. There should be no more reprehensible whines, as in the editorial pages of the *Wall Street Journal* early in this century—beginning on November 20, 2002—that the poor were "lucky duckies," because they paid no income tax and too little tax overall. No one, recalling the parable of Jesus and the rich man, considered that anyone could achieve that enviable status by simply giving away all wealth, therefore becoming a lucky duckie.

The overall proposal for a New Deal/Great Society—possibly a "Greater New Deal"—should include many of the proposals arising from those seeking the Democratic nomination in 2020. It should be presupposed that whatever is done must include effective policies to reverse climate change, to adopt a sound and humane immigration policy, and to achieve criminal justice and prison reform (including better training of all armed peace officers). These are of the utmost urgency.

Moreover, purely as a practical matter, a new progressive administration should take care to make those parts of government that affect people directly especially "user-friendly." This not only could help to offset negative attitudes toward government, in general, but it is simply the right thing to do; people should expect dignified treatment. Motor vehicle and driver license offices are among the most prominent examples of why government operations are widely despised. They affect most citizens at one time or another and too often are arduous to maneuver. Although these are state, not national, functions, the federal government can provide training and funds to ensure a high level of service to avoid creating general frustration with government.

Similarly, under the bean-counting ideology of Republican administrations, both post offices and Social Security offices have become scarce. Social Security's expenses are covered from the trust funds that are dedicated to Social Security, and the austerity that conservatives have imposed on the program's administrative expenditures, all to the detriment of the quality of service that citizens receive, should be removed. The Social Security Administration should have offices placed for citizen convenience, and they should be well-financed.

The Postal Service should be expanded, and placed once again in the Cabinet, as a Department of Communications and Fiscal Services, or something similar;: that is, it should not be expected to operate without government funding or to finance its own retirement program. Its charge would be to enhance mail and package delivery to every address under US jurisdiction, to make mini-banking services available to all (replacing the small-loan industry), to provide universal broadband, and to ensure aggressive cyber security for the country—especially for its elections. These would reinstitute and expand the old Postal Savings System and expand it by providing loan and checking services in addition to savings. The new department could absorb the duties of the FCC and otherwise enhance communication of all sorts.

In no particular order, the Greater New Deal should include Senator Warren's $50 billion to historically black colleges and universities and provide free higher education in all public institutions. Student loan forgiveness should be complete, beyond her proposals, and incorporate those of Senator Sanders. To avoid resentment from those who have paid their loans or their tuition, there could be compensatory subsidies. To avoid windfalls to the wealthy, their vastly higher income taxes should recapture their payments.

The government of the United States should become the employer of last resort. It should provide employment to every American who cannot find a better position elsewhere or to those who simply want to provide service to the public. Its functions should be to shore up—actually to upgrade—the country's sagging infrastructure and to engage in activities to improve the environment: something similar to FDR's Civilian Conservation Corps, which worked on infrastructure, forestry programs, and the like, and which planted literally more than 3 *billion* trees in its brief existence of only a decade (such a program today could be a godsend to the troubled environment). Yet when a proposal recently emerged from Switzerland that there should be a massive program to plant one trillion trees globally, as a healthy and inexpensive way to combat climate change, there were sneers that, even at the rate of a planting each second, it would take centuries to accomplish. What happened here to common sense? Why would there be only one planting a second? Any such plan would involve enormous numbers of people worldwide planting trees *simultaneously*, not one every so often. This, as with many such objections to practical solutions proposed to deal with various issues, is beyond silly.

Government agencies in a new (and green) New Deal should also provide sound job and technical training, training in civics, and other education. Coupled with this should be a vast increase in the country's minimum wage. It should be sufficient to enable a family to live comfortably and still be able to save for retirement. This was the case for Senator Warren's mother, but the minimum wage has unconscionably degraded through the years, so that it cannot prevent poverty.

This could also include some variation of Mr. Yang's UBI proposal, but possibly tied to those who are employed or who are on disability benefits. Moreover, disability benefits from Social Security should have qualifications considerably more easily met than they are currently. The conservative scare propaganda that anyone who doesn't want to work can simply "get on disability," is complete nonsense. The real scandal, currently, is that Social Security's disability benefits are so difficult to get. Almost everyone who applies is rejected; those who receive benefits usually have done so only after a very difficult process of appeal.

All this can be derided as unrealistic, even though it is vital. To be sure, it would require something that sounds partisan and perhaps is. Certainly it violates what often is asserted as the principle of sound civics: an avoidance of strong partisanship. Under modern circumstances, though, the only hope for progress is to be intensely partisan. When one party represents sound progress, and the other favors increasing concentration of wealth and rule by an elite minority, "partisanship" is not really partisan; it is common sense.

It also violates at least the unstated principles of modern political science that stresses "objectivity" at the cost of policy content. It requires "speaking truth to power," even from political scientists and even at the expense of mathematical models or ideological purity.

The political conditions in modern America have grown within the Republican Party under every one of its presidents (except Ford), from Nixon to the present. They are so extreme that the party not only nominates and elects one such as Donald Trump, it even refuses to serve as a corrective to the existential threat from his self-aggrandizing, amateurish flailing as President of the United States. One example of venom spewing from the Oval Office (July 2019) was an explicitly racist rant, via Twitter, against four members of the US House, stating that they should go back where they came from, or something to that effect (three of the four—all bright, progressive, young women of color—were born in the United States, of course). Of all the Republicans in both chambers, only four in the House had the courage to protest Trump's racism; none in the Senate was sufficiently courageous. The ineffable Lindsey Graham of South Carolina even added his own poisonous contribution, saying that everyone knew that these four members of the US House of Representatives were communists—none, though, had received any assistance from Russia's Putin, as Graham's beloved Trump did—assistance that seems to have troubled the shameless senator not at all, since it helped his candidate win the presidency.

There are also the toxic attacks, explicitly race-based, that Mr. Trump has levied against one of the most honorable, effective, and almost universally-respected members of Congress, the late Rep. Elijah Cummings. The *Baltimore Sun* responded superbly. Baltimore, the district that Rep. Cummings represents, has had troubles, to be sure. An individual member of Congress, though, has almost no way to affect those troubles. Baltimore is also a city in the United States, of which Mr. Trump, by the grace of the Electoral College, is president. A president has many tools that can be utilized to help a troubled city. He has not done so and exacerbates the troubles with reckless and racist rhetoric. Kudos to the *Sun* for applying common sense.

These conditions require absolute partisan voting. A Democratic tsunami will be required to sweep Republicans from the executive, both houses of Congress, state houses and state legislatures, and all offices and levels, including those most minor at the local level. It will require abolition of the electoral college (as several Democratic candidates, including Senator Warren, have proposed) that twice in the young century has gone against the public's will to select the two most dangerous presidents at least in modern history, if not of all time.

It also absolutely will require—as Mayor Buttigieg has proposed—reform of the judiciary. His solution would be to increase the number of justices from nine to fifteen. Five of these would be Democrats, and five Republican. These ten would choose the remaining five, who would be "nonpartisan" selections and who would each serve for a limited time. There are some attractive elements to his plan, but it certainly would not move away from the current politicized atmosphere that identifies justices by party affiliation.

Regardless, any truly objective analysis would demonstrate that a complete restructuring of some sort is essential to reform a branch that the Republicans have succeeded in corrupting. For decades, they have obstructed Democratic nominees, while selecting hard-right ideologues anytime they have the opportunity to do so. The brazen theft of a seat on the Supreme Court by Republican Senate leader Mitch McConnell was only the most obvious attack on decency that Republicans have employed in their continual chipping away of any semblance of judicial balance, independence, or even integrity. See further discussion of this in the following chapter.

A huge Democratic wave will be required to permit constitutional amendment. Difficult as it will be, amending the Constitution will be required to protect essential change, to correct rulings from a judiciary that has been corrupted by decades of conservative corruption of the system (see the history of the Federalist Society) and that makes FDR's court-packing proposal look completely insignificant, and to ensure judicial fairness. A pre-

THE COMMON SENSE MANIFESTO

requisite to such a wave likely will be for Democrats to pay close attention to language, as Republicans have done skillfully for decades, and to use language as carefully as Republicans do, but to a different end.

Republicans have been successful in manipulating language to obscure their true purposes and to mislead. (A tax on inheritances, for example, applies only to the wealthy, but suddenly became the dreaded "Death Tax.") Democrats must use language with equal care, but for the purpose of clarifying, not obscuring, and for applying common sense. When Republicans, and even conservative Democrats, condemn progressive policies as "radical," or "extreme," they need to be called out immediately.

Medicare for All, say conservatives, is an "extremist" program that Americans will never accept. A common-sense question, though, might be why a popular, superbly-functioning program cannot be expanded without suddenly morphing into "extremism"? Medicare is one of the most popular programs ever adopted, and the versions proposed would include missing elements, which would make it more popular still. Moreover, it is consistent with what all other advanced countries do and is hardly radical, except in the fevered rhetoric of American conservatives (true conservatives abroad frequently have been among the pioneer advocates of universal health care; it is common sense). The prohibition of employer-provided healthcare need not be a feature, and in any case, employers would be eager to have their employees covered at no cost to them. No Democrat should permit it to be described as "government medicine," which it most assuredly is not, nor as "government care."

Consumers would have choice that matters: a choice of healthcare providers. It is a diversionary tactic to switch the argument only to "choice" of the payment mechanism. Private health insurance requires complicated networks of providers that *limit* consumer choice. Similarly, a Green New Deal is less a radical idea than it is a common-sense solution that must be adopted if we are to survive. It is akin to people in a burning house arguing whether it is necessary to put out the fire. There is no room for argument.

Certainly, the odds against this necessary wave actually happening are great. Certainly, however, great odds against success also existed in 1932, and FDR's New Deal nonetheless triumphed, as did LBJ's domestic policy in the 1960s that even included long-overdue civil rights. The need currently is even greater—many of the gains of these great administrations are being rolled back. Whether the people's will is sufficiently strong to overcome modern techniques of organization, propaganda, and language manipulation is the question. The answer *must* be that it will happen, and the movement to impeach is a hopeful sign. The country's survival as a democratic republic is at stake, and perhaps, as extreme as it sounds, the threat is hardly confined to this country. The threat is to the existence of civilization, and to the continuance of a habitable planet.

CHAPTER VII

Republican Policies for Minority Rule

The Judiciary

O
n July 16, 2019, John Paul Stevens, former associate justice of the US Supreme Court, died at the age of 99. His lengthy judicial service included thirty-five years on the Court, the third-longest tenure in the Court's history. He was a lifelong Republican, and Republican President Gerald Ford appointed him in 1975. He also had been a voice of sanity and reason on the Court, and subsequently during his lengthy retirement.

In 2014 he published a book, remarkable for a man well into his 90s, and especially for one who had considerable experience as an associate justice on the US Supreme Court. Justices tend to be rather reticent. His title is *Six Amendments: How and Why we Should Change the Constitution.*[1] No author has ever been better qualified to write about the subject.

Stevens discusses the background and circumstances of the current twenty-seven amendments. Since 1967, there has been only one amendment added. The Twenty-Seventh Amendment "prohibiting Congress from changing its salary between elections" had been proposed over two centuries previously, in 1791, as part of the package that ultimately became the Bill of Rights.

In that half century plus since 1967, however, the Court has actively produced decisions that, he says, "have had such a profound and unfortunate impact on our basic law that resort to the process of amendment is warranted. One of those rules has changed the

---

1 John Paul Stevens, *Six Amendments* (New York: Little Brown, 2014).

character and increased the cost of campaigns for public office."[2] That was *Citizens' United*, unleashing virtually unlimited corporate and "dark money" in our political campaigns. He also is highly critical of decisions that enable judges, rather than elected officials, to be the "final authority to define the permissible scope of civilian regulation of firearms"—he would change the text of the Second Amendment to prevent further misinterpretation of its meaning. (No authority from the Founders onward for almost two centuries had ever interpreted it to prevent a state from controlling individual carry, until the great "originalist" Justice Scalia argued that it was the original interpretation). Stevens would *require membership* in a "well-regulated" state militia for any individual right to exist.

Most important, he points to the need for an "amendment prohibiting political gerrymanders," in order to provide more representation—and hence more democracy—in the makeup of the U.S. House of Representatives.[3] In light of the Court's 2019 *Rucho* ruling, calling political gerrymandering unfair, but denying the federal judiciary any role in correcting the wrong, such an amendment is even more urgent than when Stevens wrote about it.

The decades since 1967 that produced the damaging decisions that Stevens cites was the period during which the Court, and the federal judiciary as a whole, has been systematically and deliberately pushed to the right by a series of conservative Republican presidents. In 1936, President Franklin D. Roosevelt, furious at a series of rulings that undercut the New Deal, proposed to expand the Court in such a manner that its conservative members would be outvoted by new appointees. His opponents screamed that what he was proposing was unconstitutional—which it clearly was not, since the Constitution does not specify the Court's size,

2   *Ibid.*, 11.
3   *Ibid.*, 11-13.

which has varied through the years—but there can be little doubt that he was attacking the Court in an effort to push it to the left. Conservatives have condemned FDR for his attempt to "pack the Court" ever since. His plan failed, but the Court soon shifted its orientation, and began to issue rulings more supportive of the New Deal.[4]

It is difficult to resist the conclusion—common sense supports it as well—that recent decades have seen a powerful attack on the Court, and on the judiciary as a whole. This attack is less obvious than FDR's Court-packing plan (less obvious at least until Senator McConnell refused President Obama his constitutional right to appoint a justice, holding the position open to permit a Trump appointee, thereby stealing the office), but far more effective than FDR's attempt.[5] In the long-run, Republican actions also are far more destructive of judicial independence than FDR's proposal would have been. Seeming to contradict their professed discomfort with unelected officials ("bureaucrats") wielding power, the decisions that have resulted from Republican "packing" also have the effect of greatly increasing the number of occasions when decisions of a non-elected judiciary substitute for the actions of elected legislators, or of leaving in place restrictions on the majorities that select those legislators. Objective analyses can support the conclusion that the process has led to a corruption of the judiciary and a shattering of the notion of an impartial, objective, and non-partisan Court (or system of courts).

---

4   See, e.g., Erwin Chemerinsky, *The Case Against the Supreme Court* (New York: Viking, 2014), 102-103; for a brief, but fairly detailed description of FDR's plan and the fight over packing the Court, see Jean Edward Smith, *FDR* (New York: Random House, 2007), 382-389.

5   I should qualify this statement. FDR's plan certainly failed, and the failure damaged his historical reputation. On the other hand, the Court did take notice and moved, on its own, to begin to rule in the administration's favor. FDR thought he had won overall.

President Eisenhower appointed Earl Warren as Chief Justice. Warren had been both California's attorney general and its governor and had been the Republican nominee for Vice President in 1948 when Harry Truman won his surprise re-election as the Democratic president. Warren had not, however, been a judge. Regardless, he turned out to be a superb chief of the Court, judicial administrator, and leader. Most notably, he succeeded in securing unanimity in the landmark 1954 *Brown v. Board of Education* decision outlawing school racial segregation. Eisenhower was notoriously displeased about the decision in particular, and about Warren's role on the Court in general. Ike is often quoted as having remarked something to the effect that appointing Warren was the "biggest damnfool thing" he ever did.[6]

Subsequently, the Republican effort to transform the judiciary began. When Justice Abe Fortas resigned and Chief Justice Warren had announced his retirement to be effective upon confirmation of his replacement, President Lyndon Johnson was in his final year in office. Newly aroused Senate Republicans warned LBJ that that they would block any nomination that he were to make. They would, they told him, hold the position open until there was a new president, one they hoped would be a Republican. LBJ bowed to the inevitable and did not submit a nominee. The conservative hope that the next president would be a Republican was borne out, as Republican Richard Nixon narrowly won the election.

Note that this long predated the Senate's rejection of President Reagan's nomination of Robert Bork, which Republicans are fond of citing as beginning the politicization of Supreme Court nominees. Common sense scrutiny reveals that the Bork case had almost nothing in common with Republican treatment of

---

6   See, e.g., Michael O'Donnell, "Commander v. Chief," *The Atlantic* (April 2018); this is his review essay of Hitchcock's *The Age of Eisenhower* and of Liveright's *Eisenhower vs. Warren: The Battle for Civil Rights and Liberties.*

judicial nominees; it serves merely as a convenient excuse. The Democratic Senate, in Bork's case, considered him fully, held hearings, treated him appropriately (however forcefully), and rejected his nomination. McConnell treated Obama's nomination of Merrick Garland as though it had never happened. In effect, he took the unconstitutional position that the president had no authority even to send a nomination to the Senate. It was somewhat similar to what the Republican Senate minority had done to LBJ, but more overt.

Under McConnell's regime, the clear signal from today's Republicans is that no Democratic president can, or ever will be able to, place a member on the Court if they can stop it; whenever the Republicans are in charge, they will simply ignore any nomination coming from any Democratic president, and conversely, will quickly confirm any nominee, regardless of temperament or qualifications, that a Republican president might submit.

Richard Nixon, the president following LBJ, succeeded in securing confirmation of three justices (Lewis Powell, Harry Blackmun, and William Rehnquist), all approved by a Senate that Democrats controlled. The Senate rejected his nominations of Clement Haynsworth and G. Harrold Carswell. Gradually, the belief grew among Republicans that their Court nominees should have experience as judges. Such experience would mean that their records as judges would likely suggest how they would function as justices of the Supreme Court.

Certainly, such experience is not a constitutional requirement—there is no prohibition constitutionally even for a non-lawyer to be appointed to the Court, but one has never been. Some outstanding justices have previously been judges, some have not; such experience does not offer a foolproof way to predict judicial behavior. Among Nixon's appointees, only Blackmun had previously been a judge. Rehnquist was, by far, the most conservative of the three, and functioned accordingly as a justice and as the chief. Blackmun, who became the author of *Roe v. Wade*, was progressively liberal, and became a liberal powerhouse on the Court.

Perhaps it could have been expected, at least symbolically, that the beginning of a right-wing extremist takeover of the judiciary of the United States has its more formal and systematic beginning during the administration of the president whose nomination and election moved "mainstream" American politics considerably to the right. That, of course, would be President Ronald Reagan, who ultimately achieved such revered status among Republicans that he was constantly on their minds. Candidates routinely professed to be "more like Ronald Reagan" than their opponents, at least until the bombastic and ineffable Donald Trump sucked so much oxygen from the party's atmosphere that the more dignified Reagan seemed almost to have faded into a pale historical figure from an almost forgotten period.

Despite his reputation today—at least among those who do not remember, who are too young or too oblivious to know, or who simply wish to misrepresent—until he secured the Republican nomination in 1980, Ronald Reagan for over a quarter of a century had been far from a mainstream Republican. He represented the right-wing extremist fringe of the party, was simpleminded almost to the point of embarrassment, and was roundly dismissed by most politicians, including Republican powerholders, as beyond consideration precisely because of his extremism and overly simplistic solutions. His supporters were characterized as California crazies, typified by the humor of the day—sexist, classist, and ageist as it was—as "little old ladies in tennis shoes."

What only those who at the time were intimately familiar with rank-and-file Republicans sensed, though, was that the legions of more obscure, but numerous, party members found Reagan to be fascinating. His extremism was welcome, as were his simplistic proposals, and it let them speak their hearts, instead of echoing the more sedate and generally more sophisticated tone of more prominent leaders. When Reagan became the presidential nominee of a major American political party, his views—views that a mere few months previously were rightly recognized generally as unacceptably extreme—had become the base of that party's platform and astonishingly were accepted as "mainstream." Undoubtedly, those new views reflected the party's suddenly unveiled heart. It is no accident that both Presidents Carter and Ford, Democrat and Republican, respectively, felt that their greatest failure had been their inability to head off the Reagan candidacy.

At any rate, whether Reagan was involved personally or not, the atmosphere that his presidency created certainly contributed to what one thoughtful observer, Michael Kruse, has called "The Weekend at Yale that Changed American Politics."[7] That weekend was the last in April of 1982. Kruse wrote that a group of conservative students at Yale, "inspired by Reagan's ideology and emboldened by his election," audaciously brought together a group of around 200, including the most notable conservative legal scholars in the country, Justice Department officials, and judges for a three-day seminar.

However unlikely it was, that gathering led to the formation of The Federalist Society, which "has become one of the most influential legal organizations in history." Despite the society's description of itself as a non-partisan, non-political group that exists to debate rightist ideas, it is, says Kruse, "aggressively political" and from the very beginning was "steeling for a fight." As participant Antonin Scalia, then still a law professor at the University of Chicago put it, "the federal government is not bad but

---

7   Michael Kruse, "The Weekend at Yale That Changed American Politics," *Politico* (August 27, 2018), https://www.politico.com/magazine/story/2018/08/27/federalist-society-yale-history-conservative-law-court-219608 (accessed August 18, 2019).

good. The trick is to use it wisely." Robert Bork, who had just become a judge, "spoke of 'the onslaught of the New Deal.'" He argued that matters of sexual conduct and abortion should be "reserved to the states," and said specifically that *Roe v. Wade* had "nationalized an issue which is a classical case for local control."[8] The atmosphere was heady, with conservative energy expended in private discussions lasting well into the night, and introducing many who later became key players in national politics.

The Society emphasizes scholarly rigor, intensely conservative ideas and encourages bright young conservatives to become law students, graduate into the legal profession, and above all take seats on courts. This has been greatly facilitated by an influx of enormous amounts of money from conservative donors, Kochs and others.

As Kruse sums it up, "the architects of the Federalist Society have attained a level of influence on the courts they never could have imagined, in a way they never could have envisioned." He gives the Society much of the credit for Trump's victory. Without "the imprimatur the Federalist Society granted him," he almost certainly would not have been elected, nor, without him, "they almost certainly couldn't have gotten what they wanted." Trump is changing the country because of them, he said flatly.

Thus, Republican presidents, from Reagan onward, have filled the courts with Federalist Society members, conservative scholars, often ideologues, while Democrats have tended to pick moderates, for the purpose of avoiding controversy during confirmation proceedings (conservatives tend generally to be far more confrontational—nastier, if you will—than liberals or moderates, who are more likely to compromise or be reasonable). The practice generally had been for presidents to consult with members of both parties in selecting nominees.

8   *Ibid.*

As Republicans have become more and more strident and ideological, no longer do they consult with Democrats. On the contrary, the Republican Senate leader Mitch McConnell (now "Moscow Mitch" as a result of recent publicity and his consistent rejection of security measures for elections) is notorious for having stolen the final appointment of the Obama administration to the Court, keeping the position open and not even holding a hearing, for Obama's moderate nominee, Merrick Garland (of whom many Republicans previously had spoken highly). His action achieved its goal of producing an immediate opportunity for the newly inaugurated Donald Trump to nominate Neil Gorsuch.

With Justice Kennedy's retirement, another Trump nominee, Brett Kavanaugh, achieved quick confirmation (with a vote from "moderate" Maine Republican, Susan Collins, putting him on the Court), despite his clear display during Senate hearings of disrespect toward women senators, partisan rants, and an overall—and painfully obvious—lack of judicial temperament. What observer can forget his explosive bursts of anger toward "Democrats" and "the Clintons," who he charged with being "out to get him," or bitter words to that effect? Now, the Court's five conservatives, Thomas, Alito, Gorsuch, Kavanaugh, and the Chief, Roberts, are all members of the Federalist Society.

Common sense would indicate to Democrats that, if they attain full control of the executive and both houses of Congress, they must consider the recent history of the "packing" of the judiciary as a whole, and the Supreme Court in particular. High on their agenda, a prime priority in fact, must be reform of what assuredly is corruption of the judicial branch, including most visibly of the Supreme Court. It is difficult to maintain a vision of the current Court, as an impartial arbiter, or as a non-partisan body.

There have been calls for Democrats to expand the Court, to compensate especially for the "stolen" seat. That is understandable, but could—and undoubtedly would—lead to retaliation whenever an opportunity existed for Republicans to do so. That would be unhealthy, although it would be better than the current political slant. There has to be a better way.

So there is urgent reason for reform, and there have been numerous proposals. Some would require amending the Constitution, but others might be applied without that difficult task. The difficult part is to achieve true reform that does not invite a tit-for-tat retaliation whenever party majorities shift. That militates against the simplest reform, the expansion of the Supreme Court to dilute the ideological effect of recent Republican appointees. Some proposals would require term limits, 15 or 18 years, for justices, combined with a process that ensures every president one or two appointments. Other proposals have been to expand the Court substantially, and have it function in the way US Courts of Appeal do. That is, small panels of justices, rather than the entire Court, would handle most cases. This would have the advantage of less publicity to each justice, and could produce a less politically charged atmosphere for each confirmation or each case being heard.

Term limits might be arranged without an amendment. Appointments to the judiciary still would be "for good behavior," but not to the Supreme Court, itself. After a justice's term, the justice would become a judge elsewhere in the judiciary, probably on an appeals (or "Circuit") court and still be available if needed to sit on a specific case.

Whatever reform is adopted should be carefully crafted and done so that the judiciary will be rescued from ideologues, but in a manner that is fair to all concerned. Considering the recent history of the Republican Party, this would have to be devised by Democrats following a massive Democratic victory that resulted in a takeover of the executive and both houses of Congress. There could be no hope for a bipartisan solution because modern Republicans have demonstrated that they would never consent to any reform that would be fair to both parties. Unless it protected their dominance, even when they are in the minority, they would never agree. Fairness, to them, is weakness or treason, not a virtue.

As political scientist Todd N. Tucker has written, "If this sounds ludicrous, consider the following First, Senator Mitch McConnell refused to even allow a vote on Merrick Garland—completely shattering whatever bipartisan norms were left around the judiciary. Second, and even more incredibly, prominent Republicans threatened to not confirm any of Hillary Clinton's nominees had she won—not just in an election year, but *ever*. Blocking presidents from filling judicial vacancies amounts to neutering the Constitution." These were not points original to Tucker. I have made them myself in this book and elsewhere, but his succinct final argument should be repeated tirelessly: "A handful of justices pulled from the Federalist Society debating clubs can't and shouldn't get in the way of a more democratic and sustainable economy."[9]

The *Washington Post* has pointed out that the appointment process was exposed during the Kavanaugh hearings, and "it decidedly is not sober, nonpartisan review of the law. The new justice got to the court by savaging an entire political party for allegedly waging an elaborate conspiracy against him."[10] Without reform, since Chief Justice John Roberts has "long fantasized about dismantling America's most important voting rights law," the Court, with Kavanaugh in place, "could, in effect, usher in an era in which competitive elections essentially cease to exist in the United States—at least at the federal level."[11] Therefore, it

---

9   Todd N. Tucker, "In Defense of Court Packing," *Jacobin Magazine* (September 19, 2019), https://jacobinmag.com/2018/06/supreme-court-packing-fdr-justices-appointments, (accessed September 30, 2019).

10   Aaron Blake, "Pack the Supreme Court? Why We May Be Getting Closer," *Washington Post* (October 9, 2018), https://www.washingtonpost.com/politics/2018/10/09/pack-supreme-court-why-we-may-be-getting-closer/, (accessed September 30, 2019).

11   Ian Millhiser, "Let's Think About Court Packing: Yes, it's a Dangerous

is wise advice—in fact it is common sense—to forget the old norms and procedures. "Too much is at stake. Playing by the old rules while the Republicans tear them up won't cut it." The current Court is, and was deliberately chosen to be, a group of "conservative ideologues masquerading as impartial judges."[12] We need a Court, and an entire judiciary, devoted to upholding the rule of law and the Constitution, not imposing a right-wing extremist ideology.

It will be possible to effect true reform if—and only if—Democrats achieve overwhelming dominance. It is absolutely essential that this happen in order to eliminate the corruption that the Republicans have made inherent in the system. As Brian Fallon, who previously was an aide to Democratic Senate leader Chuck Schumer, put it: "Democracy simply cannot function when stolen courts operate as political shills."[13]

Gerrymandering, Filibustering, Ignoring Majorities, and More on Suppressing the Vote

If there were an attempt to provide anything like a comprehensive presentation of this section's title, this section would be enormous. Instead, it will present an unsystematic selection of Republican bad conduct. The examples here are outrageous but not cherry-picked to present Republicans at their worst. Rather, they are more or less representative of the manner in which they have conducted themselves for a quarter century

---

Tactic, But So is Permitting a Reality in which Republicans Win Rigged Elections and the Supreme Court Winks," *Democracy: A Journal of Ideas* 51 (Winter 2019), https://democracyjournal.org/magazine/51/lets-think-about-court-packing-2/ (accessed 30 September 2019).

12 Mehdi Hasan, "Pack the Supreme Court," *Intercept* (September 30, 2018), https://www.google.com/search?client=firefox-b-1-d&q=Mehdi+Hasan%2C+Pack+the+supreme+Court, (accessed September 30, 2019).

13 Philip Elliott, "The Next Big Idea in the Democratic Primary: Expanding the Supreme Court?" *Time* (March 13, 2019), https://time.com/5550325/democrats-court-packing/, (accessed October 2, 2019).

or so. This reflects not their most extreme, but rather the way they have come to conduct themselves.

Republicans, especially under leader Mitch McConnell, have so expanded the filibuster that they now apply to virtually every piece of legislation coming through the Senate. They argue that because the Founders considered the Senate the chamber for "cooling off" the overheated measures that might come from the House, they instituted the filibuster. They did not.

Until into the latter half of the nineteenth century, the term did not even refer to a legislative maneuver. It meant a group of people, private soldiers and the like, who with no official authorization conducted invasions in other countries for the purpose of fomenting revolutions. The raids were designed generally to gain wealth or power or to spread slavery.

With regard to legislation, the term came to mean a specific way of attempting to kill a piece of legislation or block another action, such as a confirmation. To filibuster is to speak at such length that the supporters of an unwanted measure will finally give up, in order to permit the Senate to return to regular business. The House does not permit unlimited debate; hence, filibusters exist only in the Senate.

Initially, there was no mechanism for halting a filibuster. Then, in 1917 during the wartime Wilson administration, calling it a national security measure, President Wilson persuaded the Senate to adopt Rule 22, which provided "cloture," stopping debate, when two-thirds of the Senate present and voting agreed to do so. It is very difficult, generally, to achieve two-thirds, so in 1975, the cloture requirement was reduced to three-fifths of the number of senators. When all 100 seats are filled, that is a vote of 60.

Originally, there were physical constraints on filibusters. A senator had to hold the floor for the entire period. The record is held by Strom Thurmond of South Carolina (a physical fitness buff, but better known as an arch segregationist) who spoke for 24 hours and 18 minutes against the Civil Rights Bill of 1957. Majority leader Lyndon Johnson was determined that the bill would pass. Thurmond, when asked later how he did it, said he didn't drink much water. There were other filibusters as well, but after nearly two months, Johnson won, and the bill passed.

By the 1970s, however, the Senate made filibusters less onerous on the chamber by permitting multiple measures to be considered simultaneously. That meant that other measures could be considered while the filibuster was underway. Ultimately, the Senate also permitted filibusters to be conducted in rotation, on a team basis, with one senator giving way to another. Then, the upper chamber made them easier still: the minority leader would simply announce the intent to filibuster against a given measure, and the measure would no longer be considered unless a cloture vote prevented it.

Thus, as filibusters were made much easier to conduct, they also were made less influential on the overall work of the Senate. Even so, they remained quite rare. They did not increase dramatically in number until the 1990s. Then, however, Republicans decided to employ them progressively more often. Mitch McConnell became Republican leader in 2006, vigorous in his determination to oppose Democratic measures. When Barack Obama became president in 2009, McConnell was suddenly notorious for doing his best to thwart the president's every move and for having as his prime goal preventing Obama from being re-elected in 2012. In that, he failed, but he completely energized the filibuster, which already had become so routine for both parties that it applied to virtually every measure under consideration. The speed at which observers came to conclude that every measure in the Senate requires sixty votes was astonishing. Even more so was their assumption that the Founders—who had done no such thing—designed it that way. There is a plausible argument, in fact, that the sixty-vote requirement for all measures is, in fact, unconstitution-al. It certainly is quite contrary to the Founders' intentions, since the only supermajority votes they mandated were for amend-ments to the Constitution, overriding presidential vetoes, expel-ling members, ratifying treaties (which requires approval by the Senate only), or the requirement for a vote of two-thirds or more for the Senate to convict impeached officials.

On August 23, 2019, Senator McConnell published an op-ed piece in the *New York Times*.[14] Observing the time-honored Re-publican practice of giving advice to Democrats, McConnell warned them against doing away with the legislative filibuster, and blaming them for having caused the extraordinary use of the filibuster to begin with. He resorted to the falsehood that, since the Senate was conceived as the more deliberative body, one of its "central purposes is making new laws earn broader support than what is required for a bare majority in the House." He cites no constitutional provision for this, because there is none; nor, until relatively recently, has a "broader support" requirement existed in the Senate. In fact, since the Senate represents states equally, and most states are relatively low in population, a huge majority of the senators can represent a fairly small minority of the population of the United States. He also slyly contributes to recent misinfor-mation regarding electoral results, when he says that "Americans have elected Republican majorities three consecutive times and counting." Technically, that is correct, in that the electoral system has produced more Republican senators than Democrats in those elections. More Americans, though, voted for Democrats for the Senate in each of those elections than voted for Republicans. That is the way the system works; it over-represents rural, often Repub-lican, states in the Senate. To say, though, that "Americans" chose Republicans rather than Democrats overlooks the built-in sena-torial bias against large states (and Electoral College bias also, it

---

14 Mitch McConnell, "The Filibuster Plays a Crucial Role," *The New York Times* (August 23, 2019), A23.

might be added). Of course, the Founders designed it that way—although who knows what they might have done had they known how populations would be concentrated as time progressed. This is not to say that the incumbents are not legitimate; merely that it should not be taken without examination that "Americans" want one thing or another because of electoral outcomes from a system that was not designed to represent majorities. If McConnell continues to have his way, the Senate will continue to ignore majorities even more. As he put it, authoritatively although questionably: "if future Democrats reduce the Senate to majority rule, we'll have lost a key safeguard of American government."

From the horse's mouth, or wherever. In the Republican view, openly stated, majority rule is to be resisted. That is why we have some of the worst income maldistribution in the world, why we have fallen behind much of the rest of the world in transportation and infrastructure, why unions have dwindled, and why policies deliberately nearly always comfort the comfortable, while they tend to make the lives of the rest of the population increasingly difficult.

- In 1999, conservatives in Missouri forced a measure onto the general ballot that would that would have required authorities to issue concealed weapons permits to a qualified applicant. The voters rejected the measure. In 2003, the Republican legislature passed a similar measure into law, overturning the expressed will of the voters. The work is cut out for the Democrats. The obstacles are great, but so are the possibilities, should common sense prevail.

- In 2018, voters in Missouri and a number of other states adopted ethics reforms through referenda. Republican legislatures quickly set about undoing the voters' reform efforts. Ethics reforms, never overwhelmingly welcomed by legislators, are especially unpopular among Republicans.

- In Florida, the voters in 2018 overwhelmingly voted to rescind the Jim Crow-influenced prohibition on voting for anyone with a felony conviction. Millions of former convicts, however, were unable to obtain voter registrations as the referendum intended. Florida's legislature and governor quickly approved legislation requiring those with felony convictions to pay all fines and court costs before they could register to vote. This effectively levied a poll tax upon them, and—since a huge proportion was poor—the requirement, as intended, continued to deny them their rights as adult citizens (and as Florida's voters desired) to cast their votes. Although this is especially brazen, it could have been anticipated. Republicans are markedly unenthusiastic about voting rights for populations unlikely to vote Republican. A large number of Florida felons in question are black, which makes Florida's Republican leaders especially happy to deny them their franchise.

- In North Carolina, Republicans won less than half of the legislative vote in 2018, but held 54% of the seats in the state's House and 58% in the state's Senate. Democrats won 50% of the state's votes for members of the US House of Representatives, but received only 23% of the seats. The state's Republicans were widely reported as having admitted that the reason they drew the maps so that Republicans would win ten of the state's U.S. representative and the Democrats only three was that they could not develop a map that would have provided Republicans with eleven seats, and the Democrats only two. In fact, as mentioned in Chapter II, they even published an article defending their position.[15] Their defense was that they believed it was better for the country to elect Republicans than Democrats, so they considered themselves to

---

15   See Ralph Hise and David Lewis, "We Drew Congressional Maps for Partisan Advantage. That Was the Point," *The Atlantic* (March 25, 2019), https://www.theatlantic.com/ideas/archive/2019/03/ralph-hise-and-david-lewis-nc-gerrymandering/585619/, (accessed August 9, 2019).

be justified in drawing such imbalanced districts. Whether such hubris is merely arrogant, or completely delusional, it demonstrates the Republican attitude toward normal considerations of fairness.

It is worth noting, that the North Carolina courts have struck down the outrageous gerrymanders that the Republicans imposed on the state. It is equally worth noting what the Republicans who control the state's legislature developed in attempting to meet the North Carolina Supreme Court's requirement that they redistrict in the interests of fairness. Their first attempt would still ensure that in a roughly 50-50 vote, eight of the thirteen U.S representatives would continue to be Republican. At this writing (mid-November 2019), it remains to be seen whether Republicans will be able to continue blocking any semblance of fairness from returning to North Carolina's legislative or congressional districts.

- Outside the south, in the upper-midwestern state that had just ousted its destructive governor, Scott Walker, Republicans began diligently to lessen the effect of the vote that had just occurred. "Early on Wednesday morning, after working through the night as the end of the lame-duck session approaches, the Wisconsin state legislature passed a set of bills that will sharply limit the ability of incoming Democratic governor Tony Evers and attorney general Josh Kaul to do the jobs that the people of Wisconsin chose them to do. The legislature did this because it is controlled by Republicans, and as much as Republicans profess to love this country and cherish the freedoms that come with living in it, one thing they cannot abide is the notion that Americans might exercise those freedoms in order to elect people that Republicans do not like."[16]

---

16 Jay Willis, "Republican Gerrymandering Has Basically Destroyed Representative Democracy in Wisconsin: What Purpose do Elections Have if Results Like These are Allowed to Stand?" GQ (December 5, 2018), https://

- "In Other Wisconsin news today, the state posted the official 2018 Assembly election results. It's a beautiful gerrymander. Dems got 190,000 more votes but Reps got 63/99 seats. Key is assuring many GOP districts get just over 50% of vote even in a bad year for the party."[17]

To be fair, both parties have drawn gerrymanders when in a position to do so. Maryland's sixth congressional district is a notorious example in favor of Democrats. Republicans, however, across the board, have drawn their maps to be overwhelming, with skill, precision, and the widest effects possible, and never miss an opportunity to do so most vigorously. Moreover, actual voter suppression—the denial of American citizens their right to vote under any pretext available—long was practiced in the south by southern racist Democrats, who, with the advent of civil rights, quickly changed from southern racist Democrats to southern racist Republicans. Now, voter suppression—elaborate ID requirements, shortened early voting periods, limited polling places in Democratic areas, voter intimidation, and the like—is largely a Republican specialty. Their zeal means that its practice is more widespread than at any time since the Jim Crow era. The people responsible for voter suppression are the same people now as in earlier times, although today they are Republicans, not Democrats.

Elaborate protections for voting rights must be made a part of Democratic programs, following any landslide election. These must include federal voter registration programs, regulation of voting procedures in all states, and encouragement of voting with "get out the vote" programs, rather than discouraging voter turnout, as bigots (such as Kansas's former secretary of state Kris Kobach) advocate. These federal protections must include

www.gq.com/story/republican-gerrymandering-wisconsin (accessed August 21, 2019).

17   Barry Burden, *Ibid.*

ample funding to all jurisdictions to safeguard elections from foreign influence; protections that "Moscow Mitch," the Republican Senate majority leader, has blocked. One can hope that a blue tsunami indeed does develop and that it proceeds inland and washes disloyal Republicans away, even in inland, mountainous, Kentucky.

In case anyone does not recognize how extreme the Republican view on the right of Americans to have fair and unsuppressed vote actually is—how far they would go to ensure that they remain in power—consider the implications of a recent study. If the study is valid, a majority of Republicans have completely discarded the restraint that their first president (and the country's best by nearly any measure) displayed during a time when Americans were actually at war with themselves. Abraham Lincoln refused to cancel the national elections of 1864, even when there were military threats, and even when at first he thought he might actually lose. Lincoln was so devoted to maintaining a democratic republic that he rejected any idea of cancelling elections, regardless.

In June of 2017, two professors conducted a study of Republican opinion. They reported their findings in the *Washington Post*. If Trump proposed that the 2020 elections be postponed to ensure that only citizens would vote, 52% of Republicans or those who "leaned Republican" said they would agree with the postponement! If Trump proposed postponement and Republicans in Congress agreed that it would be required to prevent "voter fraud," *56 % would agree.*

This would be astonishing even if massive voter fraud did exist, but there is no evidence that there is anything more than an occasional—extremely rare— improper vote in the entire country. In the rare instance that one happens, it results from a misunderstanding. I have said elsewhere that if this poll is accurate, all Americans should be aware that they—we—are directly threatened. "The Republican Party has sunk lower, and the country is in far greater danger, than even alarmists have recognized."[18]

We urgently need that blue tsunami!

Republicans: Electoral College Yes! 17th Amendment NO![19]

The Electoral College

At one time, it was commonplace to hear criticisms of the Electoral College without regard to political partisanship. Both Republicans and Democrats could be found wishing that there were some way to move to a presidential/vice presidential choice by popular vote. The issue was more one of areas: urban *versus* rural. The Electoral College gives lightly populated states far more representation than their population would warrant. A constitutional amendment would be required to eliminate it, and the amending process involves approval by three-fourths of the states.

If only thirteen states were to fail to ratify, an amendment fails (and the relevant factor here is the number of states; not their populations). If the thirteen smallest states were to vote the same way (admittedly not very likely, since Wyoming is the least populous and very conservative, while Vermont and Delaware tend to be liberal), their populations would total only 4.1% of the population of the United States and yet could block any amendment. It generally is assumed that small states would not ratify a repeal amendment, because it would not be to their interest to do so.

In any case, almost entirely through the twentieth century, there

---

18 Skidmore, *Unworkable Conservatism,* Washington: Westphalia Press, 2017, 126-127.

19 I made this argument earlier in "The War Against the Seventeenth Amendment," *Huffington Post* (April 24, 2016).

was little energy devoted to considering the Electoral College. For the most part, it had performed well. The last time it had failed to choose the winner of the popular vote was in 1888, when Republican Benjamin Harrison won the electoral vote, defeating Democrat Grover Cleveland, who won the popular vote. The electoral vote usually exaggerated majorities. In other words, the winner of the popular vote as a rule also won the electoral vote with a much higher percentage in the Electoral College than of the popular vote.

The Electoral College, however, failed in 2000. It chose George W. Bush (with assistance from five Republicans on the Supreme Court) over the popular-vote winner, Vice President Al Gore. Bush turned out to be perhaps the most reckless president who had ever been elected. He, Vice President Cheney, and British Prime Minister Tony Blair knowingly used false information to justify taking their countries into war with Iraq. The ensuing war was responsible for hundreds of thousands of deaths, enormous cultural destruction, continuing turmoil in the Middle East and elsewhere, and ultimately the creation of a guerilla force dedicated to attacking western countries and interests around the world, ISIS.

For a brief time after the tumultuous election, there was sentiment for discarding the Electoral College. Then it dwindled, as such pressure usually does. There also were contributing factors that diverted attention from reform. There had been only one Electoral College failure in more than a century; the new president was experienced, and had campaigned as if in the political mainstream. Democrats are far more willing to "play by the rules" and accept defeat than Republicans, who increasingly had become determined always to win at any cost. Moreover, 9-11 caused the usual tendency to "rally around the flag" and support the sitting president. Additionally, even the most pessimistic of observers could hardly have anticipated the torrent of violence that the Bush/Cheney administration would unleash.[20]

In 2016, the failure of the Electoral College was even worse, in that it ignored a substantial popular-vote majority of nearly 3 million votes in favor of an extremely well-prepared candidate, Hillary Clinton, handing the presidency to the totally unprepared Donald Trump, who demonstrated quickly that he was incapable of serving effectively. That also was the second such failure of the Electoral College in five elections. The president it selected, contrary to the expressed wishes of the American people, is, as of this writing, deservedly on the brink of impeachment.

Republicans, however, seem suddenly enthusiastic about the Electoral College. It is common to hear nonsense, such as: if the president were chosen by popular vote, California would always decide the winner. Mathematics, of course, does not work that way. Republican votes in California, under the Electoral College system, might as well not be cast; they would count fully in a popular-vote contest. One could equally argue that the states of the Old Confederacy would always choose the winner. Collectively, they have far more votes than California does. In fact, the two larger states, alone, Texas and Florida, have a combined vote that is considerably more than California's.

So that argument is simply wrong. What Republicans do not say openly, but what motivates them, is that they favor a system that will ensure Republican victory, even when Democrats receive far more votes than they do. Therefore, it is futile ever to count on significant Republican support to eliminate the Electoral College. Similarly, the flaw in the proposed National Popular Vote Interstate Compact, under which states agree to give their elec-

---

20   See Max J. Skidmore, *Unworkable Conservatism* (Washington: Westphalia, 2017), 151; also see the whole of Chapter V above regarding failures of the Electoral College in general, and the actions of the ruling Republicans.

toral votes to the candidate who wins the popular vote, cannot work so long as it depends upon good faith to function.

If a few more states ratify the compact, it would bring their combined total of electoral votes to 270, the number required for victory. Each state then would have agreed that, regardless of the vote in that state, its electoral votes would go to the winner of the national popular vote. If it operated as planned, it would work around the Electoral College, ensuring victory to the winner of the popular vote.

Good faith, however, is the key. Given the tactics and strategy of the modern Republican Party, it could never be counted on to keep its word. Consider what would happen if voters of a state, for example, voted Republican, but a Democratic candidate won the national popular vote. If that state were governed by Republicans, regardless of any agreement, regardless of its own laws, or even regardless of its own state constitution it could never be counted on to give its electoral votes to a Democrat. It also would have the clear legal authority, verified by the Supreme Court in *Bush v. Gore*, to do whatever the state legislature at any time decided to so, and nothing could restrain it—certainly not good faith.

The Seventeenth Amendment

As astonishing as it may seem there is a strong sentiment widespread among conservatives, especially the more extreme, to repeal the Seventeenth Amendment, the one that changed the way states choose their US senators. Previously, the state legislature made the determination; under the Seventeenth Amendment, ratified in 1913, the people choose them by popular vote. Certainly most Republicans would be unlikely to support repeal, but those who do may come as a surprise.

Those who favor eliminating the Seventeenth Amendment include many prominent Republican candidates, former candidates, and those who once held office. They include Senators Mike Lee of Utah and Ted Cruz of Texas (who said that politicians were less likely to break into your home and steal your television set before the Seventeenth Amendment. That literally is true. Televisions were rather scarce then). Former governors Mike Huckabee of Arkansas and Rick Perry of Texas (now Trump's secretary of energy) have supported repeal, as have judicial ideologues Jay Bybee, who serves as a judge on a US Court of Appeals, and the late Supreme Court justice, Antonin Scalia, a conservative icon. Quite a few hardcore ideological scholars and journalists join the chorus.

Journalist George Will, who could carry the title of the *Washington Post's* "Columnist in Charge of Silly Ideas," has written that before the Seventeenth Amendment, America thrived, and the "Great Triumvirate," Henry Clay, Daniel Webster, and John C. Calhoun graced the Senate. Under voter choice, though, the Senate seated the unspeakable Joseph R. McCarthy. Forget for the moment that it certainly is not clear whether Calhoun, the arch racist advocate of slavery as a "positive good," and an architect of secession, would be preferable to the red-baiting McCarthy, a closer look indicates that the old system also chose Senator Simon Cameron, who is famed for the supposed comment that "an honest politician is the one who when bought, stays bought," while the current system brought to the Senate such outstanding figures as William Fulbright, Lyndon Johnson, Edward Kennedy, and (if you will) Richard Russell.

The able leader Henry Cabot Lodge was chosen under both systems, as was the foul-mouthed racist demagogue, Pitchfork Ben Tillman. Both systems have sent terrible people to the Senate, and excellent ones.

In many large meetings of political scientists there are panels on "federalism." They seem in most instances to consist largely of bright, young, ideologues often adorned with bow ties who, with utmost sincerity, assume without examination that federalism is dead with the deathblow having been delivered by the Seventeenth Amendment. Because state legislatures no longer choose US senators, states no longer have a role in the government of the United States. This completely ignores a number of things, including the state role in the Electoral College that disregarded the popular vote to bring both George W. Bush and Donald Trump to Washington.

That, patently, is ridiculous. It assumes that the only way to assess a state's position on an issue is for the state's legislature to declare it. How is it any less a state selection if its people directly choose its senators than if its legislature does? Taking such a position is to assume that the people of a state cannot express that state's will, yet the people's elected representatives in its legislature can do so.

A state is far more than its legislature. It has an executive a judiciary, *and an electorate* that can express its will directly, with no less authority than the indirect expression that would come from its legislature. The states have literally the same role in the Electoral College that they had when the American people adopted the Constitution. They have the same equality of representation in the US Senate that they had before the Seventeenth Amendment. If the Electoral College fails to select a president, the states—in this case, unfortunately—still have full equality in the US House of Representatives to select the president, and in case the selection of the vice president falls to Congress, the Senate, where states are represented equally (and fully) continues to have the authority to determine which candidate assumes the vice presidency.

Even before the Seventeenth Amendment, the state had no authority to control its US senators. On rare occasions, a state would attempt to determine how its senators would vote; they failed. States were never able to instruct their senators or to recall them. In fact, one should point out to the "originalists" that the Constitutional Convention itself explicit rejected the idea that states should control their senators in favor of "per capita" voting power among them. Moreover, even before the Seventeenth Amendment, it was not extraordinary for a state's two senators to differ from one another in the votes they cast.

Those originalists should also be reminded that every US senator who voted to propose the Seventeenth Amendment was in office because of selection by a state legislature. Similarly, approval from three-fourths of the states was required to ratify that amendment; in fact, however, forty-one of the forty-eight states themselves did so, far more than required, thus expressing their collective will favorably. That would appear to pass the "federalism" criterion, however defined. States would hardly have been eager to eliminate their role or influence in the federal government.

The Founders were well aware that legislative majorities in states would shift, that they might differ between houses in the same legislature, and that a state's US senators would certainly be capable of disagreeing with one another. The argument from "federalism" is therefore completely bogus; there is no less incentive for a senator to vote "in the interests of the state" than there was before ratification of the Seventeenth Amendment.

The likelihood that the Seventeenth Amendment could ever be repealed would seem to range from almost impossible to completely impossible. How could an electorate ever be persuaded to divest itself of the power to select an important officer in the government of the United States? Why would they do so? There is no indication, of course, of a viable movement for repeal. What, then, could be the real motivation of the "repealers"? In all probability, they simply are conservatives who recognize that demographic and other trends are against them. They thus seize upon any and every method they can think of—however unlikely it might be to succeed—to restrict the power of the majorities that they fear, correctly, threaten their hold on power. Their plea to restore a vanished federal system, therefore, is actually a covert grab for power.

The opposition to the Seventeenth Amendment is related to their voter suppression practices. It would be the ultimate in voter suppression: completely denying *all* people a right to vote. Conservatives tend to believe that large voter turnouts are detrimental to their interests, and in general they probably are correct. Eliminating the vote entirely would suppress a vote completely, fulfilling one of their wilder dreams. There would (for that office) be no turnout at all! Additionally, as Republican states have demonstrated so skillfully, it is possible to gerrymander a state to enable a minority to defeat a majority. That cannot be done, though if the entire state is the district, as with a vote for a US senator. If there were no Seventeenth Amendment, a legislature gerrymandered to ensure minority (i.e., conservative) control would choose the state's US senators. With a popular vote, however, gerrymandering for that office is impossible, so the only way for a minority to prevail is to keep opposition voters away from the polls. In any case the actual motivation is less devotion to the abstraction of federalism, or even to the Constitution itself, than it is to the addictive attraction of political power.

A Note on Bullying Tactics in Order to Seize or Maintain Power

On 23 October 2019, a group of Republican House members exceeding some three dozen stormed a secure committee room in the House, where relevant committees were questioning witnesses with regard to possible impeachment of Donald Trump. The demonstrators chanted, and delayed matters, wasting some five hours of valuable time.

The committees conducting the inquiries included both Democrats and Republicans, although the demonstrators argued falsely that Democrats were operating in secret to the exclusion of Republicans. Some of the demonstrators were actually members of some of the relevant committees, so they had full access according to the rules. Since they chose not to exercise their right to attend, they clearly were more interested in creating a scene, providing the wrong impression, and getting headlines than they were in securing information. Moreover, in egregious violation of the rules, they brought cell phones and insecure devices into the secure area. Common sense indicates that it should therefore be obvious that the Republican hyperventilating about "security risks," especially "HILLARY CLINTON'S EMAILS," had never had anything to do with security, but had been designed solely to make (untrue) political points.

As for this puerile display one might assume that the entire episode was an embarrassing aberration; that it reflected actions by hotheads, or the less mature, less civilized, and consequently less influential of the House's Republicans. Unfortunately, that would give them too much credit. The demonstrators included not only Steve Scalise, the second-ranking in the House Republican leadership, but the entire fiasco had been discussed with, and received approval from, the president himself. Nor was this the first time Republicans had resorted to bullying, to breaking the rules, or throwing aside all decorum to achieve their ends. In fact, authorities with sufficiently long memories, perceptively named this "Brooks Brothers Riot 2.0"

Its predecessor took place on 22 November 2000, in Dade County, during the chaotic re-counting of the ballots in Florida following the Bush/Gore presidential election. As election officials were attempting the re-count, an unruly, shouting, mob rushed inside pounded on windows, threatened physical violence, and intimidated them into ending their efforts. The first reports followed Republican spin: these were local residents furious that Democrats were attempting to steal victory from the Republicans, they suggested. Almost immediately, though, it became clear that these were Republican operatives, working in concert. They included numerous Republican congressional staffers and others flown in for the purpose. The demonstration then became the notorious "Brooks Brothers Riot." The infamous Roger Stone claimed to have directed the effort from a nearby Winnebago; Brad Blakeman, "a Bush campaign operative," claimed that he was the one who did so. The goal of the organized rioters, he said, was plain, "never to be behind." It worked. Blakeman boasted, "we scared the crap out of them." The Gore campaign's approach was to recount, and make certain that the candidate who truly received the most ballots would be declared the winner. The Bush campaign, however, marched in lockstep, roaring that they won, and the Democrats were trying to steal the election.[21] Republican aggression, backed by a Republican chief election officer, Florida's Republican governor (who was the Republican candidate's brother) Florida's Republican legislature, and the country's Republican Supreme Court carried the day.

Recount, a television documentary and re-enactment, examined the incident; it had its premiere (HBO) on 25 May 2008. Former secretary of state James Baker was Bush's chief adviser, and oversaw the post-election activities in Florida. Baker is a thoughtful, extraordinarily able, statesman. He also is a skilled political operative. In an interview after reviewing *Recount,* he seemed almost embarrassed, remarking that he hadn't remembered being so devious, or something to that effect. One should remember, however, that in addition to being a sober and deft statesman, he is a political operator; and a Republican.

It was not until October 2019 when the Republican House members' stunt became "Brooks Brothers Riot 2.0," that the name

---

21 Michael E. Miller, "'It's Insanity!': How the 'Brooks Brothers Riot' Killed the 2000 Recount in Miami," *The Washington Post,* (15 November 2018); https://www.washingtonpost.com/history/2018/11/15/its-insanity-how-brooks-brothers-riot-killed-recount-miami/; (accessed 25 October 2019).

re-surfaced. There have been several similar incidents between 1.0 and 2.0 however, including one in the Florida Senate race in 2018. Governor Rick Scott eventually was declared the winner, defeating Senator Bill Nelson. Blakeman said of that race, "it's all being repeated," from 18 years earlier.[22]

The primary lesson here is not that Florida's electoral system is broken, although that is important, and should be a secondary lesson. Rather, it is that modern Republicans, even the most sober and thoughtful, will resort to any tactic they believe will be required to win, absolutely including physical aggression if they believe they can get away with it. Bullying is a twin of voter suppression. As America's young people become increasingly active politically as a common-sense reaction to Republican atrocities, so, too, do Republican measures designed to suppress their votes escalate. Across the country, Republican governments are making it more difficult for students, and those more likely to vote Democratic, to cast ballots. Their efforts to suppress Democratic vote are so vigorous that *The New York Times* gave it extensive attention in a front-page article, despite the plethora of news items regarding the activities building toward impeachments.[23] Common sense demands measures to counter extreme Republican tactics and strategies.

---

22   *Ibid.*

23   Michael Wines, "As Student Voter Turnout Rises, So Do Barriers to the Ballot Box," *The New York Times*, 15 October 2019.

★ CHAPTER VIII

Conservative Goal: Maximum Feasible Inconvenience

The contemporary Republican approach to government, except for police and military functions, is generally to reduce programs across the board or preferably even to eliminate them wherever possible. This tends to be the case regardless of how much pain program cuts and eliminations would cause, or how much they would lower the quality of life for most people. Generally, the only thing that makes Republicans as a group back off from their overt attacks is if they perceive that their offensives might lead to voter rebellion. This has helped keep popular and vital services, such as Social Security and the Postal Service, from being privatized—although Trump has expressed sentiments in favor of "selling off" the Postal Service, making it truly private. Their popularity has not kept them from falling victim to economic measures, however, as will be discussed shortly. Members of Congress, both Republican and Democratic, shy away from anything that possibly threatens to remove them from office or power.

Conservatives tend to avoid attacks on experiments they see as leading to privatization, even if they are more expensive than fully federal programs would be, and even (or perhaps especially) if the subsidies to private programs undercut programs that are public. Medicare Advantage is a good illustration. It costs substantially more for the government per beneficiary than standard Medicare does, but conservatives happily bear the cost as long as they believe the increased expenditure benefits "business," or leads to a reduction in government programs (especially if the ultimate result could possibly be full privatization—however much that may require government subsidies).

As if to illustrate the point, a new Trump executive order just as this is being written (the first week in October 2019), seeks to pressure more of the elderly into the privatized program Medicare Advantage (Part C). To repeat, the more people who make the shift, the more it will cost the government. Government must pay substantially more for each beneficiary in Medicare Advantage than in standard Medicare. The order bears the laughable title: "Protecting Medicare from Socialist Destruction."

Reflecting this tendency are sharp reductions in local offices that exist to serve the public. The two most striking examples are Social Security District Offices and local post offices. According to figures from the Social Security Administration, there were fewer offices (1297) in the most recent year shown, 2009, than there had been a decade previously (1340), despite an increase in population since then. An explanation could be that more functions in 2009 could be performed online than before. If that is the reason, it relies on forcing the population to turn to computers, when many members of that population are elderly, often computer illiterate, or simply less comfortable with computers than the young. Compare the 2009 figure with that only three years previously, however, when online functions had not changed materially. There still is a drop off from the 2006 figure, 1318.[1] As for 2019, SSA's answer to the question of how many offices there are is "approximately 1230 field offices." That is yet another drop,[2] despite a continued population increase overall and a higher proportion who are elderly. The figures do not have to be precise to make the point, which *Social Security News*, a blog, made in 2013:

> Since the Republicans took control of the House of Representatives in January 2011, there has been a 9% decline

---

1   Social Security Administration website, https://www.ssa.gov/history/offices.html (accessed August 27, 2019).

2   *Ibid.*

in the number of employees at the Social Security Administration. 6,493 employees lost in about two and a half years at a time when the agency's workload is burgeoning.[3]

The Social Security Administration long had a reputation for excellent service to the public, characterized by employees who are capable, accessible, and helpful. For many offices, everything not online now is done by appointment. Because of severe and persistent cuts, and efforts to drive members of the public to be content with online contacts with the agency, it often requires weeks to be able to meet with a representative. Once at an office for an appointment, the citizen often encounters crowded waiting rooms as packed as those in airports on busy routes (private businesses, too, such as airlines, when regulations weaken, tend to put profit far ahead of service, leading to considerable discomfort for their captive customers who certainly find little of advantage from "competition").

Social Security's employees still tend to be caring, able, and as helpful as possible, but their workload is heavy and the pressures on their time are considerable. This is, no doubt, by design. If people generally get unfavorable impressions from their contacts with government, they tend to be more receptive to anti-government propaganda.

Most proposals for "reform" are conditioned by the Peterson-Koch et al. propaganda that misrepresents the programs. They tend to be thinly disguised, or even overt, calls for benefit cuts or outright privatization. This does not mean that there are never reform proposals that might actually benefit the public. A number of authorities have put forth some good plans. For in-

---

3   Charles T. Hall, "Continued Decline in Number of Employees at Social Security," *Social Security News* (July 1, 2013), https://socsecnews.blogspot.com/2013/07/continued-decline-in-number-of-emloyees.html (accessed August 27, 2019).

stance, I have suggested ways in which to increase benefits while making Social Security's financing somewhat progressive, which it currently is not.[4]

Some years ago, former Senator George McGovern (now, sadly, deceased) and I developed some proposals to expand benefits, protect Social Security from the persistent attacks, and incorporate genuine reforms.[5] In recent years, I have refined those proposals. My colleague Dr. David Kingsley, who has retired from the University of Kansas School of Medicine, where he taught statistics and research methodology, and I have worked together on the proposals, and he has provided the mathematics. Most recently, we have cooperated to publish "Social Security for the Future."[6] Our recommendations include several revisions that would strengthen the trust funds. These include removal of the cap on the amount of wages subject to FICA, and a substantially increased inheritance tax to be devoted to the trust funds: 55% (15% greater than the current rate) on estates in excess of the exempted amount (in 2018, the exempted amount was a generous $11.18 million per person).[7]

We also recommend measures that would be additional drains on the trust funds. We would continue to calculate benefits based on the first dollar of earnings, but for both the employee and the

---

4   See Max J. Skidmore, *Securing America's Future: A Bold Plan to Preserve and Expand Social Security*, Foreword by George McGovern (Lanham, MD: Rowman and Littlefield, 2008).

5   See, for example, Max J. Skidmore and George McGovern, "Real Reforms to Enhance, Not Curtail, Social Security," *The Montana Professor* 18, no. 1 (Fall 2007).

6   Max J. Skidmore and David Kingsley, ""Social Security for the Future: A Fiscally Sound Proposal to Expand Benefits and Add Progressivity to the System's Funding (with Additional Suggestions for Closure of Coverage Gaps)," *Poverty and Public Policy* 9, no. 2 (June 2017).

7   "Policy Basics: The Federal Estate Tax," *Research,* Center on Budget and Policy Priorities (November 7, 2018), https://www.cbpp.org/research/federal-tax/policy-basics-the-federal-estate-tax (accessed September 2, 2019).

employer we would exempt the first $20,000 from FICA. This certainly would involve a cost to the trust funds, but the removal of the cap on the amount of wages subject to FICA would more than offset the loss. The reduction of revenue from the $20,000 exemption would be $61,819,158,121. In 2017, though, when the cap was $127,200 (as of 2019 it is $132,900), we wrote that removal would generate an additional "$286,186,902,169—a net increase of $224,367,744,048 to the trust funds. Our proposal thus would provide additional revenue of more than $224 billion per year, which should counter the propaganda regarding increased life spans, inadequacy of the trust funds, and the like."[8]

One should recognize, too, a strange anomaly in opponents' arguments. Nearly always they express great concern over increasing life spans (many of their models, in fact, presuppose a biologically-dubious assumption of ever-increasing human longevity that builds in greater stress on the trust funds based solely on the year in which they base their calculations—when all other factors are identical). First, common sense would question whether it is a biological possibility that human longevity can increase without limit. Second, there is a question of basic data: one wonders if these apparently sophisticated opponents simply do not follow the news, or if they are deliberately distorting the facts.

Actually, in the last few years, the American lifespan has not been increasing. Rather, while longevity for women has remained the same, *for white men, it has been declining.*

Under our revisions, the vast majority of workers would see an increase in take-home pay, without an increase in income tax. The change would also lower the cost of doing business for most employers and would introduce a measure of progressivity into the financing of Social Security, removing the regressive features of the current law.

---

8   Skidmore and Kingsley, 1.

We also recommended expanding Social Security to ensure that it becomes a complete retirement system. We would provide "Family Credits" that would give coverage for caregivers of dependent children six years of age or under or homebound family members. These coverages would come without requiring FICA payments and would recognize the importance of caregivers in our economy and social structure. All these changes should come with sharp increases in the minimum wage, indexed to inflation, to provide an income that is above the poverty line and sufficient to support a family.

Because of the system's self-funding, we strongly recommend removal of the costs of administration from the normal appropriation process; the money comes from the trust funds, regardless. This would add efficiency and rationality and should have been done long ago. Applying the normal appropriation process merely has provided an opportunity for conservative austerians to shrink the system, close district offices, reduce employees, introduce delays and inconveniences, and make the system function to provide a maximum of inconvenience to the people.

Our suggested changes meet the standard of common sense. As we say in our article, "macroeconomic trends during the past half century have been greatly beneficial to the most affluent members of society while they have reduced a large share of the lowest income earners to an existence that should be unacceptable in a democracy with an abundance of wealth and resources." In addition, "globalization and advancing computerization of the workplace have resulted in a rather rapid disappearance of adequately paying jobs. Unfortunately, the government has not stepped in to provide for the well-being of citizens harmed by radical trends of the past few decades that have resulted from neo-liberal economic practices." There can be little doubt that, to put it as gently as possible, "along with economic restructuring, political reconstruction occurring in the United States since the early 1980s has tilted government activities strongly in favor of the upper-class." All the while, social programs designed to assist citizens have progressively weakened. "During the decade of the 1980s, traditional defined benefits retirement programs were replaced by 401(k) defined contributions retirement systems. With the decline of union representation in the U.S. workforce, the age of generous benefit programs, bargained for collectively, disappeared."[9] The disappearance of so many Social Security offices is merely the overt public face of conservative austerity.

A persistent pattern is to reduce service to the public, to create annoyances, such as long lines and inaccessible facilities. The purpose is to generate unhappiness with specific government services that, conservative ideologues hope, will generate hostility to the very idea of government activities. This will reduce support for government programs, they believe, and lead to increasing privatization. Ultimately, many conservatives advocate the complete withdrawal of government from activities that enhance the welfare of the people, forcing them to avail themselves of profit-making private services and fostering an anti-government atmosphere that will remove regulation and eliminate taxes.

The "privateers" tend to ignore the many difficulties inherent in shifting from government to the private sector. To make a profit, private organizations must charge more than government; they cannot match the value government provides. Moreover, government is capable of making service the top priority and has no real need to maximize income.

Social Security, of course, is the classic example of a target for conservative attacks. Its superb functioning and popularity have not protected it from lengthy and lavishly financed negative campaigns by its opponents, but they recognize that they have obstacles to remove. The programs are popular, benefit nearly

---

9   Ibid., passim.

everyone, and have been wildly successful. Thus, they conduct massive propaganda campaigns aimed at convincing the public that Social Security and Medicare are "unsustainable," that private investments are better, and that current generations can keep their programs while gutting them for their children and grandchildren. Fortunately, the public generally has not been persuaded, and supporters now also conduct their own informational campaigns. They have analyzed and publicized the nature of the misinformation coming from conservatives—and from the conservatives' (sometimes unknowing) henchmen, the "moderates." The truth is out there, to borrow from the *X Files*, so that there now can be hope that the public is even less likely now than before to accept Republicans' ideologically-oriented rants as valid.

Conservative ideologues attempting to be bipartisan or nonpartisan began the effort that the Republican Party eventually took over as its own. This happened quickly, especially after Ronald Reagan—who as late as the end of the 1970s had been dismissed by all but ideologues—won the Republican nomination in 1980 and then assumed the presidency.

The beginning of the organized effort was likely the beginning of the constant repetition by former actor Reagan during the 1950s, when he gave "The Speech" (his own term) around the country as a spokesman for the General Electric Corporation. Subsequently, there have been massive efforts by the Koch Brothers and others, such as Peter G. Peterson, an anti-Social Security zealot billionaire investor who had briefly been Richard Nixon's secretary of commerce. Peterson founded and funded a plethora of organizations, such as the Concord Coalition, the Committee for a Responsible Federal Budget, the Peter G. Peterson Foundation, and the like, all dedicated to the ultimate elimination of "entitlements." Peterson had a genius for working with and gaining support from mainstream figures that he misled into believing he was only interested in "good government and fiscal responsibility." His many efforts succeeded in raising public doubts about the sustainability of Social Security and Medicare. Happily, while such efforts from the right have reduced public confidence in them, they have not reduced the enormous popularity of these essential programs.

Despite snide comments about "snail mail" and condemnation from Donald Trump, who ominously says that the Postal Service must be "restructured" and is on an "unsustainable path," US mail is part of the fabric of American life. It has been since the beginning. Although at times, there certainly have been problems, postal services in the United States have been historically a remarkable government success. A closer look demonstrates that the successes have even been dramatic.

Both in colonial times and in the early Republic, mail revolutionized communication and became a model for the world. "Mail" had existed for centuries and in many other places, but not in such a systematic manner as in the American colonies and then in the United States. It tended elsewhere to be beyond the reach of average people, unreliable, and generally based on private attempts to make some kind of arrangement to get someone to carry a message somewhere.

Americans have always been mobile, and not static, as in more traditional societies. Had they not had the mail, family members could have lost touch with one another forever. Early travel in America was arduous. There were few roads, and those that existed were hardly functional until well into the twentieth century. Railroads and boats left large sections unserved, and roads were hazardous, slow, uncomfortable, and often impassable. Nevertheless, because of the mail, it was possible for family members to remain in contact with one another, despite dispersal. In many countries, when a son (or rarely, a daughter) moved away, the parents had to assume that they may never have news again of their child. In America, because of the mail, there could continue to be communication.

Mail in the United States even had the effect of breaking down society's reluctance to see women outside the home. When post offices opened, women often would collect mail, as did men. At times, there were efforts to keep the sexes separate within postal facilities, but the change in how society viewed women had begun.[10]

The US mail today is an example of treating everyone equally, without regard to social class, urban or rural status, or distant and isolated or centralized location. It is a clear example of national unity, of "we're all in this together." Perhaps that helps explain the opposition. Conservatives, almost by definition and regardless of how they adopt rhetoric that denies their attitudes, tend strongly to favor programs that favor those of wealth. They continue to pour more hardship upon the disadvantaged and are uncomfortable with true national unity. They often fear that those who are less successful may pay "too little tax." Worse, they may even want to vote!

Without question, other forms of communication have emerged that now share part of the mission formerly exercised exclusively by the mail. Also without question, the country's post offices have felt the blows from conservative axes, just as Social Security offices have. The goal is the same, whether the issue is postal services, Social Security, Medicare, or some other program. It is to make governmental services progressively less convenient

10 Although the Postal Service may not be a "hot topic" today, there are a several excellent histories that are interesting as well as enlightening. See, e.g., Devin Leonard, *Neither Snow Nor Rain: A History of the United States Postal Service* (New York: Grove Press, 2016) and Winifred Gallagher, *How the Post Office Created America* (New York: Penguin, 2017).

and less accessible, in the hope that the private sector can absorb everything and pour profits into the coffers of the already wealthy.

In spite of other, newer services that perform some of the same functions, the post office remains essential. It is an organization devoted exclusively to public service (despite Republican efforts to force it to be self-sustaining or even to run at a profit), and is perhaps the only government agency that has continuing day-to-day contact with most members of the public. For those who cannot leave their dwellings, such as some with certain disabilities, the letter carrier may be the only regular contact with anyone connected to government. Such contact can be lifesaving. Some years ago, I worked with the police department of an affluent suburban community to develop a cooperative effort with the local postal service. If letter carriers, who often had some knowledge of the living conditions of the people along their routes, noticed an unexpected accumulation of mail, for example, they would notify the Police Department, who then could check and ascertain whether the resident needed assistance.

This is an instance of how, in spite of Republican pressures, the Postal Service can put service above profit. Regardless of advertising from competitors, the USPS is the only delivery service in the United States that can ship to post office boxes and the only one that will see to it that every address in the country, no matter how remote, can have access to mail or packages. Moreover, it does this efficiently and at reasonable, uniform rates—regardless of delivery costs. Remote locations anywhere in the country are not penalized; they remain American, wherever they are.

Even so, local post offices demonstrate a trend similar to that of Social Security offices, and that bears repeating. Because of Republican policies, they are becoming fewer and more difficult to locate. The Postal Service does not make comprehensive data available, but there is no doubt that the long-term goal of conservatives is to shrink, privatize, and eliminate government involvement in the moving of mail.

The conservatives are correct that the Postal Service has been losing money. The great recession that began under George W. Bush created a burden that it has not been able to overcome despite a vigorous package business. That recession, in itself, should have been a corrective to conservative economic notions, since it followed Bush's enormous tax cuts. According to conservative dogma, the cuts should have ushered in prosperity and economic growth. Instead, disaster followed them. The economic shambles, though, did little or nothing to alter the conservatives' ideological commitment to bad economics. They failed to practice minimal common sense. Beyond that, however, lies a basic question that it seems no one has thought to ask. Why should a government agency run at a profit or even be expected to break even? Government under a democratic republic exists to provide protection and service, not to grow wealthy at the expense of the people.

To add to the other economic burdens, Republicans have gleefully pressed upon the Postal Service a requirement that it prepay decades of retirement benefits for employees. Congress imposed that mandate in 2006 and created troubles for the mail that no other agency faces. That requirement may not be the only reason the Postal Service loses money, but the billions of dollars it requires annually surely makes it among the foremost. Again, why should any agency fund itself? The 2006 act seemed almost designed to create insurmountable obstacles. Because of this law, the Postal Service cannot undertake any of the new services that would seem almost a requirement for an agency that delivers packages. It cannot provide notary services or wrap packages and is forbidden from shipping alcoholic beverages—services that the private companies can provide.

Senator Bernie Sanders supports removing all these restrictions and permitting the Postal Service to "expand into digital services and 'offer a non-commercial version of Gmail.'"[11] Long before she began running for president, Elizabeth Warren called for the Postal Service to begin offering banking services.[12] As a presidential candidate, she has called again for such an expanded role. One of the benefits would be to provide needed services to many who now have no access to them, and also to drive the unspeakable payday loan industry, which preys on the poor, out of business.[13] She also has a plan to provide access to broadband coverage across the US, including rural areas, and would allocate $85 billion to combat the "deep digital divide" in the nation.[14]

A resuscitated and greatly expanded Postal Service would be the perfect vehicle to accomplish all these ends, and more, such as perhaps absorbing the functions of the FCC and certainly enforcing a newly modernized version of the Fairness Doctrine. A new progressive government could restore the Post Office to the Cabinet and open numerous additional local post offices to provide easy access for all Americans. For historical reasons, it probably would be best to restore the title "Post Office," adding something along the lines of "Financial and Internet Security

---

11   Jake Bittle, "Bernie Sanders Is to Deliver a Commonsense Plan to Save the Postal Service," *The Nation* (June 7, 2018), https://www.thenation.com/article/bernie-sanders-commonsense-plan-save-postal-service/(accessed September 10, 2019).

12   John Nichols, "Why We Need a Bank at the Post Office," *The Nation* (February 11, 2014), http://www.campaignforpostalbanking.org/news/why-we-need-a-bank-at-the-post-office/ (accessed September 10, 2019).

13   Hannah Levintova, "Elizabeth Warren Has Another New Plan—And Wall Street Isn't Going to Like It," *Mother Jones* (July 18, 2019), https://www.motherjones.com/politics/2019/07/elizabeth-warren-plan-private-equity-postal-banking/ (accessed September 10, 2019).

14   Shirin Ghaffary, "American Has a Terrible Digital Divide. Elizabeth Warren had a Plan for That Too," *Vox* (August 7, 2019), https://www.vox.com/recode/2019/8/7/20757705/elizabeth-warren-broadband-digital-divide-broadband-access (accessed September 10, 2019).

Services." A new Department, relieved of the burdensome requirement to prepay billions of dollars in retirement costs, could provide expanded (and speedy) mail and package delivery. Additionally, it could be in charge of Internet services, creating high speed broadband coverage accessible anywhere in the country, ensuring net neutrality, and—especially important these days—maintaining national security against foreign hacking.

Along with electronic communication, the new department should assume full banking services especially geared to those of low income or even moderate means: checking, savings accounts (generally to be re-deposited in non-profit credit unions), small loans, and all the services that low-income Americans need and often do not have available. The Post Offices could do much of the paperwork that flows between citizens and the government: passport applications, voter registration (authorized by a new law requiring uniformity in procedures), and the like.

As soon as possible, it should also develop a unit to protect American electronic communication security, guarding it against interference, especially from abroad, and especially with regard to elections (the Post Office, historically, has maintained a vigorous and effective law-enforcement unit, Postal Inspectors, so there is precedent). This unit should work with a re-energized Federal Election Commission (FEC). Under Trump, one should note, the FEC cannot function because he has refused to appoint members and thus has too few even to operate. Unfortunately, this is all-too-characteristic of Trump's approach across-the-board to government agencies.

As knowledgeable persons might expect, his Republican Party has not called him to account on this or apparently even taken notice of his dereliction of duty. His supporters often argue that this is a way to reduce government expenses. A similar argument would be that one can kill bedbugs by burning down the house, except that the bedbugs actually would be killed, while government expenses do not go down.

From 1911 until 1967, the Post Office Department maintained a Postal Savings system quite successfully. It provided security for small depositors, helped enhance confidence in government programs, and brought much money out of hiding by citizens who distrusted banks. The department deposited its receipts in local banks, helping local economies. There thus is a precedent in the United States that once had such a system in place, as many other countries continue to have.

State offices form another major point of contact between citizens and government. These include motor vehicle licensing and drivers' license offices, as well as those performing other functions. They are often sources of major frustrations for the public. Although these are functions of the state and not the national government, many citizens do not have clear conceptions of the difference, and therefore form negative opinions of all government services. This situation has evolved haphazardly, but can be reformed simply, and at the same time ease burdens on the public while improving the public perception of government services. The federal government could offer grants to states to have such offices adequately staffed with efficient and helpful procedures and to ensure that personnel receive sound training not only with regard to the technical aspects of their jobs, but also on how to deal effectively and pleasantly with the public. This would be a simple—and common sense—improvement across the board.

★ CHAPTER IX

Common Sense Action Appendix

T his appendix discusses programs that a new progressive administration—and, one can hope, officials in a new progressive era—should consider implementing as soon as they can be designed soundly and passed into law. As officials consider crafting and implementing new programs, they would be well advised to study program development and implementation under LBJ.

After the awkward rollout of "Obamacare"—albeit short-lived and then well implemented; after the lengthy and extremely tormenting beginning of George W's Medicare Part D (the drug benefit), also now well administered; after the horrid display of presidential incompetence in New Orleans regarding Hurricane Katrina and the even worse incompetence coupled with shocking lack of concern Trump displayed for Puerto Rico and the disaster of Hurricane Maria, LBJ's performance should shine like a beacon, but has been largely ignored. Consider his flawless implementing of the whole of Medicare, his superb handling of Hurricane Betsy (also in New Orleans), and his equally superb handling of the great Alaska earthquake. For equal inspiration, consider Republican Theodore Roosevelt's handling of the disastrous San Francisco earthquake. Learn from the best of the past; do not continue distorting it, and do not ignore the valuable lessons it teaches.[1]

These action items are given in no particular order, and the list is not exhaustive. Each of these would be a substantial step forward.

---

1   See, e.g., Max J. Skidmore, "Anti-Government is Not the Solution to Our Problem, Anti-Government IS the Problem: Presidential Response to Natural Disasters, San Francisco to Katrina," *Journal of Risk Hazards, and Crisis in Public Policy,* 3:4 (December 2012).

The motivation for progressive Democrats—and for American politics in general—should always be the one that Abraham Lincoln said motivated his new Republican Party (that was in the party's too brief period of greatest purity): Republicans, he said were "for both the *man* and the *dollar; but in cases of conflict, the man *before* the dollar.*"[2] To put it in more modern language: the political system should provide protection for human rights and for property, but if there is conflict, human rights should *always* be paramount. Conservatives will oppose this as upending what they believe to be the natural order of things. What it really upends, is the order of things as wealth has structured them.

Some of the items below are repeated for emphasis; all are important. Taken together, they would make America not only much more responsive to people's needs—and more democratic—but much more humane as well. Also keep in mind Professor Kelton's comment that any program that is technically feasible can easily be afforded. Each of these programs should therefore be designed for maximum quality and service, not to satisfy budget hawks. Design them for effectiveness, not minimum costs.

Items:

- On an emergency basis, implement a "Manhattan Project" of measures to combat climate change; re-create the Civilian Conservation Corp in a modern version, including a fully fleshed out Green New Deal with a continuous program of massive tree planting and a wide array of environmental improvements. The original CCC in its brief existence planted some *three billion trees.* Such a program today, preferably ad-

---

2   Quoted in Heather Cox Richardson, *To Make Men Free: A History of the Republican Party*, New York: Basic Books, 2014, xiv; Richardson's work is one of the two most insightful work on the party's history. The other is the 2nd edition of Lewis Gould's *The Republicans: A History of the Grand Old Party*, New York: Oxford, 2016.

opted by all countries, could make an enormous contribution to efforts to combat climate change.

- Implement an upgraded version of FDR's Economic Bill of Rights.[3] Make government the employer of last resort, and include as rights all the proposed measures, such as universal housing, quality health care, and income maintenance.

- Eliminate the Electoral College. It presents a danger to America's democratic republic, having gone against the popular vote in two recent elections. It also authorizes state legislatures to choose electors, regardless of a state's laws or even a state's constitution, something Florida's legislature planned to do in 2000 until the Republican majority on the Supreme Court made it unnecessary. Replace the Electoral College with a direct popular vote. This should employ run-off voting, ranked-choice voting, or some other measure to ensure that winners receive a majority of the vote. This, of course, could only occur after massive waves of progressive votes at all levels that made possible an amendment to the Constitution.

- Restore the Post Office Department to the cabinet and re-open post offices throughout the country. Remove requirements that currently prevent the Postal Service the Post Office from offering full shipping services and that require it to break even and to pre-fund retirements; also remove restrictions that would prevent the new Post Office Department from engaging in banking services, and other services pertaining to communication; then re-structure the new department to implement and supervise universal wideband accessibility, while empowering the department to ensure secure electronic communication. Protect Americans' communications with the most advanced technology and procedures and, provide an unparalleled law-enforcement unit to guard electronic

---

3   See epigraph to Chapter VI for a list of the rights.

communication, secure elections, and absorb (and retaliate against) any cyber attacks, especially those from abroad. Provide banking services (where possible in cooperation with non-profit credit unions), making it the Department of the Post Office, Financial, Communication, and Internet Security Services. This new department could also supervise a renewed and modernized Fairness Doctrine.

- Immediately embark upon an emergency program of complete infrastructure modernization, including widely-available, inexpensive, high-speed rail throughout the country, speedy mass transit (free or at least affordable), accessible throughout all congested areas. Upgrade and weather-proof all utilities. Provide innovative and inexpensive individual transit; adopt requirements for energy efficient vehicles and appliances, and renewal of roads and highways. Reduce or eliminate highways where appropriate, because of more efficient transit provisions.

- Wipe out all student debt (with tax credits for those who have paid off student debts), make higher education free at all public institutions, provide massive assistance to HBCUs, and provide equity grants to make living expenses affordable for students. If quantitative easing can be applied to save corporations, the same mechanisms can be applied to erase student debt; citizens deserve relief no less than commercial enterprises.

- Adopt comprehensive immigration reform, including border security and citizenship for dreamers.

- Attack severe income inequality. Adopt tax reform, including a wealth tax. Adopt heavily progressive income taxes that impose large marginal rates and that affect those at lower levels lightly, if at all. Progressively reduce the number of billionaires, with a goal of eliminating that level of ultra wealth as incompatible with the existence and adequate functioning of a democratic republic. No one should feel oppressed because of a prohibition of wealth beyond $999+ million. Raise the minimum wage to the point at which the head of a family of four who makes minimum wage at a full-time job earns enough to be above the poverty level. Work diligently to resuscitate America's labor unions, and maintain union-friendly policies. Re-energize the Consumer Financial Protection Bureau, and prohibit mandatory arbitration clauses.

• Reform Social Security to expand benefits, making it a full retirement system with somewhat progressive funding, and include coverage for those family members who provide childcare, and who care for other family members who are homebound by disabilities.

• Adopt universal health care Medicare (fully public) or fully nationalized Medicaid available to all, with a parallel national health service patterned upon Veterans Administration (or even expand the VA) for any of those who prefer. Care should be available to all who are in the United States. . This could also be done by reorganizing the Public Health Service, restoring its earlier status and expanding it. Construct a network of hospitals across the country, especially in rural areas, and make full health care available to all. Make certain that these facilities and their personnel are established not for economic reasons, but specifically, and solely, to provide health care of the highest quality; to all who seek it.

• Provide relief for those who have been bankrupted or severely harmed by enormous healthcare costs.

• Adopt public funding of elections, eliminating all private funding. Renew the Voting Rights Act. Adopt national voter registration with nationally uniform standards of eligibility (Article I, Section 4 provides the authority). Encourage voting and cease, and effectively outlaw, all voter suppression. Adopt voting by mail, patterned on the Oregon practice.

- Reform the federal judiciary including creation of a new Supreme Appellate Court to assume appellate functions of the current politicized Supreme Court. Provide for fair selection of judges, compensate for stolen seats, and for decades of court packing.

- Mandate paid family leave.

- Eliminate privatization of government functions at all levels: no more private prisons, privatized license offices, etc.

- Provide federal assistance to local and state governmental offices so that all services are widely accessible, provided with courtesy and efficiency, and designed to maintain the dignity of both the employees and those being served.

- Declare corporations to be business concerns without the rights of citizens (this would not, despite allegations, deny newspapers, television, etc., free-speech rights; the First Amendment assures them, specifically mentioning the press). Make it clear that commercial speech is distinct from the free speech that the First Amendment protects, and that spending money is not exercising free-speech rights.

- As soon as possible, admit Puerto Rico and the District of Columbia (with accommodations for the 23rd Amendment) as states. Provide Puerto Rico with sufficient assistance to overcome the vast neglect over decades (especially the unconscionable treatment from the incompetent Trump administration), and eliminate the commonwealth's debt.

- Adopt and enforce a rigid code of ethics (applied with especial rigor to presidents and vice presidents), forbidding public employees from enriching themselves, or engaging in any outside or self-serving business activities.

- Eliminate the OLC opinion that a sitting president cannot be indicted, and make it clear by appropriate legislation that every official is subject to the law. Make sure, however to retain clear protections against political attacks or coups.

- Implement national firearm registration, and adopt sensible measures of firearm control based on rational (and historical) interpretations of the Second Amendment. Counter the objection that the Second Amendment guarantees an individual right of open or concealed carry, and the further objection that America's gun culture precludes any sensible regulation. America has lived with the Second Amendment ever since it adopted the Constitution, and it had effective gun control until recently, when an NRA-influenced, and Republican-dominated, Supreme Court gutted it. As for gun culture, other countries with a similar heritage have dealt rationally with the issue. Australia and New Zealand responded rapidly and effectively to control firearms after massacres—demonstrating the irrationality of America's cowardly impotence on the subject. Canada, with rather widespread firearm ownership controls its guns effectively, while the USA, its southern neighbor, cowers under NRA influence and judicial irrationality. Responses in Norway and elsewhere also should suggest effective methods of gun control.

CHAPTER X

A Selective Appendix

Quick and Easy Reference to Decades of Republican Malfeasance[1]

Richard M. Nixon

- In his presidential race in 1968, Nixon conspired with leaders of South Vietnam to "monkey wrench" the Paris Peace Talks, intending to ensure that the war and the killing continued until after the election, to prevent an "October Surprise" peace that might assist Vice President Hubert Humphrey, his opponent. Treason could be a common-sense interpretation of this.

- As president, Nixon adopted a racist "southern strategy" to assure Southerners that he would "lay off the pro-Negro crap."

- He was literally a criminal president, causing a psychiatrist's office to be burglarized and causing a break-in of the offices of the Democratic National Committee in an aborted attempt to plant listening devices in the offices of the Democratic National Committee in the Watergate Hotel (the famous "Watergate scandal").

- He maintained an "enemies list" and used government resources against those who angered him. He used government officials for his political gain and was instrumental in covering up his crimes.

- Republican officials—then still capable of putting country and principle above party—joined Democrats in forcing him to resign the presidency.

---

1   See Chapter I for more detail.

- Prior to that, however, President Nixon exercised strong leadership in combatting environmental pollution. He signed legislation creating the Environmental Protection Agency and treated it seriously. His Republican successors, unfortunately, tended to consider industrial profits, and profit in general, to be more important than the environment. They went so far as to dispute, and continue to reject, scientific opinion regarding climate change. They set out to weaken the EPA, often by appointing hostile directors (Justice Gorsuch's mother, for example, Anne Gorsuch Burford) to keep the agency leashed. Under Trump, the appointment to head the EPA went to an Oklahoma attorney general who made his reputation bringing lawsuits against the agency. Both administrators, Reagan's Gorsuch Burford and Trump's Scott Pruitt, were forced out by major scandals.

- At the state level, Republicans functioned similarly. Michigan, for example, in order to save money, shifted water sources to the city of Flint, thus leading to the mass poisoning of residents. Those residents were predominantly black. They continue to suffer.

Spiro T. Agnew

- Spiro T. Agnew was Nixon's Vice President; both were elected narrowly in 1968 and re-elected in a tremendous landslide in 1972. At first, Nixon had assigned him as liaison to the cities and states because of his experience as a county executive and as governor. That ended quickly when Nixon recognized his incompetence. He then became Nixon's political hatchet man, doing for Nixon what Nixon had done when he was Eisenhower's Vice President. Political wits called him "Nixon's Nixon." It was Agnew, under Nixon's direction, who began the Republican war on the news media. He succeeded in creating the false myth of "the liberal media" that Republicans have kept alive for decades by gleeful repetition.

- Agnew is also distinguished for his corruption, becoming only the second Vice President to resign (John C. Calhoun was the first), and the only one to be forced out on a plea bargain to keep from going to jail. A *Washington Post* columnist called him "Trump before Trump."[2]

Ronald Reagan

- Ronald Reagan began his presidential campaign—the beginning of the "Reagan Revolution"—employing the "Southern strategy" with a vengeance, but disguising it so that the racist message was confined largely to willing hearers in the South; he opened his campaign near Philadelphia, Mississippi. Reagan was a master of symbolism and knew exactly what he was signaling to racists by selecting the notorious location where the Klan had murdered civil rights workers.

- Doing his best to turn Americans against their own government—a rather unpatriotic move for one who portrayed himself as the patriotic embodiment of the United States—after some gracious words for President Carter, Reagan declared in his inaugural address that government was the problem, not the solution. As president, he worked consistently to shrink non-military government and slash Social Security. (Because of a huge outcry from citizens, he was limited in what he could do and promised to avoid future attacks; he kept his word.) He demeaned government workers and shifted taxes downward, away from the wealthy and toward the less affluent. Thus began the enormous increase in income disparity, which most Republican presidents, beginning with Reagan, have made far worse. The United States, according to the most recent figures, is worse than roughly

---

2   Richard Cohen, "Spiro Agnew was Trump Before Trump," *Washington Post* (September 3, 2018), (accessed October 9, 2019).

THE COMMON SENSE MANIFESTO

three-fourths of the world's countries with regard to income inequality.[3]

- Persistent and plausible rumors have suggested that Reagan followed Nixon's lead in seeking political gain by sacrificing the country's interests. In Nixon's case, he sought to prolong the Vietnam War, heedless of its slaughter, in order to prevent an advantage to his political opponent. In Reagan's case, not definitely proven, but suggested by circumstantial evidence, he allegedly signaled to the Iranians who had stormed the US embassy in Teheran that the captives should not be released while Carter was in office. Carter had been negotiating for their release. Senate Republicans blocked funding for an investigation into these allegations, so the truth has not been disclosed. The timing, however, is more than suspicious: the Iranians released the hostages *exactly* as Reagan took office. Moreover, although Reagan had asserted forcefully that he would never negotiate with terrorists, he went far beyond negotiation and actually supplied the Iranians with arms that they could turn around and use against Americans. He then used the funds from the arms sales, illegally, to support right-wing revolutionaries in Latin America. This was the notorious "Iran-Contra" scandal that could certainly have been grounds for impeachment; however, his time in office was nearly over.

- The supplying of weapons to America's declared enemies was so bizarre that it lends credibility to the charges that he promised to assist them, if they did not release the hostages until Carter left office. One can imagine the roaring calls for impeachment on the grounds of treason if a Democratic president had done anything remotely similar.

---

3   Central Intelligence Agency, *The World Factbook*, n.d., https://www.cia.gov/library/publications/the-world-factbook/rankorder/2172rank.html? (accessed October 9, 2019).

- Beginning a Republican practice of rejecting measures to protect the environment, Reagan reversed Carter's energy program and his environmental efforts. He symbolized his disdain for "tree huggers" by removing solar panels from the White House that Carter had installed, even though they worked perfectly.

- Reagan also contributed strongly to the degradation of American politics, deliberately or not, by effectively clearing the way for the rise of talk radio and the creation of Fox News, which became essentially an arm of the Republican Party. His Federal Communication Commission halted the Fairness Doctrine. Congress passed legislation to re-institute it, but it fell victim to a Reagan veto.

- The Reagan administration, judging by indictments and convictions, was one of history's most corrupt, dwarfed only by the current one under Trump.

George H. W. Bush

- Bush ran a venomous campaign against Michael Dukakis and succeeded in demonizing the word "liberal." Previously, it had been one of the most honored words in American politics. More troubling, his campaign advertising adopted thoroughly racist themes, as characterized by the "Willie Horton" emphasis.

- Bush issued pardons for a number of Iran-Contra figures, some of whom had not yet been tried and therefore would never be interrogated. He may have been trying to ensure that no adverse information would emerge about him, but in any case, it is clear that his pardons had the result of suppressing information that should have been made public.

The Clinton Years

- Republicans loathed Bill Clinton, and sought to destroy his presidency. If anything, their hatred of Hillary Clinton was even greater. Early in Clinton's time in office, both parties generally recognized that it was vital to reform America's healthcare delivery system. The Clintons put forth a plan, and numerous Republicans were cooperating with Democrats to enact it. Then, Bill Kristol, a top aide to former Vice President Dan Quayle, sent a memorandum to every Republican in Congress, both senators and representatives. The gist was to kill healthcare. If reform were to be enacted, it should be under a Republican president. No Republican, it said, should cooperate with the Clintons on healthcare. None did. Many Republicans had been working across the aisle; they ceased to do so. By the time a Republican president was in office, Republicans had become anti-healthcare ideologues, and there was no more prospect of progress.

- Beyond that, they sought to expel Democrats in general from public life. House Republicans, following the firebrand Newt Gingrich, succeeded in driving Democratic Speaker Jim Wright out of Congress. Additionally, they whipped up a spurious furor over the "House Banking Scandal." There was no real "bank" and only members' personal money was involved—there were no public funds at risk—but despite all that, the noise they generated contributed to a Republican takeover of both houses of Congress.

- All the while, Republicans were moving further to the right, becoming far more tribal, and becoming more and more dedicated to power, rather than to the good of the country.

George W. Bush and Richard Cheney

- George W. Bush was elected president, despite narrowly losing the popular vote, by virtue of clever tricks in Florida, disputed vote counting, and a Republican majority on the US Supreme Court. In retrospect, in view of the very close vote in Florida, the Democratic candidate, Vice President Al Gore, had no chance. The Florida State Legislature, gerrymandered and Republican-dominated, was planning to choose the Republican slate of electors, thus electing Bush, *even if a recount showed that Gore had won!* According to the Court in *Bush v. Gore*, that would have been legal. There is no constitutional right of citizens to vote for presidential electors, and regarding electors, a state's legislature can do whatever it chooses, in spite of votes or anything to the contrary in the state's own constitution.

• Florida Republicans, therefore, were fully prepared to ignore the state's voters, if it came to that, and to choose Bush anyway. This is an illustration of the mindset that has become common among today's Republicans. It also illustrates a flaw in the Constitution that should be corrected. Elimination of the Electoral College would accomplish this.

• The Bush-Cheney administration took the United States into a war that was a disaster for all involved. It was clear that Iraq, the country Bush invaded, had nothing to do with the attacks on 9/11, but Bush and Cheney maintained otherwise. They searched for non-existent weapons of mass destruction. A British intelligence worker, motivated by conscience and attempting to head off a brutal war, leaked a top-secret memorandum that revealed that Bush and British Prime Minister Tony Blair were aware that the reasons they had stated to support the war were false. But the war came. Many Bush advisers had been part of the Project for a New American Century (PNAC), which had sought to pressure President Clinton into invading Iraq—years before 9/11—demonstrating that the invasion was planned regardless of the rationale employed to justify it.

- Bush and especially Cheney were furious regarding the opposition to their war plans. Ambassador Joseph Wilson journeyed to Africa to determine whether it was true, as Republicans alleged, that Iraq's Saddam Hussein had sought to purchase yellowcake uranium for nuclear weapons. It was not, and he revealed that it had not happened. This so outraged Cheney and his aides that the identity of Wilson's wife was leaked to the press. His wife, Valerie Plame, was an undercover agent for the CIA, working on keeping nuclear weapons out of the hands of America's enemies. With her cover destroyed, her career was ruined, her life was in danger, all with whom she worked abroad were put in harm's way, and America's interests were decidedly damaged. She returned home unharmed, but her agents disappeared. If this were not treason, it came very near. Cheney's top aide and assistant to the President, I. Lewis "Scooter" Libby, was convicted of perjury and obstruction of justice as a result. Bush commuted his jail time, but left his $250,000 fine intact. Trump pardoned him.

- Although Bush's official propaganda persuaded many voters that Republicans were more "efficient" than Democrats and that they "got things done," it became clear that it was all smoke and mirrors. The Bush administration demonstrated massive incompetence when faced with the ravages of Hurricane Katrina in New Orleans. Incompetence, common sense would make clear, is more a Republican phenomenon than not. And why not? Why should Americans expect a party that says "government" cannot be effective to be effective? Certainly, there were good examples to follow: LBJ faced similar circumstances in New Orleans from Hurricane Betsy, and performed superbly. LBJ, however, had confidence in government and knew how to make it work. He was on the ground, working effectively, within 24 hours; Bush looked down from an airplane and flew on. If Bush were even aware of LBJ's precedents, he ignored them.

- Adhering to relatively recent revisions to Republican ideology, the Bush administration enacted huge tax reductions for the wealthy. Ideologues argued that this would bring prosperity. Instead, following soon thereafter came the worst financial disaster since the Great Depression. Bush attempted to help with a financial stimulus, including the Troubled Asset Relief Program (TARP), but it was left to President Obama to secure a far greater stimulus (although still too modest), which halted the descent into a full-blown depression.

- No one should ever forget that Bush, however benign he may be thought to be in comparison with the unspeakable Trump, put the United States of America on record as being in favor of torture. This invited international ridicule, coming from the country that officially was founded on the principles of the Declaration of Independence, and had presented itself as a beacon of human freedom and humane values. He adopted extremist views in violation of human rights and the rule of law, and otherwise raised doubts about the principles that are the foundation of a democratic republic. For instance, he was cavalier about right to counsel, and lawyer-client privilege, and was quick to fire U.S. attorneys who would not conduct official investigations into the spurious Republican fantasy of widespread voter fraud.

Republican Malfeasance During the Obama Administration

- Mitch McConnell, the Senate Republican leader, notoriously said early in the Obama presidency that his duty was to ensure that Obama would be a one-term president. He failed. Unfortunately, he succeeded in so institutionalizing the filibuster and applying it to virtually all legislation that it became widely accepted that to be passed, a bill would have to clear the 100-member Senate by sixty votes.

- Republicans in general did not move to challenge the racist lies that political operatives, including one New York real-estate developer, Donald Trump, spread about Barack Obama; for example, that he was born abroad and thus not a "native-born citizen" or (nonsensically) that he had a "colonial mentality."

- Speaker of the House John Boehner invited a foreign head of government to address a joint session of Congress without clearing it with the State Department or even informing the administration. The fact that it was Benyamin Netanyahu of Israel, an ally, did not excuse the unconstitutional act. He came here explicitly (and unwisely) to undercut the foreign policy of a sitting US president. Republicans certainly would not have countenanced such an affront to a Republican in the White House.

- Similarly, Tom Cotton, a wild-eyed and extremist Republican senator from Arkansas, arrogantly composed a letter that he, along with forty-six Republican colleagues in the Senate, signed. He sent it to the leaders of Iran, talking down to them and telling them to ignore President Obama's foreign policies. Again, regardless of strict definitions, Republicans would screech with indignation had Democrats done such an inappropriate thing during a Republican administration.

Donald Trump

- What can one say about Trump? Any catalogue of his malfeasance would be huge and repetitive. He leaves government agencies unstaffed, to America's great danger. He deliberately appoints agency heads who work to subvert the missions of the agencies, and he maintains the Federal Election Commission with too few members to function—making it impossible for the FEC to hold him to account.

- Whatever his personal views—and on many matters, it is doubtful whether he has a view at all, other than to favor what is useful to him at the moment—Trump has explicitly fostered white nationalism. His "good people on both sides," his immigration cruelties, and his blindness to the evils of racism all broadcast bigotry and excuse hatred and murder. Rather than serving as president for all, he condemns large segments of the population. He encourages right-wing extremism in general, with all the racism and violence that comes with it. His version of a "Southern strategy" makes those of Nixon and Reagan appear mild by contrast. His disregard for women is legendary, open, and obvious.

- He conducts foreign policy from ignorance, believing it to be better to make decisions without being influenced by facts, because of his "great and unmatched wisdom." The result is policy by impulse, completely lacking in wisdom.

- He lies constantly. Lying apparently comes as naturally to him as swimming to a fish. Even many of his supporters have learned to dismiss most of what they hear him say, considering it unimportant.

- Trump conducts business by Twitter, calling his tweets "official policy." Judicious use of Twitter could be a major advance in connecting with the people, such as Kennedy's use of television or FDR's use of radio. Trump's consistent lack of discipline or sense of the appropriate, however, makes it highly dangerous. Any random thought—or positive reaction to misinformation from, say, a Tucker Carlson or a Sean Hannity—that pops into his head (his great brain) tends to pop immediately out of his fingers, becoming "official." Again, this is policy by impulse, and Trump's impulses are often illogical, bigoted, and dangerous—and always uninformed.

- Trump's incompetence is—or should be—legendary. One would hope that his time in office would forever put to rest the absurd argument that a president should be a businessman, "because businessmen know how to do things." Despite Republican propaganda, his inability to pass legislation is extraordinary, except for the tax cut, and no modern Republican president could ever fail under any circumstances to get a tax cut through a Republican Congress. George W. Bush even managed to sign one just as he was taking the US into a major war—probably a first in human history. It is unclear what the circumstances were that have led to Trump's complete failure to rebuild Puerto Rico following Hurricane Maria. Certainly lack of concern is a factor, but so is his general incompetence. George W. Bush's incompetent response to Hurricane Katrina was a major factor in the decline in the reputation of his administration, and as clumsy and ineffective as the bush response to Katrina was, it was far better than Trump's to Maria. Characteristically, however, Trump trumpets his failure there as a huge success and says Puerto Ricans should be "grateful."

- He antagonizes allies and believes alliances exist only to "take advantage of America." At the same time, he allies himself with our antagonists, being especially drawn to tyrants.

- He even betrays allies. He impulsively gave approval to Turkey to attack the Kurds, who fought against ISIS as our major ground troops. He is thus demonstrably untrustworthy and has made that clear both at home and abroad.

- Trump openly and illegally calls for assistance from Russia, and subsequently from other countries, to help his own personal political fortunes.

- He mocks the disabled, demeans anyone who is inadequately deferential, and causes children to be ripped from the arms of their parents. He hopes to be able to shoot refugees when they approach a moat (or moot) separating the US from Mexico, one filled with snakes, alligators, and other unfriendly beasts.

- He openly enriches himself and his family from foreign governments, despite clear constitutional prohibitions.

- He chooses unqualified and inadequate aides, then fires them, and tends to listen only to himself or television commentators who say what he wants to hear.

- He insists on the utmost loyalty, but refuses to be loyal in return.

- He violates every norm of conduct. He knows nothing about how to be president, and perhaps worse, does not care what is or is not appropriate.

- He is a bully, and that affects everything he does.

- He rejects fact, attacks the free press, and ignores the values of democracy and a free society.

- It bears repeating that, if there is anything that Trump's performance has made clear, it is that he cannot be trusted (just ask our allies, the recently betrayed Kurds).

- Sadly, the same can be said for Republican leaders. "Moscow Mitch" McConnell, for example, the Senate Republican leader, has blocked measures to secure American electoral procedures intended to protect the process from meddling by our enemies. It is hardly surprising that opponents now speak unkindly of #MoscowMitchMcTraitor.

- Trump is a danger to the United States and the world. The Republican Party has been completely complicit and is equally dangerous. He, needs to be removed from power, as does the entire Republican Party—at all levels.

★ CHAPTER XI

Appendix on Common Sense Self-Protection

Fighting is Wrong: Learn to Fight

I n a civilized world, part of the social contract is that government is responsible for providing safety. It stands as a shield against foreign threats, against dangerous products and environmental pollutants, and against threatened harm from domestic sources such as criminals. Self-protection thus should not be required.

Unfortunately, nothing in this vale of tears is perfect. Threats to our well-being have never been completely eliminated, despite the efforts of government even when it is at its best, so it always has been prudent to be prepared. This does not mean to be paranoid, but to be alert. Even less does it mean that victims should be blamed for being victims. Being inadequately prepared may place one at greater risk, but in no way should anyone infer that full blame should be laid anywhere but at the feet of bullies and oppressors.

Small-government ideologues who call themselves "conservatives" have brought about conditions that increase risk for the people. Recent Republican measures have considerably reduced environmental protections. Even the air we breathe and the water we drink can no longer be free from reasonable suspicion that it may be harming us. Unless policies change the situation will assuredly become worse. Protecting yourself against these threats may even be impossible. Nevertheless, we must all be alert to protecting ourselves as much as possible from pollution, contaminated food, environmental pathogens, and unhealthy lifestyles.

Vigilance, vaccination, prudent precautions regarding sanitation, and the like are essential.

There are also other threats that are more immediate, and certainly more dramatic. Under pressure from the National Rifle Association, Republicans—some gleefully, and others reluctantly—at all levels of government have rushed to do the bidding of arms manufacturers and the NRA to welcome rapid-fire, enormous capacity, high velocity weapons, and other weapons of varying characteristics into public, as well as domestic, spaces.

Common-sense controls on firearms have been so reduced by mis-interpreting the Second Amendment—mis-interpretations accepted by a newly-compliant Supreme Court, overturning tradition and advancing the NRA's apocalyptic dreams—that the deadliest weapons are available virtually anywhere, to virtually anyone. The fanatic cry of NRA spokesman, the ineffable Wayne LaPierre, that "only a good guy with a gun" can afford protection, is ridiculous; the preposterous proposition advanced by NRA henchmen that "the more guns, the less violence" not only offends common sense, but has made the United States the country most widely known for death by firearm.

It is too bad that it is not possible to prosecute the agents of death as war criminals; they are indirectly responsible for more slaughter than overt terrorists. Deaths include not only suicide, domestic violence, police and vigilante shootings of unarmed civilians—largely black males, vengeful killings by individuals and general adherents of the gun culture, and the setting of worldwide records by the United States as the country with the most frequent mass murder of innocents, most often committed by racist ideologues.

There was recently a request from deep within the NRA that made it quite obvious that when there are too many guns available, a "good guy" who has one is hardly sufficient to protect anyone.

LaPierre attempted to persuade the NRA to provide him with a six-million-dollar mansion for protection against alleged threats on his life. By so doing, he implicitly admitted that he considered his protection to require far more than his ability to carry a gun. Thus, his solution to individual protection is not conceal-carry; it is to have a fortified (luxury, of course) mansion. Admittedly, that would probably be more effective than NRA slogans, but it is so absurd and so expensive that the NRA turned down his self-serving request.

Other countries have adopted sensible gun-control measures. There is no reason why the United States cannot do so as well. The Second Amendment has been part of the Constitution ever since ratification of the Bill of Rights, and until recently did not preclude effective action at either state or federal levels. Rationality can return to gun-control policies when it returns to American politics, and it also will require far better training and supervision of police so that they can defuse tense situations, and not automatically reach for a firearm if they become nervous. That will require an enormous blue tsunami, and subsequent progressive victories at the polls.

Firearms aside, the culture is becoming more accepting of violence. Even the president of the United States notoriously urges his supporters to give vent to their fury, going so far as to say he will pay their fines should they be prosecuted. Although his supporters have no more chance of having him actually pay fines than do tradesmen who through the years have complained that he refuses to pay them, such rhetoric from high office can only be pernicious.

Common sense indicates that, at a minimum, citizens should be aware of the value of voting for a major party. They should understand the laws governing them, and what agencies can assist them if necessary. They should know of the elected officials who make policy and how to communicate with those officials. They should know what situations to avoid, what actions to take in any situation they are likely to encounter, and they should know how to respond to actual physical assault. Obviously, there is little that you can do to fend off a bullet if someone is making you a target. The best strategy is to anticipate, and, if at all possible to avoid it and not to be in a dangerous situation. It is decidedly *not* to carry a firearm. In a situation of mass shooting, having a firearm could at times be of help, but it is far more likely that the one who is armed will be the first to be shot.

Domestic situations, and personal situations in general, must be improved. What could be more sad, or more deserving of remedy, than personal relations that contain plausible elements of fear? Relationships of trust must replace those of danger. Remedies must involve broad and widespread education in empathy— and in common sense. They also may involve appeals to shame and decency. For better or worse, they also should include development of skills in self-defense. Consider the truth that, sadly, remains in the comment often attributed to Margaret Atwood: Men are afraid women will laugh at them; women are afraid men will kill them.

Physical skills are important, and they can be developed more easily than often assumed. Mental skills, though, are at least equally important. There are a number of works on self-defense that can be helpful. Looking only at one source: that newspaper of record, the Grey Lady herself, the *New York Times*, reveals that even there in that staid venue, there have been numerous articles through the years on self-defense for women.

Men should not make the mistake of dismissing these as "merely women's articles." Techniques that are valuable for women are equally valuable for men. Regardless of how formidable a man may be, he can always encounter someone more formidable. Regardless of how formidable a man may be, under the right conditions he can be bested by a smaller, weaker, victim who is determined, trained, and willing to do what is necessary without hesitation. Being prepared for self-defense requires both men and women to be able to function well when threatened by someone larger and stronger. Women, too, should be admonished not to assume that they are helpless when facing someone regardless of size and strength. Albeit in different ways, women can be equally formidable with men.

In an aptly-titled article, "Like a Tupperware Party, With Punching," The *Times* in 2012 discussed self-defense courses for women. The author, Linda Himelstein, noted that such courses are most successful when presented in an appealing manner, not merely as self-defense. She quoted Lisa Skvarla, the head of "the American Women Self Defense Association and a creator of Girls' Fight Night Out" that it is necessary to "do something" to make women want to attend classes. Leanne Brecklin, a criminologist, conducted research that supported this; she found that "sharing women's success stories" is an effective tool. "Fighting back," Brecklin noted, "is not only possible but also effective." Courses can be aimed specifically toward certain groups, such as Jerrett Arthur's "Mothers Against Malicious Acts," which teaches not only self-protection, but also "protecting one's children" (Jarrett has a black belt in Krav Maga, the self-defense art of the Israeli military).[1] Her organization is called MAMA. That would be far better on a ball cap than the MAGA (Trump's "Make America Great Again") slogan that often infects them today.

The world has been shocked in recent years by publicity from India. It took many outrageous acts before the dangers to women in the subcontinent received publicity outside its borders. Especially in certain areas, such as Delhi, sexual harassment has been

---

[1] Linda Himelstein, "Like a Tupperware Party, With Punching," *The New York Times*, (July 26, 2012), E 5.

rampant for decades, if not centuries. The euphemism "eve teasing" covers everything from catcalls, to rape and murder.[2] The New Delhi police force for a decade or so has been offering free instruction to girls in the city's public schools and universities. Women police constables are the instructors, and the courses include effective techniques from various martial arts. They also offer Summer and Winter camps for women, and "gender sensitization" courses for boys, "a lawyer-led course that teaches men how to help women in trouble and how to be more respectful to them in public spaces." A woman instructor, a constable, said it aims to develop feelings of responsibility among men for their conduct, so that they will "feel responsible towards girls and women."[3]

The first thing the Indian girls learn is contrary to their cultural deference. They scream to attract help. Then, they fight. As a result of the increase in publicity, even internationally, and of newly-energized women's organizations, women are beginning to be heard. Indian women now are coming forth to file complaints, and sometimes they find officials willing to listen, and to act.

In early 2019, the *Times* published an article cautioning women not to succumb to fear, but to be prudent when traveling. The safety tips included many common-sense recommendations (carry wedges for door stops to keep doors securely closed, etc.), and among them are "learn to defend yourself."[4] This is so im-

2   I learned about this national shame—certainly a vicious cousin to another vicious practice, bride-burning—when I lived in India as a Distinguished Fulbright Lecturer, and was CEO of a large research library in Hyderabad, the American Studies Research Centre; this was before these pernicious practices were widely known outside of India.

3   Maria Abi-Habib, "'Men Treat Us Like We Aren't Human.' Indian Girls Learn to Fight Back," *The New York Times* (April 16, 2018); https://www.nytimes.com/2018/04/16/world/asia/india-girls-self-defense.html; (accessed November 6, 2019).

4   Tariro Mzezewa and Lela Moore, "'Don't Succumb to the Fear' Women Share Travel Safety Tips," *The New York Times* (March 26, 2019);

portant that it can hardly be overstressed. Women should learn to use any available object as a weapon. They should trust their instincts, and not hesitate to summon help. They should not be frightened to be alone, and they should continue to travel!

In a vivid presentation of personal experience learning to fight, the *Times* published, "Beth Ditto is 'Feeling Self-Defensive' and Fights Back." The core of the course it describes seeks to eliminate women's feeling of powerlessness. It concentrates on a few key techniques for breaking free, and teaches striking back. "Eyes! Knees! Groin! Throat!" becomes the chant, stressing the most effective—and devastating—targets that also require the least skill. "'As a fat person, rolling around on the ground, I think that's really cool, too,' Ms. Ditto Said." [5]

For anyone who wishes to see examples of fighting techniques that enable women to defeat men—anyone who can tolerate scenes of extreme violence, that is—there is an extraordinary film, *Atomic Blonde*. Ignore the title, and concentrate on the inspired performance of the superb Charlize Theron. She typically immerses herself in her roles, and this instance is no exception; she trained vigorously for many months, all the while seeking realism regarding the fighting techniques that are most appropriate for women.

She found them, and presents them thoroughly. A surprising amount of the film consists of her character successfully fighting off attackers. The fighting is realistic; in no way does she escape unscathed. An early scene shows her weary, exhausted in fact, in a tub of ice water with floating ice cubes, soothing her bruised and battered body. As the review in *The Guardian* put it, there are "some terrifically good one-on-one combat scenes—much

---

https://www.nytimes.com/2019/03/26/travel/safety-tips-female-solo-travel.html; (accessed November 9, 2019).

5   Alexis Soloski, "Beth Ditto is 'Feeling Self-Defensive' and Fights Back," *The New York Times* (November 3, 2019), ST 4.

more continuously and realistically shot than the rest of the film—crunchily horrible extended punch-ups in which Theron establishes some serious martial arts chops."[6] A personal note may be appropriate here. I was impressed by Theron's performance, and I have studied martial arts for more than a half century, having earned advanced black belts (5th and 6th degrees) in several styles. The *Guardian* review I cite here also used the word "prurient" to describe the bathtub scene, but that is nonsense. The scene graphically demonstrated the damage that combat inflicts upon the human body, was integral to the material, and contained not a hint of the erotic.

The most effective of the numerous self-defense training courses primarily for women, at least according to reputation and descriptions of the training, may be Model Mugging (note: I know it only by reputation, and have not personally observed any of their sessions). It involves sound training, with hard and vigorous pummeling of well-padded instructors. It seems to be scientifically grounded, and philosophically appropriate. Although Model Mugging is not a martial art itself, it seems to be compatible with various forms of martial arts training, and would seem to be highly effective in developing skills specifically in self-defense. As a public service, Model Mugging has posted a rather extensive list of self-defense articles.[7]

Among numerous books on self-defense, one especially designed for women is noteworthy. Shelley Klingerman's *Vigilance* takes a holistic approach.[8] Quite appropriately, she sets the scene, discusses not only the need to be vigilant, but what it involves. She

6   Peter Bradshaw, "Atomic Blonde Review—Charlize Theron Punches Up Hyperactively Silly Thriller," (August 9, 2017); https://www.theguardian.com/film/2017/aug/09/atomic-blonde-review-charlize-theron-punches-up-hyperactively-silly-thriller; (accessed November 10, 2019).

7   See "Self-Defense Articles," *Model Mugging* http://modelmugging.org/self-defense-articles/; (accessed November 10, 2019).

8   Shelley Klingerman, *Vigilance*, Indianapolis, Niche Pressworks, 2019.

warns that it is essential to be prepared to face fears; waiting until one is in a dangerous situation is ineffective. Fear paralyzes, but knowing what to do can be a protection against its debilitating effect. Training can enable one to discard any thought of being "ladylike," and—however off-putting it may be to some—instead to be "a warrior." She calls upon her readers to "join the community of bad-ass women," and launches into her first chapter, perfectly summed up in its title, " Prepare—Prevent—Protect."

Klingerman's book is rich in detail, and strong on connection to actual situations. She outlines everyday objects that can be used as weapons, she gives useful pointers on personal protection and prudent measures to take to reduce danger while abroad or at home in familiar surroundings. There is far too much to summarize, but it would be well for her book to be widely read and heeded.

Beyond that, there are measures that every adult citizen should be able to take to make dramatic improvements in everyday lives. Vote for candidates who are concerned for the people, rather than for their own re-election or for their contributors.

Vote a straight ticket. Make that ticket a major party. Make that party one that does not tolerate (let alone advocate) grabbing children from their parents at the border. Vote to remove from office anyone who does not advocate firearm control, who does not insist on control of law-enforcement violence, and who does not move effectively to protect the rights of all people, especially women. Vote consistently to reject any party that overtly or implicitly rejects the rights of women to make their own choices, whether for reproduction or any other phase of personal conduct.

Direct your vote to the destruction of any party that will not move toward all measures that will improve the lives of constituents. Above all, vote to incorporate humanitarian and humane

THE COMMON SENSE MANIFESTO

values into government, and remove all officials and members of any party that has been complicit in institutionalizing cruelty.

Targets of voters who will vote accordingly, you know who you are. Perhaps you will join many others of your party, willingly step aside, and retire from politics.

Index

Abrams, Elliott, 20

Ackerman, Spencer, 41

Action items, 236-241

Affordable Care Act, 51, 93, 116, 134, 235

Agnew, Spiro T., 7, 244

Alaska earthquake, 235

Albert, Carl, 9

Alston, Philip, 99

Ambrose, Stephen, 11

American Economic Review, 112

American institutions, fragility of, xiii, Chapter I

"American Way," x

"Anti-Government is Not the Solution to Our Problem Anti-Government IS the Problem: Presidential Response to Natural Disasters, San Francisco to Katrina", 235 (n1)

Armitage, Richard, 26, 250

Ash, Michael, 113-114

Ashcroft, John, 33

Assault on Reason, The, 79

Assault, responding to, 260

Atlantic, The, 60, 61 (n5), 78

Attacks on 9/11, 32

Atwater, Lee, 20

Atwood, Margaret, 260

Austerity, 110-111, 113-114, 123, 178

Baby bonds, 177

Baltimore Sun, 182

Banking services, 237-238

Bankruptcy, see Warren, Elizabeth, 239

Baker, Dean, 113

Baker, Peter, 6

Baker v. Carr, 61

Barr, Bob, 24

Barr, William, 3, 27
  Misrepresenting Muller Report, 3, 27

Beirich, Heidi, 40

Bernal, Andres, 133

Biblical inerrancy, 117-119

"Biblical Literalism and Constitutional Originalism," 104 (n 14)

Biden, Joseph, xviii, 37, 173, 175

Bill of Rights, 259

Billionaires, 238-239

Blackmun, Harry, 191

Blair, Tony, 25, 55, 249

Blum, John Morton, 130

Blumenthal, David, 132

Boeing crashes, xxi

Boehner, John, 36, 252

Book of Jerry Falwell, The, 117

Booker, Cory, 163, 177

Border wall, 48

Bork, Robert, 190-191

Bowker, Betrenia, ix

Bowles, Erskine, 114, 126-127

Boys on the Bus, The, 67

Black males, unarmed, killed by police, 258

Brennan, Thomas, 105 (n16)

"Brexit," xiii

Brown v. *Board of Education of Topeka,* 190

Brownback, Sam, 154

Buchanan, James, 62

Budget balancing, 135

Burlington, Vermont, 162-163

Burr, Richard, 10

Bush, George H. W., xiii, 20-21, 110,
    Demonizing "liberals," 247
    Pardons suppressed vital information, 247

Willie Horton campaign, 20

Bush, George W., 16, 25-29, 53-56, 57, 62, 79, 88, 134, 230, 235, 248, 249, 254
    Advocating torture, 251

Bush v. *Gore,* 44. 62

Business experience, not qualifying, 254

Buttigieg, Pete, 183

Cable news, 70-71

California, 76

Calhoun, John C., 245

Cambridge Journal of Economics, 114

Canada, 241, 259

Card, David, 112

Card and Krueger Study, 111-112, 126

Carlock, Greg, 133

Carlson, Tucker, 253

Case Against the Supreme Court, 189 (n4)

Cassidy, John, 114-115

Carswell, G. Harrold, 191

Carter, James E. (Jimmy), 12-14
    Energy policy, 247
    Installed solar panels on White House, 15
    Likely Republican delay of prisoner release, 246
    Only full-term president who had no Supreme Court appointment, 13

Centers for Disease Control (CDC), 166

Chaffetz, Jason 34

Charlottesville protest, 47

Chenault, Maj. Gen. Clair, 5

Chenault, Anna, 5

Cheney, Richard, 12, 25-29, 55, 56, 135, 348, 250

Chemerinsky, Erwin, 189 (n4)

Chernobyl, xx

CHIP program, 86

Children, separating from parents, x, 254-255

CIA, 25-26

Citizen influence, 259, 265-266

Citizens United v. *Federal Election Commission*, 62, 188

Civil Rights Act of 1964, x, 133

Civil rights movement, x

Civil War, U.S., xiv, xv, 49, 94

Civilian Conservation Corp (CCC), 180
    Planting of *three billion* trees, 236

Clarke, Richard, 33

Clarridge, Duane (Dewey), 21

Climate Accords, xiv, 174

Climate change, 133, 173-175, 178,

"Manhattan Project" needed for, 236

Clinton administration, terrorism warnings by, 33

Clinton, Hillary, xviii, 10, 42, 46, 48, 56, 57-58, 65, 75-90
    "Basket of Deplorables," 78
    Demonization of, 49, 65-66
    More stress than Trump on jobs, 49

Clinton, William, 20, 21-22, 83, 90, 110, 134, 249
    Republican hatred of unprecedented, 248
    Scandal and impeachment, 23-24

Colbert, Stephen, 79, 167

Communication, security of, 237-238

Confederate monuments, 47

Conceal-carry, inadequate for protection, see La Pierre, Wayne, 259

"Constitutional Interpretation," 105 (n15)

Consumer Financial Protection Bureau (CFPB), 163-164, 171

Conway, Kellyanne, 79

Cohen, Michael, 45

College Republicans, ix

Comey, James, 73-74

Commerce Clause, 51

Commercial speech, distinct from free speech, 240

Confederate states, former, 76

Congress, ix

Congressional Budget Office (CBO), 110-111

Conservatism (conservatives), American, xi, Chapter I, 51, 96, 100, 111, 141
    Conservative interpretations, 105
    Rejection of Lincoln's "man before the dollar," 236
    Relationship to right-wing extremism, 39-43
    Unworkability of, xii, 106

Constitution of U.S., 104-105, 147, 259
    On electoral college, 43-44, 237

Conventional Wisdom, 97, 109, 123, 126
  "Censorship: Who Needs It? How the Conventional Wisdom Restricts Information's Free Flow," 125 (n2)
  Coinage of term, 97 (n8)
  Effect on economics profession, 112
  Krugman: different from serious thought, 166
  Need to disregard, 151
  Responding to right-wing propaganda, 164-167

Cordray, Richard, 171

Cornyn, John, 79

Corporations as people 50, 240
  Role of, 129-130

Corruption, x
  Records set by Reagan, until Trump, 247

Cotton, Tom, 35, 252

Cousins, Norman, xix-xx

Crapanzano, Vincent, 116

Creation stories, 118-119

Criminal justice and prison reform, 178

Crouse, Tim, 67

Cruelty, 49-50, 266

Cruz, Ted, 10, 35

Cummings, Elijah, 182

Daily Kos, 38

Dayton, Ohio, 43

"Deafness Before the Storm," 32

Debt, student, 171, 180, 238
  See Sanders, Bernie; see Warren, Elizabeth

Democracy, 163

Democracy, threats to, xi, xiii, xiv, 61-62, 63

Democracy in Chains, 92

Democratic Party, ix, x, 57, 88, 134
  Confirming Ford as VP, thus refusing to "steal the presidency," 8-9
  Gains in 2018 elections, 103
  Senators defying conservative propaganda on Social Security, 164

Democratic wave, need for, 63, 103, 182-183, 205, 207, 259

Democrats, Southern, ix

Depression, xiv, 2

Desegregation, racial, ix

DiMaggio, Anthony, 39, 48

Disabled, the, subject of Trump's mockery, 254

Discourse, public, deterioration of, 71-72

District of Columbia, statehood for, 240

Dukakis, Michael, 20

Economic Bill of Rights, 102, 143-144, 169, 175, 237

Economic Policy Institute, 110

Economics profession, 112

Eichenwald, Kurt, 32-33

Eisenhower, Dwight, 79, 92, 94, 95, 147. 190

El Paso, Texas, 43

Electoral College, xiii, xiv, xix, 4, 43-44, 49, 50, 56, 57, 65, 67, 76-77, 182, 201-202, 237, 249
    Ignoring nearly 3 million votes for Clinton, 42
    Recent failures of, 208-209
    Republican newfound affection for, 43-45, 207-210
    "Rigged" for Trump, 45

Election, 2016, xiii, xxi, 56, 57. Chapter III

Elections, 2018 mid-term, xiv

Elections, public funding of, 239

Election interference, x, xiii, 36, 37, 56, 57, 88-90
    Expanded Post Office Department to counter, 237
    McConnell's blocking of measures to prevent, 255
    Normalization of, 51
    Republican ignoring of, xxi, 29-30, 38
    Trump's request to Russians for, xviii

Empathy, development of, 260

Energy efficient vehicles, 238-239

Environment, threats to, xiv

Environmental protections,
    recent Republican threats to, 257

Ethics, 240

Euro Zone, 128

European Union, xiii

Executive order, ix

Fair Game: My Life as a Spy, My Betrayal by the White House (Plame), 26 (n 29)

Fairness Doctrine, 16-17, 247

Falwell, Jerry, 120-121

Falwell, Jerry, Jr. 117, 120-121

Family leave, paid 176-177, 240

Farrell, John A., 5-6

Fascism, American, 39-43, 48

FBI, 73-74

Federal Aviation Administration, xxi

Federal Election Commission, 48, 252

Federal Highway Act, 94

Federalists, 102

Filibuster, 198-201, 251

Firearms, 241
    Proliferation of in U.S., xxi, 258

First Amendment, 240

Florida, 56, 57, 88, 89
    Legislature of willing to overrule voters, 45, 237, 249

Flynn, Michael, 59, 88

Ford, Gerald, 4, 8, 11-12, 21, 98, 187

Fortas, Abe, 190

Founders, 101, 104-105, 188
Strengthened, not weakened, national government, 107

Fourteenth Amendment, 34-35

Fox News as arm of Republican Party, 16-17, 36, 79

Free College Plan, 171

Freedom Dividend, see Yang, Andrew

Friendly Fascism, 48

Fukushima, xx

Fundamentalism, xii, 91, 103-121
Constitutional, 104-107
Relation to originalism, 103
Economic, 107-115, 136
Religious, 115-121

Funding, 47-48, 107-109
For the US, "anything that is technically feasible is financially affordable," (Kelton),133-134

Galbraith, John Kenneth, 97 (n8), 123

Garland, Merrick, 37, 191

Gerrymander, xi, 60-62, 188. 198
Examples, 202-205

"Get Over It? Why Political Influence in Foreign Affairs Matters," 52 , 52 (n 55)

Gillibrand, Kirsten, 83, 163, 177

Gingrich, Newt, 21-22, 248

Gore, Albert, Jr., 54-55, 58, 79, 88, 249

Gould, Lewis, 236 (n2)

Government, "user-friendly," 178-179

Government as employer of last resort, 236

Government functions, privatization of, 240

Graham, Franklin, 121

Graham, Lindsey, 182

Grant, Ulysses S., x

Grassley, Charles, 9

Great Recession, 163

Greater New Dean 178

Green Apollo Plan (Warren), 174

Green Marshall Plan (Warren) 174

Green New Deal, 133, 174

Gross, Bertram, 48 (n 54)

"Growth in a Time of Debt," 112, 126

Guardian, The, 99

Gun control, sensible, 259

Gun, Katherine, 25, 55

Haldeman, H. R., 6

Haley, Nikki, 98

Halperin, Mark, 81

Hamilton, Alexander, 102, 147

Hannity, Sean, 253

Harding, Susan Friend, 117

Harmonization, 116-119

Harrington, Michael, 97

Harris, Kamala, 35, 163

Haslam, Bill ("Tennessee Promise"), 170

Hatch, Orrin, 86

Haynesworth, Clement, 191

Healthcare in America, 50, 86, 92-93, 162-165, 239, 248
    Irrationalities and inadequacies of, 155-158

Heart of Power, The, 132

Heim, Joe, 117

Herbert, Bob, 14

Herndon, Thomas, 113-114

Hiltzik, Michael, 110-111

Hise, Ralph, 60-61, 61 (n5)

Historically Black Colleges and Universities (HBCUs), 238

Hocevar, Carl J., xx-xxi

Holan, Angie Drobnic, 76

Homeland Security, Department of, 41

Horwitz, Morton, 103

House Banking Scandal, 248

How Democracies Die, xi

House or Representatives of U.S., 48, 102

Huffington Post, 133

Human Rights Council, UN, 99

Humphrey, Hubert H., 4

Hurricane Katrina, 31, 235, 254

Hurricane Maria, 31, 128, 235, 254

Hussein, Saddam, 55

Immigration reform, 238

Impeachment, 96, 141

"In Context: Hillary Clinton and the 'Basket of Deplorables,'" 78

Income inequality, 225-226, 238, 246

Inflation, 137-141, 152

Infrastructure, 175-176, 238

Inhofe, James, 33

Inslee, Jay, 173-174

Interstate Highway System, 94

Intelligence agencies, 56, 57

Iran, xiv, 13, 37
    Republican letter to leaders of, 35

"Iran-Contra," 17-19, 246

Iraq War, 25, 31-32, 55
    Disaster of, 249
    False justification for, 208-209

ISIS, 55-56

Israel, 36

Jefferson, Thomas, 99-102, 105, 145, 147
    And "living Constitution," 105 (n16)

Jackson, Andrew, 9, 20, 102

Johnson, Boris, xiii

Johnson, Gary, 57

Johnson, Lyndon B., x, 4-6, 93, 98, 191, 235, 250
Passion for health care, 132
Successful because he "muzzled economists," 133

Judicial review, 102

Judiciary, 102, 183
Corruption of, 63, 189, 192-198
Reform of, 195-198, 240

Kansas, 110, 154

Kansas City Star, 148

Kavanaugh, Brett, 10

Keefe, Linda, 97, 98

Kelton, Stephanie, 133-134, 137-141, 152, 175, 236

Kennedy, Anthony, 9

Kennedy, John F., 97, 98

Kessler, Glenn, 34

KGB, x

Kingsley, David, 164, 222

Klein, Naomi, 60 (n 4)

Klobuchar, Amy, 176

Knightly, Keira, 25 (n 27)

Kobach, Kris, 2-5

Koch Brothers, 153-154

Koch, David, 153-154

Kristol, Bill, 248

Krueger, Alan, 112

Krugman, Paul, 112, 126, 170
Serious analysis more progressive than conventional wisdom, 167

Kurds, Trump's betrayal of, 254

Laffer, Arthur, 154

Language, importance of precision, 140, 184-185, 201-202

LaPierre, Wayne, 258
Request to NRA for secure (luxury) mansion rejected, 259

Lauer, Matt, 81-82

LBJ, see Johnson, Lyndon B.

Legislative procedure, 96, 251

Legislatures of states, authority of, 43-44

Levitsky, Steven, xi-xii

Lewis, Sinclair, 67

Lewinski, Monica, 23-24, 82-83

Lewis, David, 60-61, 61 (n5)

Libby, I "Scooter," 26, 250
Bush commutation of jail time, 27
Trump pardon of, 27, 28

"Liberal media," fake news from Republicans, 244

Lies, Incorporated: The World of Post-Truth Politics, 114 (n22)

Life expectancy decline, 166, 223

Lifestyles, unhealthy, need to guard against, 257

Lincoln, Abraham, x, 14, 95,
  Man before dollar, 236

Local and state government,
  assistance to, 240

Longevity, see Life expectancy
  decline.

Louisiana, 110

Los Angeles Times, 98-99, 110

MacDonald, Dwight, 97-98

MacLean, Nancy, 92

Madison, James, 102

Maher, Bill, 84

Majority rule in America, status
  of, Chapter II

Making of the President, The, 67

Manhattan Plan, 175

Marshall, John, 102, 105

Mass murders in America, 42-43,
  50

Mass transit, 238

"Maybe It's Time to Admit that
  the 'Grotesque Caricature'
  of White Evangelicals is the
  Reality," 119

Mayer, Jane, 19

McCain, John, 10, 119

McCarthy, Joseph, 31

McCarthy, Kevin, 38

McCullough, David, 14

McConnell, Mitch, 10-11, 29-30,
  34, 37, 50, 75, 183, 189, 191
  Devotion to minority rule,
    201, 205-206
  Normalizing filibuster, 251
  Obsession with blocking
    Obama, 38, 251
  Rejection of accepted
    standards, 47
  Routine blocking of measures
    for election security, 255

McGovern, George, 222

McManus, Doyle, 19

"Me Too" sea change, 82

Media Matters, 114 (n22)

Medicaid expansion, 51, 93, 239

Medicare, xvii-xviii, 93, 137, 235,
  239
  Part C, "Medicare Advantage,"
    155
  Republican move toward
    privatization, 219
  Part D, 107-108, 134-135,
    235
  Effective against southern
    segregation, 122, 132
  Cost not an issue, 127

Mental skills, 260-265

Mercer University, 119

Michigan, 45, 49, 57, 89

Military expenditures, 135

Minimal government, 130-131

Minimum wage, 110-112, 125-
  126, 239

Milbank, Dana, 30

Mississippi, 14

Mitchell, Marcia, 25 (n 27)

Mitchell, Thomas, 25 (n 27)

Modern Monetary Theory, 133, 166
  Anything technically feasible is financially affordable, 134
Modern Political Economy, Chapter V, 145
  "Modern Political Economy and Public Policy," 125 (n1)
Mondale, Walter, 21
Morone, James A., 132
"#MoscowMitchMcTraitor," see McConnell, Mitch
Movement conservatives, 106
MSNBC, Chapter III
Mueller Report, 3, 27, 56, 57

Nader, Ralph, 56, 57, 88
National defense as symbol, 90-91, 102
National Defense Education Act, 95, 147
National Popular Vote Interstate Compact, 210-211
National Review, 2
National Rifle Association, xxi, 40, 43, 241, 257, 258
NBC, 58
Nemo iudex in causa sua ("no man should be a judge in his own case"), 129 (n5)
Neo-Nazi groups in America, 40-41

Netanyahu, Benyamin, 36, 252
New Hampshire, 89
New Deal, ix, xviii
New Jersey, 111, 126
New Orleans, 31, 235
New York Times, xi-xii, 14, 25, 31, 32, 40, 41, 51,112, 163
  Right-wing ideas influencing Social Security coverage, 164-167
New Yorker, 2, 97, 114-115
New Zealand, 39-40
NFIB v Sebelius, 51
NIIP (National Influenza Immunization Program), 11-12
Ninth Amendment, 106
Nixon, Richard M., x, 2-9, 17, 21, 98, 191,
  Positive parts of record, 244
  Sabotaging Paris Peace Talks, 5-7, 243
  Southern racist strategy, 243
  Watergate, 243
Nixon, Ron, 41
North Carolina, xi, 45, 60-61
  Supreme Court of, 61
Norway, 39
Novak, Robert, 26
Nuclear proliferation, xiv
Nuclear threat, xix-xx

Obama, Barack H., 9, 36, 51, 93, 109, 123, 164, 189, 251

Racist untruths about by Trump, 34, 46, 252

Republican hopes to impeach, 34

Right to make Supreme Court appointment denied, 37

Solar panels on White House, 15

Obamacare, see Affordable Care Act

Ocasio-Cortez, Alexandria (AOC), 174

Office of Legal Counsel (OLC), 241

Official Secrets Act (Britain), 25, 55

Opponents, prosecution and persecution of, x, 2, 25, 49, 69-74

Originalism, 103, 104-105

O'Rourke, Beto, 173-174

Other America, The, 97

Paine, Thomas, xv-xvi

Paris Peace Talks, see Nixon

Payday loan industry, 231

Pelosi, Nancy, 103

Pence, Mike, 74

Pennsylvania, xi, 57, 89, 111, 126

Peterson, Peter G., 221, 226-227

Pharmaceutical industry, 93, 134

Philadelphia, 111

Phelps, Hollis, 119

Physical skills, 260-265

Plame, Valerie, 26, 250

Police, killings of unarmed civilians (largely black males) by, 258

Need for better police training, 259

Political skills for self-protection, 265-266

Polio, 93

Policy recommendations from Democrats, 158-164

Politico, 68

Pollin, Robert, 114

Post Office Department (see also Postal Service), 237

Postal Savings, 232-233

Postal Service, expand and restore to cabinet, 179, 231-232, 237

Postal Service, Republican efforts to privatize, 219-222, 227-229

Reduction in number of offices, 155, 220, 229-230

Restrictions on, 230-231

Poverty in America, Chapter IV, 98-99, 102, 110, 122-123

Powell, Lewis, 191

Power, misuse of, see Republican Party

Preamble to Constitution, 106

Presidents, Pandemics, and Politics, 94 (n 4)

Press freedom, Trump's attacks on, 255

Privatization, 240

Project for a New American
Century (PNAC), 249

Propaganda, 91, 201-202, 254
Right-wing propaganda in
mainstream media, 164-
167

Protecting Children and Mothers,
94

Protestant Ethic, 115-116

Public service, 229

Public Health Service, 239

Puerto Rico, 31, 128, 235, 254
Statehood for, 240

Putin, Vladimir, 59, 88

Rabin-Havt, Ari, 114 (n22)

Rail, high speed, 238-239

Reagan, Ronald W., 4, 12-19, 20,
21, 98, 110, 135, 141, 192-
195, 226
Arms to enemies, and likely
delaying of prisoner
release, 246
Began widening of income
disparity, 245
General attacks on
government domestic
programs, 245
Opened campaign with racist
symbolism, 14, 245
Killed Fairness Doctrine,
16-17
Provided arms to enemies of
US, 17-19
Removed solar panels from
White House, 15

Shifted taxes toward the less
affluent, 245

Quayle, Dan, 248

Radio, FDR's use of, 253

Regimes, dictatorial, xiii

Regulation, 128-129, 130

Reinhart and Rogoff Study, 112-
115, 126

Reinhart, Carmen, 112, 126

Reitman, Janet, 41

Religion Dispatches, 119

Religious fanaticism, 55, 91

Republican Party, ix, x, xi-xii,
Chapter I, 39-43, 57, 59, 60-
61, 108, 147, 182, 235-236,
248
Bullying tactics, 214-217
Belief that only they can
legitimately hold office, 61
Blocking measures for
election security, 255
Clandestine invitation to
foreign leader to undercut
president, 252
Climate Accords, rejection of,
xiv
Complicity with Trump
endangering America, 255
Decades of demonization of
Clintons, 49
Deliberately making
government offices
inconvenient, Chapter
VIII

Efforts to sabotage ACA, 116

Elephant logo, xii-xiii

Energizing violent groups, 42

Malfeasance of, Chapter X

Minority rule, devoted to,
Chapter VII

NRA influence on, 258

Ideological nature of,
growing, 91, 140

Income redistribution
upward, 225-226

Incompetence of, 31-32, 250,
254

Lame-duck attempts to
inhibit Democrats, 45

Rejection of majority rule, 43-
44, 62, Chapter II

Routine refusal to confirm
nominations by
Democrats, 191

Science, rejection by, xiv

Tax reductions for wealthy,
251

Threats to deny appointments
to HRC if elected, 48

Threats to environment, xiv

Willingness to adopt extreme
practices, 47

Willingness to cancel
elections if Trump
recommended, 206

Willingness to overrule
any tradition if to their
advantage, 45, 255

Republicans: A History of the
Grand Old Party, The, 239
(n2)

Rehnquist, William, 191

Reuters, 36

Reynold v. Sims, 61

Rhetoric, political, 91, 101-102,
107

Rhode Island, 121

Richardson, Heather Cox, 236
(n2)

Right-wing extremism, 39-43

Roe v, Wade, 192

Roberts, John, 51, 61-62

Rogers, Katie, 52 (n 55)

Rogoff, Kenneth, 112, 126

Rohrabacher, Dana, 38

Roosevelt, Franklin D. (FDR),
70, 102, 140, 175, 180
Court packing, 183-184, 188-
189

Roosevelt, Theodore (TR), 92,
235
The "Republican Roosevelt,"
130

Rose, Charlie, 81

Rove, Karl, 79

RT, 59, 88-90

Rumsfeld, Donald, 12

Rucho v. Common Cause, 61, 63,
188

Russians (see also Election
interference), x, xiii, 28, 29,
56, 58, 58 (n2), 62, 72-73, 88,
182
Republican recognition of
while ignoring, 38
Loss of influence as symbol,
91

Ryan, Paul, 38, 112

San Francisco earthquake, 235

Salk, Jonas, 93

Sanders, Bernie 57, 85, 88, 162-163, 172, 180, 231

Sandalow, Terrance, 105 (n15)

Sarandon, Susan, 89

Science, rejection of, xiv

Second Amendment, 188, 241, 258, 259

Securing America's Future, 164

Self-defense, Chapter XI

Separation of church and state, 122

Senate of U.S., procedures of, 47

Serving the Word: Literalism in America from the Pulpit to the Bench, 116

Seventeenth Amendment, Conservative opposition to, 210-214

Sexual harassment, 82-83

Shelby County v. *Holder*, 63

Shierholz, Heidi, 110

Sick, Gary, 18

Six Amendments: How and Why we Should Change the Constitution, 187

Skidmore, Max J., xi (n 1), xvii (n 6), 94 (n 3), 125 (n2), 235 (n1)

Skills (mental, physical, and political) for protection, 260-266

Skocpol, Theda, 94

Slavery, 101

Slavery, southern fears of national power as threat to, 29

Smith and Tuttle, 104 (n14)

Smith, R. Jeffrey, 41

Smith, Peter J., 104

Social contract, 257

Social Security, xvii, 92-93, 106, 122, 137, 148-149, 164, 181, 239

  Disappearance of offices, 155, 220-221, 226, 229-230

  "Reform" proposals mostly attacks, 221, 225

  Republican efforts to privatize, 219-221, 227-229

  Right-wing themes influencing mainstream coverage, 164-167

  Sound proposal for expansion, 221-225

"Social Security for the Future," 164

"Southern Strategy," 4, 14, 98

Solar panels on White House, 15

Sommer, Jeff, 165 (n10), 166

Southern Poverty Law Center, 40

Spending money, distinct from speech, 240

Spy Who Tried to Stop a War, The, 25 (n 27)

Sputnik, 95

"Squad," the, 47

State offices, 233

Stein, Jill, 56, 57-58, 59, 88

Stevens, John Paul, 187

Stevenson, Adlai, 80

Stewardship Theory (TR), 105

Stolen seat, (also see Supreme
  Court), 9, 37, 183
  Threat of future thefts, 48

Sunstein, Cass, 103

Supply-side economics, 110

Superman, x

Supreme Appellate Court, 240

Supreme Court, xi, 61-63, 102,
  104, 105, 183, 187, 191, 192-
  198, 241
  Partisanship of, 63, 258

Taft, William Howard, 105

TARP, 251

Taxation, relation to income, 110

"Taxpayers' money," 110, 137-
  141

Tax policies, 178, 223, 238, 250,
  254

Television, 70
  JFK use of, 253
  Policy source for Trump, 255

Third parties, 56, 57, 88-90

Three Mile Island, xx

*To Make Men Free: A History of
  the Republican Party*, 236 (n2)

Today Show, 81-82

"Thomas Jefferson and the Living
  Constitution," 105 (n16)

Torture, 251

Tree planting 180

"Tricky Dick," see Richard M.
  Nixon

Truman, Harry S., ix, 14, 190

Trump, Donald J., x, xi, xiii, 8, 13,
  16, 20-2, 48, 56, 57, 58, 65,
  68, 69-74, 96, 98, 141, 147,
  164,175-176, 254
  Allies, antagonizing of, or
    betraying, 254
  Appointees, qualifications
    disregarded, 255
  As international symbol for
    white supremacy, 39
  Attempt to use executive
    orders to obtain funds, 47
  Bullying, 255
    Attacks on women of
      color, 182
  Complaints by about being
    mistreated, 42
  Corruption, reputation for, 2
  Culmination of Republican
    policies, 1
  Danger to US and world, 255
  Efforts to sabotage ACA, 116
  Electoral college overruling
    popular vote to select, 42,
    50
  Environmental sabotage, 244
  Fascist symbols, adoption
    of, 40
  Impulse, policy by, 253

Inaugural address as white nationalism, 79
Inaugural crowd, smallness of, 81
Incompetence, 254, 255
Institutionalized cruelty of, 49-50
Lying, 252, 253
Mental deterioration of apparent, 45-46, 68-69
National defense, loss of power as symbol, 91
Neglect of Puerto Rico, 128, 235
Norms, routine violation of, 255
Nuclear explosion to ward off hurricane, xxi
Pardon of Libby, 27
Praise of neo-nazis, 47
Press freedom, attacks on, 255
Racist lies, 252
Request to Russians for election assistance, xviii, 87, 175, 254
Request to Ukrainians for election assistance, 175
Reluctance to fill positions, 48, 252
Science, rejection by, xiv
Security violations by, xviii
Southern strategy of uniquely pernicious 253
Twitter, business by, 253
Tyrants, attracted by, 254
Uniquely unprepared, 45
White nationalism, fostering of, 252

Willingness to ignore elections, 45, 45 (n52)
Women, disregard for, 253
Trump, Tiffany, 79
Tur, Katy, 2, 66-75, 87
Turkey, 254
Tuttle, Robert J., 104
Twenty-Fifth Amendment, 7-8
Use of to replace VP Agnew, 8-9
Twenty-Seventh Amendment, 187
Twitter , Trump's use of as policy tool, 253
Tyler, John, 9

Ukraine, 36, 175
Unbelievable, 66-75
Unions, need to resuscitate, 239
United Kingdom, xiii
United States v. *Libby*, 27
Universal basic income (UBI), see Yang, Andrew
Universal programs preferable whenever possible, 122-123, 136
University of Massachusetts, 126
Unworkable Conservatism, xi, 100, 141, 145, 153
"User-friendly" government, 178-179
USSR, xiii
Utilities, upgrade and weatherproof, 238

Vaccines, 93-94

Van Buren, Martin, 9, 20

Vanity Fair, 32

Venezuela, 92, 93

Veterans Administration, 239

Veto, 102

Voter fraud, 206

Voting Rights Act, 61-63, 239

Voter registration, 239

Voter suppression, xii, 78
Need to outlaw, 240

Voting in America, Chapter II, 76, 200-207
Importance of voting for major party, 259
The irrelevance of "deserving" to win, or "likeability," 53-54
Voting by mail, 240

Vox, 78

Violence, 39, 43, 46-47, 49, 69-72
Republican energizing of violent groups, 42
Trump encouraging atmosphere of, 259
See also right-wing extremism
See also opponents, prosecution and persecution of

Wall Street Journal, 178

Wallace, George C., x, 4,
Electoral strength in northern states, 49

War on Poverty, 98

Ward Republics, 100-101, 146

Warren, Earl, 190

Warren, Elizbeth, 163, 167, 170-173, 177, 178, 180, 183, 231, 239

Washington Post, 30, 34, 38, 41, 98, 117, 206

"Watergate," 6-7, 21, 243

"We Can Pay for a Green New Deal," 133 (n9)

"We Drew Congressional Maps for Partisan Advantage. That Was the Point," 61 (n5)

Wealth tax, 238

Weber, Max, 115

Weinberger, Caspar, 21

Weisberg, Jacob, 23

Weiss, Andrew, 58

Welfare, constitutional authorization of, 106-107

Wellesley College, 90

What Happened?, 75-90

Wheaton College (Illinois), 119

White House solar panels, 15

White supremacy; white nationalism (see also right-wing extremism), 39-40, 79

White, Theodore, 67

Windrem, Robert, 58 (n2)

Williams, Roger, 121

Wilson, Joseph C. IV, 25-26, 250xs

Wilson, Valerie Plame, 26

Wired, 41

Wisconsin, xi, 45, 49, 89

Women's March on Washington, 80

World Affairs, 125 (n1)

World War II, xiv, 2

Yang, Andrew, 167-170, 181

Ziblatt, Daniel xi-xii

Zinke, Ryan, 79